Brighter Thinking

The Sun King: Louis XIV, France and Europe, 1643–1715

A/AS Level History for AQA Student Book

David Hickman

Series Editors: Michael Fordham and David Smith

CAMBRIDGE
UNIVERSITY PRESS

University Printing House, Cambridge CB2 8BS, United Kingdom

Cambridge University Press is part of the University of Cambridge.

It furthers the University's mission by disseminating knowledge in the pursuit of education, learning and research at the highest international levels of excellence.

www.cambridge.org
Information on this title: www.cambridge.org/9781107571778 (Paperback)
www.cambridge.org/9781107571792 (Cambridge Elevate enhanced edition)

First published 2016
First Edition 2016

A catalogue record for this publication is available from the British Library

ISBN 9781107571778 Paperback
ISBN 9781107571792 Cambridge Elevate enhanced edition

Additional resources for this publication at www.cambridge.org/education

This textbook has been approved by AQA for use with our qualification. This means that we have checked that it broadly covers the specification and we are satisfied with the overall quality. Full details of our approval process can be found on our website.

We approve textbooks because we know how important it is for teachers and students to have the right resources to support their teaching and learning. Please note, however, that the publisher is ultimately responsible for the editorial control and quality of this book.

Please note that when teaching the A/AS Level History for AQA Student Book course, you must refer to AQA's specification as your definitive source of information. While this book has been written to match the specification, it cannot provide complete coverage of every aspect of the course.

A wide range of other useful resources can be found on the relevant subject pages of our website: www.aqa.org.uk

Contents

About this Series

Cambridge A/AS Level History for AQA is an exciting new series designed to support students in their journey from GCSE to A Level and then on to possible further historical study. The books provide the knowledge, concepts and skills needed for the two-year AQA History A-Level course, but it is our intention as series editors that students recognise that their A-Level exams are just one step on to a potential lifelong relationship with the discipline of history. The book is thus littered with further readings, extracts from historians' works and links to wider questions and ideas that go beyond the scope of an A-Level course. With this series, we have sought to ensure not only that the students are well prepared for their examinations, but also that they gain access to a wider debate that characterises historical study.

The series is designed to provide clear and effective support for students as they make the adjustment from GCSE to A Level, and also for teachers, especially those who are not familiar with teaching a two-year linear course. The student books cover the AQA specifications for both AS and A Level. They are intended to appeal to the broadest range of students, and they offer not only challenge to stretch the top end but also additional support for those who need it. Every author in this series is an experienced historian or history teacher, and all have great skill both in conveying narratives to readers and asking the kinds of questions that pull those narratives apart.

In addition to quality prose, this series also makes extensive use of textual primary sources, maps, diagrams and images, and offers a wide range of activities to encourage students to address historical questions of cause, consequence, change and continuity. Throughout the books there are opportunities to critique the interpretations of other historians, and to use those interpretations in the construction of students' own accounts of the past. The series aims to ease the transition for those students who move on from A Level to undergraduate study, and the books are written in an engaging style that will encourage those who want to explore the subject further.

Icons used within this book include:

Key terms

Speak like a historian

Voices from the past/Hidden voices

Practice essay questions

Taking it further

Chapter summary

About Cambridge Elevate

Cambridge Elevate is the platform which hosts a digital version of this Student Book. If you have access to this digital version you can annotate different parts of the book, send and receive messages to and from your teacher and insert weblinks, among other things.

We hope that you enjoy your AS or A Level History course, as well as this book, and wish you well for the journey ahead.

Michael Fordham and David L. Smith Series editors

PART 1: THE SUN KING 1643–1685

1 The Regency, 1643–1661

In this section, we shall look at the beginning of Louis XIV's reign and the situation in France when he came to the throne aged four. We shall look at how the government was established that ruled in France until Louis took personal control of affairs in 1661. The Regency years were marked by armed conflict, so we shall also examine the wars and civil wars of this period in French history. We will look into:

- the French monarchy in 1643: the legacy of Richelieu and Louis XIII; the establishment of the Regency
- the minority of Louis XIV: the roles of Anne of Austria and Mazarin; the Parlement of Paris, unrest and opposition; the Frondes
- France and Europe: the rise of French power at the expense of the Habsburgs; the treaties of Westphalia and the Pyrenees
- the condition of France at the accession of Louis XIV in 1661: politics, economy and society.

The French monarchy in 1643

The legacy of Richelieu and Louis XIII

Louis XIII was king of France 1610–1643 and married Anne of Austria. After 23 years of hoping for an heir and four still births, the couple produced Louis in 1638, prompting calls of a miracle birth.

Voices from the past

Richelieu

Figure 1.1: Richelieu

Armand Jean du Plessis de Richelieu was French Chief Minister 1624–1642. He founded France's navy and promoted colonies. His **Testament Politique** celebrated enhancing Louis XIII's glory and power, and boasted that the monarch was leaving France:

'in the highest degree of glory and reputation which it has ever had.'[1]

Key terms

Huguenots: French Protestants, influenced by the writing of theologian Jean (John) Calvin.

Key terms

Chambres de l'Arsenal: a court that usurped the parlements' authority.

parlements: law courts, *not* parliaments. The Paris Parlement was the biggest; its jurisdiction covered at least a third of France. In this book where we simply say 'Parlement', we mean the Paris Parlement.

Lit de justice: a session when Parlement met in the king's presence, thereby deterring opposition.

The noble family of Habsburg: held the Holy Roman Empire crown for nearly 300 years. They acquired Spain; Philip IV was son-in-law to Habsburg Emperor Ferdinand III.

Richelieu's achievements included defeating **Huguenot** revolts. The 1629 **Edict of Grace** permanently weakened the Huguenots' ability to rebel, depriving insurgents of cities and fortresses.

He developed state **propaganda**. Countless **Académie Française** (formed 1635) pamphleteers defended and glorified Richelieu. A royal printing press presented government opinion as fact.

Richelieu frequently circumvented judicial procedure. His **Chambres de l'Arsenal** quickly tried and removed royal opponents. He weakened the **Paris Parlement** and its right to **remonstrance** (protest) against royal edicts. Louis XIII used **lits de justice** to override remonstrances and force through an **edict** preventing discussion of state affairs without his permission. This limited remonstrances to just three: one regarding judicial legislation and two regarding financial legislation. By 1643, state affairs were the Crown's legislative prerogative.

Royal infringement of parlementary liberties by 1643 included:

Actions:	**Consequences:**
Handpicked judges Extensive use of **commissaries** (special royal representatives) **Intendants** supervised judicial affairs and civil cases.	Lost prestige and revenue Sovereign courts overruled
Richelieu exploited the **office system**, selling government service jobs and threatening to create and sell more.	Undermining the value and status of existing judicial and administrative posts.

Richelieu increased royal power in the provinces of France by extending government administration to Dauphiné, Burgundy and Provence. He increased Intendant use and powers. These hand-picked officials were only employed for three years. They supervised army billeting, used troops to enforce taxation and suppress revolts and took over the **assiette** (the basic assessment of the main direct tax, the **taille**) in 1642.

France and Europe by 1643

Richelieu wanted to:

- weaken **Habsburg** power to limit possible incursions along France's eastern border
- take the province of Alsace
- frustrate the ambitions of Spanish king Philip IV.

He therefore took France into the **Thirty Years War** against Spain and the Habsburg Holy Roman Emperor in 1635. Territories captured included:

- Arras
- Artois
- Alsace
- Rhine bridgeheads
- Roussillon
- Perpignan.

This laid foundations for French European dominance.

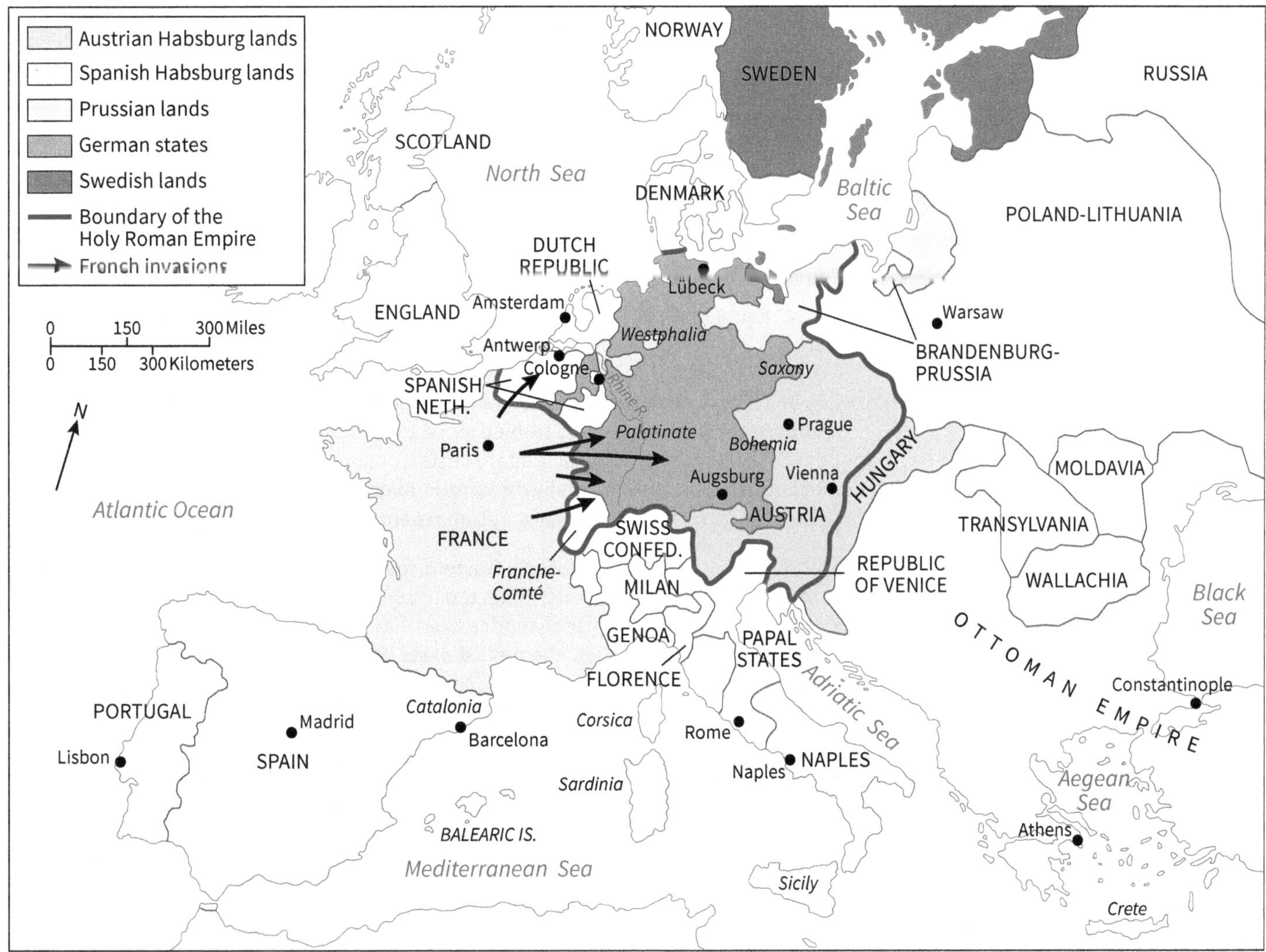

Figure 1.2: Europe during the 30 Years War

ACTIVITY 1.1

Look up and clearly define:

- Huguenots
- Edict of Grace
- Académie Française
- Chambres de l'Arsenal
- Paris Parlement
- remonstrance
- lit de justice
- intendants
- offices
- taille
- pays d'états

ACTIVITY 1.2

List the key elements in Richelieu and Louis XIII's legacy. After studying later chapters, revisit this question and see whether you still take the same view. Annotate your list, commenting on how further study has changed your opinion.

Catholics and Huguenots

By 1643, the monarchy's natural devout Catholic supporters were disconcerted by ongoing Huguenot religious freedom and conspiracy (in Languedoc) and a Protestant war against Spain (led by the United Provinces, Brandenburg-Prussia and, from 1630, Sweden) that increased poverty.

By 1643, even government and royal-family members opposed the war and royal policies:

- Brigadier-General the Duc de Bouillon had negotiated for peace with Spain and helped Louis **Bourbon** lead insurgents from Lorraine, Champagne, Sedan and **Spanish Netherlands**, defeating royal troops at La Marfée in 1641.
- Louis XIII's brother Gaston d'Orléans repeatedly tried removing Richelieu. In 1641–2, he plotted Richelieu's murder and negotiated peace with the Duc de Bouillon, Louis XIII's favourite the Marquis Cinq-Mars, and Olivares.
- Anne of Austria, Louis' wife, confessed to treasonable correspondence with her brother, the **Cardinal** Infante Ferdinand of Spain.

Despite Cinq-Mars' execution in 1642, aristocratic rebellion remained a threat. Louis XIII absolved other conspirators (including Gaston, the Duc de Bouillon and Anne of Austria), allowing those exiled to return home after Richelieu's death. This invited future rebellion, as did Louis' will. This stipulated that war must continue until a decisive outcome, thereby extending the biggest cause of royal unpopularity and instability.

Taxation

Royal treatment of parlements had created conditions for habitual radical opposition and revolt:

- In 1641 Aix and Rouen's parlements openly defied royal policy, rejecting new **chambres de requêtes** (sessions with judicial officials that examined petitions for cases going to magistrates).
- In 1643 Parlement significantly delayed and modified plans to extend **Intendant** control over taxation.
- By 1643, parlements and tax payers were both alienated. Taille and troop **'subsistence'** tax levies had trebled since 1620. Indirect taxes had more than doubled. So too had annual military costs, consuming nearly 75% of expenditure.
- Richelieu's war was financially disastrous. Averaging about 25 million **livres** annually, government expenses outran revenue and debt interest spiralled.

Taxation collection was corrupt and wasteful; over 75% of 19 million livres of **gabelle** (an indirect tax on luxury goods) collected in 1641 was lost. Tax evasion was widespread. Much of France remained grossly undertaxed. France's newly acquired and often semi-autonomous territories, the **pays d'états** (Brittany, Burgundy, Dauphiné, Languedoc, Normandy and Provence), comprised one third of France, but paid just 10% of all taxes.

Voices from the past

Mathieu de Morgues

Mathieu de Morgues was prominent among the pamphleteers who actively opposed Richelieu's religious and foreign policies. Initially supportive of Richelieu, he became disillusioned and emerged as a leader of the **dévot** (religious) faction. This was a loose grouping of people who supported monarchy and Roman Catholicism and opposed:

- French participation in the Thirty Years War
- Richelieu's tyrannical power.

Morgues demanded Richelieu's overthrow:

'all good Frenchmen, open your eyes to see what a miserable condition you are in; open your minds to foresee the great desolation that menaces you. Do not permit a puny man, sick in body and mind, to tyrannise over the bodies and minds of so many sane persons.... Cast off these ... evil instruments.'[2]

Subsequently, revenue was increasingly dependent upon:

- High-interest rentes (loans). Interest rates between 20% – 33% broke both the 5.5% legal limit and fiscal common sense.
- Office sales. By 1642, the number of these administrative posts was around 40,000, more than the administration required. This increased salary and pension costs and transferred tax collection to notoriously dishonest officials.

By 1643, revenues from rente and office sales approached 700 million livres. Other problems were caused by Richelieu:

- burning old Treasury accounts
- ignoring the **chambres des comptes** (sovereign courts specialising in financial affairs)
- secretly paying financiers (nearly 172 million livres).

This prevented proper auditing, debt control and trust in royal fiscal management.

By 1643, open revolt had erupted against royal taxes in Orléans. No scope remained to increase taxation without risking further revolt.[3]

Richelieu left a rapacious taxation system which unduly burdened those least able to pay. This threatened civil war, as Richelieu himself foresaw in 1641:

'If Messieurs of the council continue to allow tax farmers and contractors the freedom to treat the king's subjects according to their unruly appetite, then it is certain that a disorder similar to that in Spain will happen in France.'[4]

France's army in 1643

Richelieu's army was not disciplined, big or good enough to conclusively defeat its enemies.

- Troops were often unpaid, and prone to looting and extortion.
- Corrupt commanders (and some Intendants) often cheated **muster rolls** (troop number lists used to calculate pay) by borrowing other regiments' troops, temporarily recruiting peasants or retaining dead soldiers on pay rolls.

French dominance over its territories was incomplete. Habsburg invasion of Corbie (1636) – 80 miles from Paris – and Spain's invasion of Languedoc (1637) left France craving security. Lorraine remained occupied, but disorderly and resentful. Local brigands attacked and tied down French soldiers. French troops engendered hostility, plundering so much property and food that many women were reportedly reduced to eating their own children.

Richelieu's and Louis XIII's reported achievements were fairly exaggerated in reality. Much maligned though Mazarin has been, he did not initiate the key problems he faced after 1643 – but as we shall see, he did intensify them.

Richelieu and Louis XIII left behind them:

- financial and social disorder
- an unpopular, unwinnable war
- enormous debt
- the foundations for aristocratic, parlement and mass revolt.

The establishment of the Regency

When Richelieu died in 1642, Louis XIII's health was already failing. Internal tuberculosis left him contorted and emaciated. By April 1643, Louis XIII's death was only a matter of time, but the issue of his **succession** created many problems.

ACTIVITY 1.3

Look up and clearly define:

- Spanish Netherlands
- maîtres des requêtes
- paulette
- Cours des Aides
- chambres des requêtes
- gabelle
- rentes
- chambres des députés.

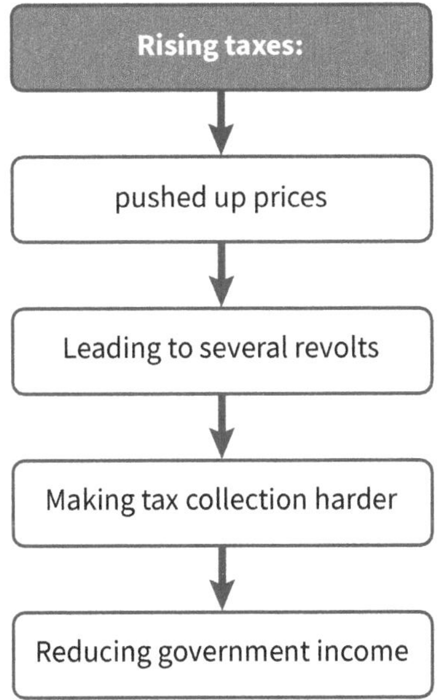

Figure 1.3: Richelieu's financial legacy

ACTIVITY 1.4

Look up and clearly define:

- subsistence tax
- Lorraine.

ACTIVITY 1.5

Draw up spider diagrams summarising the problems Richelieu left in the areas of:

- religion
- politics
- finance
- defence.

The old king's son, also Louis, was only four, so too young to rule. Louis XIII's brother Jean Baptiste Gaston had repeatedly plotted against Richelieu and been a co-conspirator with Cinq-Mars. Louis' wife Anne of Austria had also been treacherous and distant. Louis had been reportedly reluctant to sleep with her, preferring close emotional attachments with men.

The king's priority was to protect his young son's interests and avoid power falling into the wrong hands or worse still, a power struggle developing into a civil war. He thus devised a will that denied Anne, Gaston and other political players the opportunity to assume power after his death. This established a Council of Regency that essentially ensured that Anne could not take full power as **regent** but should be controlled and guided by it:

'the office of Regent is a trust of great weight, upon the due discharge of which depends the welfare and glory of the kingdom; and as it is possible that the Queen can have the requisite knowledge to conduct the course of great and important events, which is acquired only by long experience, we have thought good to name a Council of Regency, by the advice of which, and under her Majesty's authority, state affairs shall be resolved by a plurality of votes'[5]

Louis' will struck a careful balance, curtailing different individuals' power without denying or inflating it. Louis refused to name either Gaston or Anne as regent, but included both as council members. He also insisted that:

- Anne could not change Regency Council members, unless one died.
- State policies required a majority vote in this council, thereby reining in his wife's power.

As a further precaution against Anne trying to dominate, Louis insisted that the Regency Council should include trusted allies in the following roles:

Who:	Role:
Prince Condé Henri de Bourbon	Royal household head
Gaston d'Orléans	**Lieutenant General**
Pierre Séguier	Chancellor – this was not a financial role, but judicial, controlling the parlements
Claude Bouthillier	Finance superintendant
Léon Bouthillier (Comte de Chavigny)	Foreign minister
Cardinal Jules Mazarin	Council member in charge of all ecclesiastical issues.

Louis XIII overestimated his ability to determine events after his death through his will. French constitutional law prevented a king from binding his successor to any **decree** or will, as each king had the full authority of the crown. He also underestimated Anne of Austria's ability to disregard his last wishes regarding her status and to gain support. Anne was astute and active, not apathetic. In establishing Louis XIV's regency and her prominent role within it, Anne was very much her own woman with her own agenda. Nothing would prevent her son from being the future king of France and from her having a leading role as regent. To achieve this, she asked the Duc de Beaufort to guard her sons and courted the support of the powerful Condé family, especially the Duc d'Enghien, who commanded the army. In addition, she 'was the first to kneel in homage to her son Louis XIV', thereby conveying her leading role in serving the new king.[6]

Anne was certainly not prepared to be side-lined and denied her rightful leading role as her son's regent. She immediately set about overturning her late husband's will that restricted her power. To do this, she:

- covertly prepared the ground to overturn Louis XIII's will; five days before he died, Anne made it clear to Paris Parlement lawyer Omer Talon that a lit de justice on her son's behalf could be in the offing regarding her husband's will
- led Louis to a formal lit de justice session with the Paris Parlement for removing the restrictions placed on her authority by her late husband; this was just four days after his death
- placed Louis on the throne of state in the Parlement hall of justice and took a seat to his right
- surrounded herself with potential power rivals Gaston, the Prince de Condé, the Duc de Vendôme (both illegimate sons of Louis' Bourbon grandfather Henri IV) and other peers and dukes; this reinforced the idea that Louis' rule under her tutelage was popularly supported
- used her son Louis to initiate the request to overturn his father's will; Anne taught him to say "Gentleman, I am come to show you my affection; my chancellor will tell you the rest".

Anne also wooed the Paris Parlement by:

- offering it an advisory role about the welfare of the state during the rest of her regency
- removing the need for magistrates to swear new oaths of loyalty
- offering magistrates the chance to reduce the regency council from a ruling body to an advisory role.

Since the regency council left by Louis XIII contained so many of Richelieu and Louis XIII's ministers, Anne's appeal to the Paris Parlement seemingly offered a win-win premise for Crown and Parlement alike. The Paris Parlement perceived, and was encouraged to perceive, that it now had the opportunity to curb Richelieu and Louis XIII's more 'despotic' policies. This idea also appealed massively to Gaston and Condé.

Anne overturned constraints upon her power by using the ultimate propaganda smokescreen during Louis XIV's lit de justice. To this end, she employed Chancellor Séguier to persuade the Paris Parlement to dissolve Louis XIII's will. Séguier did not speak as if was representing Anne, but her four-year-old son Louis. He brilliantly deployed the language of shock and reason to win magistrates' hearts and minds. He flagged up warnings about the stability of royal **sovereignty** in the event of authority being divided (as in Louis XIIII's proposed Regency Council).

He also reinforced Louis XIV's natural **dynastic** right to be king by presenting the concept that 'The King never dies' – the idea that, even though an individual king dies, the institution of monarchy survives because as soon as one king is dead, his heir is immediately the rightful king. Thus the natural way for royal authority to live on after Louis XIII's death was through his son, as Louis XIV, who would naturally need his mother's protection. Séguier claimed that 'seeds of royal virtue' guaranteed 'the rebirth of the dead king in the person of his king the son'.[7]

Paris Parlement Avocat Général Omer Talon also strongly supported Anne in helping to overturn Louis' will. He reinforced Louis' dynastic Bourbon right by claiming that he had taken 'public possession of the throne of his ancestors'.[8]

These interventions effectively made the Paris Parlement's nullification of Louis XIII's will and approval of Anne as sole regent a done deal. Contrary to her deceased husband's explicit wishes, she was enshrined as regent with all restrictions upon her power quashed. The regency council was to be an advisory board, not a ruling body. This meant that Anne, as according to ancient and natural **royal prerogative**, would be left to take charge of the young king and the business of state.

Anne immediately set about her own reshuffle of the royal administration. On the evening after the successful lit de justice, she invited Cardinal Jules Mazarin to be her closest adviser and chief minister. She had a strong personal bond with him and met with him in her private cabinet for two hours each evening to be briefed on foreign policy.

Jules Mazarin had succeeded Richelieu as Louis XIII's Chief Minister in 1642 and remained in the post under Louis XIV until his own death in 1661. Born Giulio Mazzarini in Italy, he was a former French secret agent and Cardinal in the **Roman Catholic** Church. In 1640 he had defused a dangerous situation in Savoy, where the regency of Louis XIII's promiscuous sister, Duchess Christine (and thus French influence in the duchy), had been challenged. He had helped to unmask the Cinq-Mars conspiracy.

Mazarin tactfully enabled Anne to believe that she was in control, claiming that 'she was born to govern'.[9]

Anne surrounded herself with ministers she could trust. She disgraced Chavigny and with Mazarin's support and recommendation, enlisted as her inner council:

Person:	**Role:**
Pierre Séguier	royal expert on judicial matters
Patricelli d'Hémery	Finance Minister
Michel Le Tellier	Secretary of State for War

Here was a recipe for continuity of royal policies, not change. Séguier had been Louis XIII's Chancellor. D'Hémery and Le Tellier were Mazarin's friends and yes-men when it came to the key issue of extending the war. Crucially, the royal **council of state** existed in a purely advisory role. Although it was party to official decisions made by Anne and Mazarin, it was entrusted to merely ratify policies which Anne and Mazarin and their inner council had formulated in advance. Anne's regency council deftly included **princes of the blood** with posts that flattered their egos but denied them any central political role. Gaston was maintained as the Kingdom's Lieutenant General and Condé was offered a general's role on the frontline. Only rarely were they consulted on basic state policies made by Anne and her chief advisers. This was intended to give Anne and Mazarin's rule a veneer of legitimacy and a measure of control, by 'associating illustrious names with the regency, without granting a corresponding responsibility'.[10]

The minority of Louis XIV

The roles of Anne of Austria and Mazarin

Anne's tenure as regent lasted until 1653. Mazarin's role as Chief Minister lasted until his death in 1661.

Anne was widely perceived to be under his spell, if not in his bed. He had certainly formed a very close relationship with her, giving her jewels and signing letters to her 'Yours to the last breath'.

Together, they were supposed to:

- prepare Louis XIV for his future rule as king
- continue Richelieu's war
- tap extra revenue to fund this campaign
- prevent the princes of the blood from seizing power.

In only the first of these roles did Mazarin and Anne have any definite success. Mazarin played a leading role in mentally conditioning Louis for personal rule. In 1644, he enlisted Hardouin de Péréfixe (Archbishop of Paris 1664–1671) to tutor Louis and instil in him a strong grasp of his Divine Right and prime him for taking a strong and active future role. History lessons gave Louis a secure grasp of public laws and right, alongside the importance of order and resolute action to overcome successive challenges. According to Geoffrey Treasure, Louis also learned that, as the peak of a pyramid of counsel and command, his role was 'primarily to perform decisive actions'.[11] Louis translated Divine Right theories daily from Latin. This helped to cultivate his appetite for personal rule:

'The profession of a king is a majestic, noble and delightful one ... a king should delight in his calling ... homage is due to kings; they may do as they please.'[12]

Buoyed by improving French military fortunes and the prospect of securing substantial territorial gains, Anne committed herself to continuing the war against Spain. In 1643, she rebuffed Spanish overtures for peace, even though she was the daughter of Philip IV (Spanish King until 1655). Louis XIII's will had stipulated that this must continue until a decisive outcome. Mazarin also wholeheartedly supported the war. The Duc d'Enghien's (Condé's son) victory over Spain at Rocroi in May 1643 increased Mazarin's ambitions. War was continued at great detriment to royal finances and popularity, as explained below.

For all the problems he inherited, Mazarin made them considerably worse, especially royal debt and opposition to royal policies. Like a compulsive gambler, he decided that conquering additional territory was important enough to risk borrowing more money. The results were disastrous:

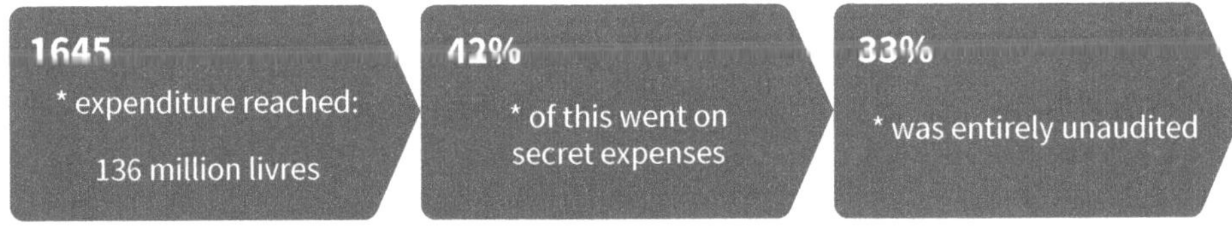

Figure 1.4: French state expenditure under Mazarin

Instead of acting like an accountant and cutting back expenses while raising income, Mazarin acted like a gambler and borrowed 115 million livres. Lenders were getting more worried and could only be persuaded to hand over the cash by being given high interest rates of 15%–20%.

The security for this was royal revenues until the end of 1647. Concerns about financial mismanagement mounted and were entirely well founded.

With debts exceeding 100 million livres and no conclusive military victory in sight, Mazarin left D'Hémery a nigh on impossible job of trying to balance the books. His efforts made Mazarin and the regency the fulcrum of increasing opposition:

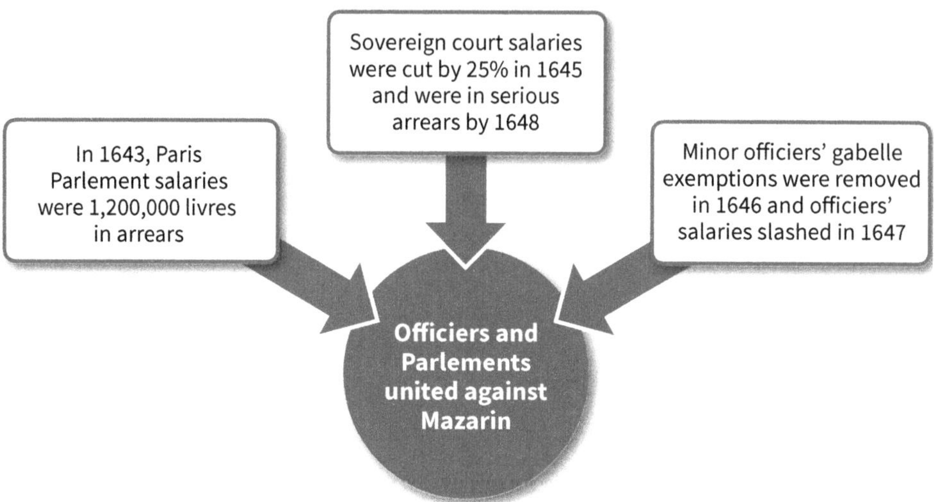

Figure 1.5: Reasons why the Paris Parlement and officiers united against Mazarin

Mazarin's blindness to rising socio-economic hardship also made him an increasing source of hate among tax payers. Subsequently, royal control of taxation deteriorated. By 1648, taxation had soared to three times its 1630 figure. Payment arrears increased, as did:

- troop use to enforce collection
- riots
- attacks on collectors; by 1645, serious tax revolts had affected Arles, Draguignan, Marseille, Gascony, Pardiac and Dauphiné.

Anne and Mazarin tried but failed to contain aristocratic ambition. In 1646, Condé's son (the Grand Condé) inherited the royal household headship and royal council seat. His brother-in-law, the Duc de Longueville, was admitted to the council in 1648. Mazarin aimed to divide and rule *les grands* (important aristocrats) by promising everything to everyone without actually delivering. This antagonised *les grands*, as did Mazarin's mismanagement of French internal affairs.

Indignant at their lack of promised central and provincial political power, an aristocratic gang led by the Duc de Beaufort conspired to murder Mazarin during 1643–44 in '**l'affaire des importants**'.

The plot included:

- The Duc de Vendôme: coveting the admiralty and governorship of Brittany, he promised to pull Mazarin's moustache off.
- Augustin Potier, Bishop of Beauvais: his ambition was to be chief minister.
- The Marquis of Châteauneuf: he wanted to be restored to favour after being sacked by Richelieu.

Government spies detected the conspirators. Beaufort was imprisoned and others sought voluntary exile. But a renewed aristocratic revolt was only a matter of time:

- Beaufort escaped from jail in 1648.
- Châteauneuf and Potier continually tried to turn other nobles and Parisian judges against Mazarin and Anne.
- The Count of Chavigny, the former secretary of state, constantly schemed to undermine Mazarin and secretly negotiated with the Cardinal's enemies in the sovereign courts of Paris.

The aristocracy was neither prepared to be excluded from office nor to accept Mazarin as Chief Minister, far from it. Mazarin's selection as Chief Minister ignited xenophobia, intrigue, resentment and vitriol. Mazarin became a lightning rod for an irreversible trend of personal attacks on himself and Anne. This is shown by the 5,000–7,000 **Mazarinade** pamphlets that swept across Paris during the **Frondes**.

Hostile pamphleteers habitually referred to Anne as Mazarin's whore and focused upon Mazarin's low birth, greed, lechery, scrounging – and alleged shameful personal tastes. They also condemned him for financial mismanagement, **embezzlement** and misleading the regent, as well as capturing her affections with love potions.

Mazarin was hated for extending the war for personal gain and united opposition, as explained in the next few sections.

Anne's courting of Paris Parlement support for overturning Louis XIII's will had whet the appetite of magistrates for remonstrance. They now sought a leading advisory role to help scale back Louis XIII's policies. When neither of these things proved forthcoming, royal **constitutional powers** were attacked. Anne was something of a pushover for the Paris Parlement. When she stated her intention to have a lit de justice to enforce registration of a forced loan scheme on the richest Parisians, in September 1644, Talon disparaged her authoritarian approach:

'It was an extraordinary and unparalleled act for a king who was still a minor to hold a lit de justice and to have edicts verified by the exercise of his absolute power.'[13]

After a fierce backlash against the 1645 lit de justice, Anne made no formal attempt to overrule the Paris Parlement until January 1648. Conversely, the Paris Parlement became increasingly willing to defend various vested interests (people who were well served by the current system and would defend it against any proposed changes) and taxpayers, as we will now see.

Key terms

Frondes: French for 'sling' (used by Parisian crowds to smash the windows of Mazarin's supporters) and the name for the unrest overall.

Voices from the past

This January 1649 Mazarinade entitled *The Guard at the King's Bed who Tells All* was typical in alleging an affair between Queen and Cardinal:

'People can't doubt it any longer, it's true that he shags her'.[14]

The Parlement of Paris: unrest and opposition

From 1643, Paris Parlement's unrest and opposition involved blocking and challenging:

- finance raising measures
- judicial reviews
- lits de justice.

Dates:	Government action:	Paris Parlement opposition:
July 1643	Ordered **Cours des Aides** to register intendants' new fiscal powers.	Remonstrance, forcing modifications Persuaded Cours des Aides to: a) alter the edict b) demand control of embezzlement cases.
March 1644	Introduced the **toisé** (a tax on houses built near Paris' walls) Referred appeal cases to royal councils, not Parisian sovereign courts.	Omer Talon: a) questioned lost appeal revenue b) warned of riots and provincial parlement resistance unless appeals were heard by the Paris Parlement, forcing the tax's withdrawal.

Dates:	Government action:	Paris Parlement opposition:
July 1644	Resumed toisé collection; royal guard companies assessed property fines Placed all litigational cases under Royal Council control Anne accused Parlement's enquiry and requests chambers of causing tenant riots and disturbances in Paris.	United condemnation of authoritarian taxation Radicals: proposed arresting toisé collectors refused to register it forced its suspension Remonstrances against loss of appeals Mathieu Molé (Paris Parlement President from 1645) accused Anne of slander Appeal and enquiry judges encouraged riots, forcing 90% tax reductions and exemptions.
March 1645	Revived the toisé Arrested Jean-Jacques Barillon (Parlement President until 1645) for demanding guarantees against this.	Immediate protests ended its collection and attempted enforcement Parlement refused to approve any future fiscal expedients, stirred by taxpayers' support and martyr Barillon's death in jail.
1645	Proposed taxing royal domains Used a lit de justice to enforce registration and 18 other financial edicts.	Judges: refused registration created a 'veiled veto', converting the tax to a voluntary levy denounced royal tyranny encouraged Paris merchants to close shops rather than pay, forcing the tax's suspension.
1646–7	Tried enforcing Parisian goods' **tariffs**.	Cours des Aides' rejection and insistance on **exemptions** Parlement: questioned its legality without its authorisation insisted upon registering all future indirect taxes limited the tax to 200,000 livres – well below its estimated 450,000 potential.

Table 1.1: How royal financial policies stirred Paris Parlement unrest and opposition.

Criticising procedure became Parlement's way of obstructing royal judicial interference and cutting D'Hémery's power over judicial reviews:

- 1645: Molé protested against the exiling of parlementary judges for alleged treason
- 1645 and 1647: Judges remonstrated against Intendants
- 1647: Magistrates challenged intendants' role in higher courts and prohibited special commission and royal council appeals.

Magistrates became increasingly willing to fight for various supposedly oppressed vested interest groups, including:

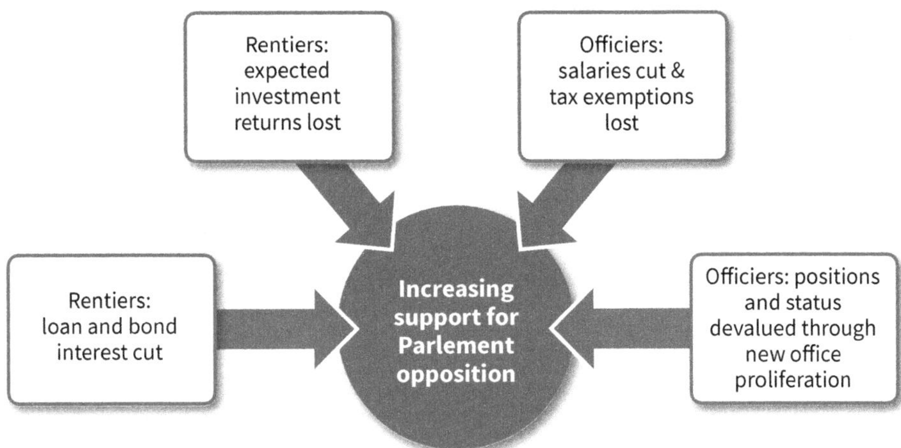

Figure 1.6: Who supported Parlement's increasing opposition to Mazarin and why

In 1644, Parlement rebuffed D'Hémery's attempted tax on Paris' wealthiest merchants, switching the tax onto ***traitants***, hated government tax collecting and office selling financiers.

Royal control was deteriorating:

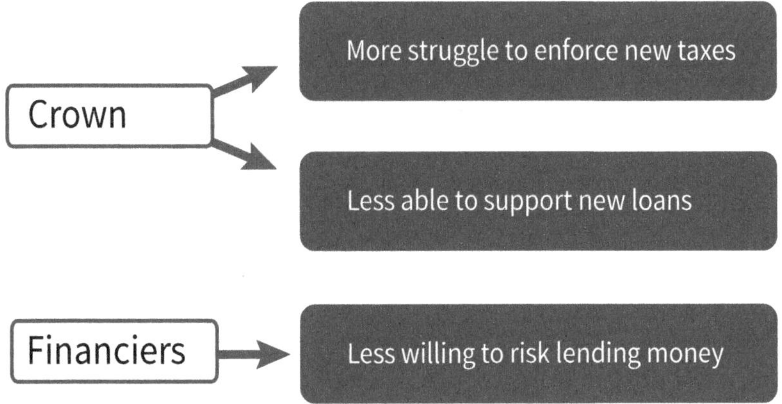

Figure 1.7: Deteriorating royal control over finances by 1648

By 1648:

- Military expenses were up
- Powerful people were alienated
- Social discontent was increasing
- Money-raising was harder.

Anne decided to help Louis XIV hold a lit de justice in Parlement in January 1648. This ordered judges to register new financial edicts and accept:

- new office sales, including 12 new **maîtres des requêtes** (royal judges attached to the King's council)
- Parisian food and wine purchase taxes, tariffs and alienated royal domain tax (alienated domains were lands such as Burgundy whose rule had been transferred to dukes as a form of **patronage**)
- the **franc-fief tax** (on non-nobles who owned property previously in the hands of the nobility), including arrears from 1634.

Anne hoped for magistrates' submission, but miscalculated:

- A lit de justice from a **minority** king seemed like illegal bullying.
- Mazarin was preoccupied by war.
- Government-financier confidence was shattered.
- Judges condemned the edicts; Talon stated they were unlawful without sovereign court examination.

Molé was also shocked at the regency's temerity and neglect of public interest. He denied that Parlement had to submit to the King's personal decree. While not refusing to register the edicts, magistrates persistently amended them, rendering them unviable:

1648:	Actions:	Results:
January	Magistrates banned the proposed alienated royal domain tax. Anne asked whether judges meant to deny the principle of royal absolutism.	Parlement became more radical.
March	Parlement remonstrated and amended the proposed tariff (making it useless).	Parlement found that it could successfully oppose the King.
April	The crown refused to modify and withdraw any edicts. It offered controversial **paulette** renewal terms, for offices to be hereditary. These exempted the Paris Parlement and demanded four years' salary.	Magistrates and officers refused to be divided on the issue and united in denouncing the renewal terms as unlawful.
May	Members of the three sovereign courts and Paris Parlement met together in the **Chambre St Louis** in the **Palais de Justice**. The regency declared this meeting illegal, but still received a list of 27 demands, including: • the paulette's renewal on usual favourable terms • D'Hémery's and intendants' removal • a greater governmental role for the Paris Parlement (regarding office creation, taxation and royal finances) Judges said any tax not registered by them was invalid, forced a 12% taille reduction and insisted on 25% future reductions.	Mazarin: • backed down • replaced D'Hémery with Marshal de la Meilleraye in July 1648 • accepted the Chambre Saint-Louis proposals, reducing the taille and abolishing intendants (except in frontier provinces).

Table 1.2: Unrest and opposition from the Paris Parlement in 1648

Voices from the past

Omer Talon

Parlement's Advocate-General Omer Talon observed:

'Monsieur D'Hémery … established the annual right advantageously for the Parlement of Paris, without any forced loan; with regard to all the other sovereign courts, he cut their salaries for four years. This royal declaration offended all the honest people of the kingdom, either because they received a notable financial prejudice or because of jealously at receiving different treatment from the Parlement of Paris'.[15]

Talon also blamed Mazarin's failure to conclude the war for virtually bankrupting the state:

'There is no cash in the Treasury to meet all these expenses, but only promises and letters of financiers who pay in monthly instalments the sums they have promised. The war plans were drawn up on the assurance of these undertakings. Nevertheless, those who have promised to make these loans do not have cash at hand … As for any credit, it is a matter of public knowledge that the financiers have none'.[16]

Discussion point

1 **What do you think were the principal causes of Louis XIV's financial difficulties?**

Anne and Mazarin had alienated what should have been their natural, conservative, royalist judicial allies and had been outthought and outfought by their opponents in 1648.

Parlement's overt defiance characterised the demands made by the Chambre St-Louis deputies on 3 July 1648:

'No new taxes are to be imposed except as a result of edicts and declarations verified in the sovereign courts which have cognisance … There may be no reduction in the salaries of office holders, no reduction of annuities … except as a result of edicts … properly verified by the courts on a free vote'[17]

All this ruined royal finances. Having consumed the current year's and the following two years' taxes, Mazarin stopped paying bonds and debts.

With war continuing and virtual royal bankruptcy, the situation was explosive.

The spark that ignited matters came in August 1648. Magistrate Pierre Broussel assumed new powers assessing tariffs and investigating:

- gabelle collection
- tax farmer contracts
- royal financiers.

The Frondes

The Frondes were rebellions and civil unrest (1648–53) aimed at:

- overthrowing Mazarin
- personal political gain
- overcoming socio-economic hardship.

This included two major (and one localised) campaigns:

August 1648 and March 1649	Fronde of the parlements
January 1650–February 1653	Aristocratic Fronde
1652–1655	Ormée Fronde, Bordeaux.

ACTIVITY 1.6

Look up and clearly define:

- officiers
- toisé
- Parlement
- franc-fief
- Chambre St-Louis
- Palais de Justice.

ACTIVITY 1.7

Write short biographical notes on:

- Patricelli D'Hémery
- Omer Talon
- Mathieu Molé
- Pierre Brussel.

ACTIVITY 1.8

1 Produce a profile of Mazarin.

2 Create a spider diagram explaining Louis XIII's will and how Anne nullified it.

3 In a two column diagram, show:

   a the financial and political situation Mazarin inherited in 1643

   b how he made things worse.

4 Produce a timeline of Paris Parlement unrest and opposition in this period, regarding:

   a finance raising measures

   b royal judicial reviews

   c challenging lit de justice use.

The Fronde of the parlements

After the (former Duc d'Enghien) Prince of Condé's victory against the Spanish at Lens in August 1648, Mazarin chose to confront Parlement. He intended to arrest Parlement members in a victory ceremony at Notre Dame Cathedral on 26 August. Some magistrates were seized, others escaped. Respected government critic and Paris Parlement magistrate Pierre Broussel's arrest ignited furious protest. A Parisian mob, angry at rising grain prices, rallied to his defence, shouting 'Long live the King, death to Mazarin'. They erected barricades, mobilised a middle-class/artisan militia and forced royal guards to retreat. Paul de Gondi, assistant Archbishop of Paris, led a crowd to the royal palace demanding Broussel's release.

When Anne refused, armed crowds prevented Chancellor Séguier from reaching the Palais de Justice to forbid parlementary debate on the arrests, forcing him to hide in a cellar until the next day. Within two days, Broussel and other judges were released.

Further royal humiliation occurred on 22 October 1648. With Mazarin forced into the background, Gaston and Condé accepted the Chambre Saint-Louis programme. This abolished:

- intendants and extraordinary commissioners
- new office sales
- royal abolitions of parlement decrees
- new forms of taxation assessment and collection
- **lettres de cachet** (letters signed by the king imposing edicts, preventing assemblies and imprisoning individuals without trial).

Parlement's registration of this programme two days later coincided with the Treaty of Westphalia, overshadowing any positive news.

Mazarin and Anne:

- fled Paris with the court for Saint-Germain (20 miles away) on 5–6 January 1649
- approached Condé to attack Paris.

When rumours of this spread, nobles offered to fight for Parlement, including:

- Condé's brother Armand, Prince of Conti
- dukes Longueville and Beaufort.

On 9 January 1649, Parlement:

- dubbed Mazarin 'an enemy of the king and state'[18] who had **usurped** royal authority
- demanded his exile.

An expanding aristocratic **coalition** assembled by Gondi pledged military support to Parlement nine days later, including Charles of Lorraine and Duc de Bouillon and Duke D'Elbeuf. Gondi also coordinated resistance with Aix and Rouen's parlements.

War started soon after. Condé-led royal troops besieged Paris. Conti then sent a letter, purportedly from Mazarin, inviting Habsburg invasion through the Low Countries, but lost Charenton's **garrison** to Condé.

Royal authority remained highly precarious. General Turenne (Bouillon's brother) joined the rebels. Gondi, Bouillon and D'Elbeuf continually incited public disorder and requested Spanish aid to overthrow Mazarin.

January 1649 saw Louis XIV's uncle, England's and Scotland's King Charles I beheaded – a worrying parallel.

Divisions between aristocrats and parlementary royalists weakened the revolt. Loathing extremism, disorder and regicide, Molé actively pursued a compromise, agreeing the Peace of Rueil (March 1649). This confirmed all concessions won by

ACTIVITY 1.9

Look up and define 'lettres de cachet'.

ACTIVITY 1.10

Create a spider diagram showing the terms and significance of the Peace of Rueil

ACTIVITY 1.11

Create a timeline of the main events of the Frondes of the Parlements and add short notes commenting on what you think were the key developments.

Parlement in July and October 1648 and withdrew anti-Mazarin parlementary declarations.

In summary, the Peace of Rueil:

- bought the crown time; when Louis XIV came of age a year later, concessions could be revoked
- ended the war
- allowed Louis XIV's return to Paris.

The aristocratic Frondes

By spreading to Provence, Guyenne and Bordeaux, the Frondes awakened latent aristocratic ambitions:

- Beaufort wanted Brittany's governorship.
- Bouillon wanted control of Sédan.
- Conti wanted disgraced troublemaker **Madame de Chevreuse**'s return.

Gondi and other aristocrats plotted against Mazarin, denouncing the Peace of Rueil as cowardice.

Mazarin tried to divide Parlement and the aristocrats in 1649, by offering:

- magistrates the chance to put prominent Frondeurs on trial
- to pay **officiers'** salaries and **rentiers'** interest.

But he could not stop:

- confrontation between Guyenne's governor and magistrates
- Normandy's courts defying tax farmers
- royalist troop expulsion from Dauphiné
- civil war between Alais' governor and Aix's Parlement.

Condé also was not satisfied. He refused to fight unless he received a leading political role. Mazarin tried to divide rival factions by secretly dealing with Gaston and Gondi, who offered to protect Paris in exchange for Cardinal nomination (this happened in 1652, when Gondi became Cardinal de Retz).

Mazarin threw caution to the wind by arresting Condé, Conti and Longueville (January 1650). His risk-taking backfired. Parlement condemned:

- arrests of princes of the blood royal family members
- violation of Rueil's guarantee of individual freedom against unjust punishment.

This led to the union of parlement and aristocratic Frondeurs on 30 January 1651:

'We the undersigned, recognise from experience the prejudice which the King and the State receive from the detention of Messieurs the princes of Condé and of Conti and the Duc de Longueville ... Cardinal Mazarin is notoriously the author of their detention, and the cause of the disorders which have followed it. He arrested them in order to delay a general peace, and by their arrest hoped further to secure the authority which he had usurped during the Regency. His conduct exposes France to the misfortunes which foreign and civil war can cause a State exhausted of men and money, and there can be no hope of seeing an end to war while he remains in government.'[19]

The three prisoners' wives then instigated aristocratic revolts:

- The Duchesse de Longueville recruited Marshal Turenne, provoked risings in Normandy and signed a peace pact in return for Spanish financial and military help to release her husband and brothers and overthrow Mazarin (April 1650).

- Claire-Clémence de Maille-Brézé (Condé's wife) led resistance in Guyenne, Burgundy and Berry. Subsequently, Bordeaux's parlement joined Condé's supporters against royalist governor Epernon.
- Conti's wife encouraged revolt in Champagne.

Mazarin recalled war-frontline troops, to little avail. Whole areas like Touraine and Bordeaux ceased paying taxes, leaving Mazarin dependent upon high-interest loans.

By October 1650 Burgundy and Bordeaux were recovered, while Turenne was defeated at Rethel. But Turenne's initial Spanish-backed capture of Rethel revealed the Crown's continuing fragility. Mazarin opposed Gondi's Cardinal appointment; by January 1651, Gondi had joined Gaston and Broussel and Molé in opposing Mazarin.

Parlement petitioned Anne, demanding the prisoners' release and Mazarin's dismissal and exile. Mazarin had stirred a hornet's nest of anti-royal resistance.

Facing united opposition, Anne agreed. Mazarin left France in February 1651. He had won a few battles, but lost the war. Aristocrats and magistrates had united against him, accusing him of arresting the princes to boost his own corrupt power and prolong war with Spain, to France's great detriment.

Mazarin, then, not monarchy, was detested. Unlike Mazarin, Anne succeeded in out-thinking the regency's opponents. Parlement and public thanked her for removing Mazarin and agreeing to exclude all foreigners from power. Gondi surrounded the Palais Royal with troops after hearing that Louis had been removed. Anne invited crowds to file through his bedroom (as he feigned sleep) to verify his presence. She created an inner council of Mazarin allies (Lionne, Le Tellier and Servien) to work in his interests, build bridges with magistrates and undermine the unity of Mazarin's enemies. Anne's calculated compliance successfully sowed seeds of Frondeur division.

Condé also alienated allies by:

- making himself Guyenne and Berry governor (controlling 25% of France)
- ignoring other aristocrats' ambitions
- opposing Gondi's Cardinal-bid
- opposing Mademoiselle Chevreuse's marriage to Conti, thereby antagonising the Chevreuse family.

Louis ended his minority and recalled Mazarin in September 1651. Armed resistance would now be against Louis, not Mazarin. Condé now lost battles and allies by:

- accepting Spanish military and financial assistance (November 1651)
- committing war crimes, massacring Parisians (April 1652)
- quarrelling with Turenne who changed sides, restored royal control over Anjou and defeated Condé at Faubourg Saint-Antoine (July 1652).

The Regency's survival in 1651 thus owed as much to aristocratic accident as it did royal design.

Mazarin also contributed to rebel defeat by:

- persuading Anne to give Gondi his Cardinal's hat
- sending troops to defend La Rochelle (November 1651)
- successfully buying off Spanish ally the Duke of Lorraine by June 1652
- choosing a second exile (August 1652–February 1653).

Mazarin's exile transformed public opinion, enabling a popular consensus to build for peace. This was disastrous for Condé, as was Paris' negotiated surrender to Turenne. Mazarin bribed Condé's former ally Gaston to leave Paris. By September 1652, the aristocratic Fronde was finished in Paris, as was Condé, who left to fight for Spain. A month later, Louis made an uncontested entry into Paris and reminded Parlement that it could not obstruct royal edicts.

Parlement registered this compliantly: it would not challenge a royal authority that was being exercised by a divinely appointed king. With the parlement and aristocratic Frondes over, Louis faced few obstacles in extending his authority, at least centrally.

Ormée Fronde

Bordeaux's Ormée Fronde (1652–1653) showed that beyond Paris, more protracted struggles lay ahead. Led by utopian Christophe Dureteste and prompted by a fourfold rise in taxation since 1632, artisan and small business Ormists attacked noble and magistrate timidity, seized power and prepared to fight for fair taxation and health-care for the poor.

They were overthrown in summer 1653. As collapsing wine and bread trade caused starvation, Mazarin conspired with local magistrates to send troops to Bordeaux. Dureteste was tried and executed, and the last remnants of Frondeur resistance shattered.

ACTIVITY 1.12

1 Research and write one paragraph each on the Fronde role of:
- Condé
- Conti
- Duchesse de Longueville
- Duchesse de Chevreuse
- Christophe Dureteste.

2 Make notes on the individual roles played by Anne, Mazarin and Condé in helping end the aristocratic Fronde.

3 Briefly summarise the Ormée Fronde causes and events.

France and Europe

The rise of French power at the expense of the Habsburgs, 1643–1648

Before 1643, French security had been threatened, but Spanish threats repelled. In 1636, the Spanish had invaded Burgundy from their base in Franche Comté before being forced to retreat. The Spanish had also retaken Valtelline in northern Italy in 1637. By 1643, the tide had turned in France's favour with Arras, Roussillon and Perpignan all taken.

From 1643, French forces were getting the upper hand against the Habsburgs. This was just as well, as Anne had brought Mazarin into the regency council for his perceived skill in international relations and to secure optimum foreign policy advantages for France.

ACTIVITY 1.13

Mazarin survived the Parlement and aristocratic Frondes. Discuss whether you think this was due to:

- luck
- his political skills
- the regent's political skills
- something else entirely?

Mazarin was far more successful in fighting his enemies abroad than his enemies at home. His foreign policy was increasingly successful after 1643 from a military perspective. Mazarin's foreign policy was increasingly successful after 1643 from a military perspective. His first three years as Cardinal saw French victories against the Emperor and Spain orchestrated by Condé (Duc d'Enghien). In 1643, Condé killed over half of Spanish forces at Rocroi. He then followed this up by:

- pushing onwards towards the **Palatinate**, in order to deal with the threat to France's eastern border posed by Habsburg ally the **Elector**-Duke of Bavaria
- defeating the Bavarians in the Battle of Freiburg in 1644
- occupying the key fortified town of Phillipsburg.

This strengthened French border security along the Rhine and helped to prevent Habsburg attack. Turenne's occupation of other key fortifications and towns, including Worms and Mainz, also tightened French control of the Rhine.

Gaston's appointment as French army commander in Flanders in 1644 also helped to enhance French power at Habsburg expense. His campaign to take towns on the way to Dunkirk bore fruit, with the surrender of Gravelines (1644) and the occupation of Courtrai, Mardyck and Furnes thereafter. Condé also boosted France's north-eastern security at Spanish expense by capturing Ypres and Dunkirk in 1646. Dunkirk was a major port linking the North Sea and English Channel, so its loss significantly weakened Spain's naval threat.

Key terms

Palatinate: a territory on the Rhine, part of the **Holy Roman Empire**. Its Count was one of the imperial electors. Formerly the emperor of the Holy Roman Empire had been elected by a group of nobles called the electors. By the 17th century the crown was the hereditary possession of the Habsburgs, but the title of 'elector' remained.

Elector: a German prince entitled to take part in choosing the Holy Roman Emperor.

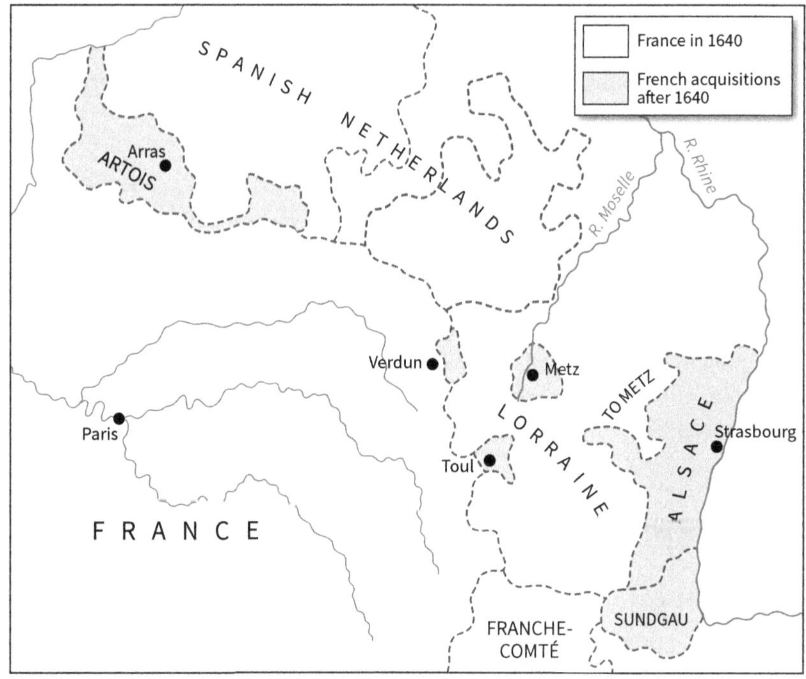

Figure 1.8: France's gains on its north-eastern frontier 1643–59

Mazarin also shrewdly strengthened France's position against the Habsburg threat. By sending French troops to support Catalan and Portuguese rebels against the King of Spain, Mazarin tied up enemy soldiers and left Spanish King Philip IV facing the threat of political disintegration in the Iberian Peninsula. Mazarin also built up support for France's allies in the war.

He negotiated the Peace of Brömsebro between France's ally Sweden and Denmark in 1645. Sweden had been fighting Denmark since 1643, which caused it to divert troops away from fighting the Habsburgs in Germany. Mazarin's negotiated peace and alliance with Denmark enabled Sweden to again fully focus its resources upon fighting the Habsburgs in Germany and support French interests. As a result, Turenne was able to link up with Swedish commander Wrangel and invade Bavaria in 1646.

Mazarin subsidised George Rákóczy, Prince of Transylvania, thereby securing him as an ally. Rákóczy promised to lend military support to the Swedes in Germany and to a rebellion against Habsburg Emperor Ferdinand III in Hungary. This strengthened French power by diverting and tying down Habsburg troops from the war with France.

The Cardinal arranged the marriage of a French princess, Marie de Gonzague-Nevers (daughter of the Duke of Mantua) and Polish King Wladislaus IV. This strengthened the potential threat to Ferdinand III's Empire along its north-eastern border.

Mazarin further increased French power by pushing back Habsburg-Bavarian troops at Nordlingen in 1645. Turenne's invasion of Bavaria in 1646 temporarily removed the Habsburgs' main ally from the war. French military supremacy was confirmed by the crushing defeat of the Imperial-Bavarian army at Zusmarshausen in May 1648. This enabled French invasion of Austria, threatening Vienna and Prague's capture. Habsburg power and threats to France seemed a distant memory.

By 1648, Mazarin's foreign policy showed some military successes. With Habsburg forces crushed at Lens and Spain's army near disintegration, Mazarin undoubtedly put France in a strong negotiating position. What can be disputed, however, is the speed and extent of Mazarin's end product from the war. Mazarin had taken too long to achieve peace, squandered the opportunity for conclusive forms and left France's vulnerable frontier security incomplete.

The Peace of Westphalia, 1648

After negotiating since 1644, France signed the Westphalia peace with Habsburg Emperor Ferdinand III, German princes and Sweden, in October 1648. Much was gained for France, but Mazarin was never thanked for this. Westphalia had taken too long to achieve and coincided with Parlement's registration of the demands of the Chambre Saint-Louis. This deprived Mazarin of the diplomatic glory he craved, as he lamented:

'You must admit that it requires a commitment to the very limit and a quite extraordinary zeal to redouble one's effort in public service – as I do – when one is treated so badly and at a time when it would seem possible to say without vanity that my efforts are beginning to bear fruit.'[20]

Mazarin had something of a point. France's exhaustive military effort had been fairly well rewarded. French control was confirmed over Metz, Toul, Verdun and bishoprics of Lorraine, along with Moyenic, Baccart and Rambervillers, also in Lorraine. France's eastern border security and Rhineland presence was strengthened by the gains of Breisach and the right to garrison Philippsburg.

This gave some security against Habsburg attacks from Franche Comté. French possession of Pinerolo was also confirmed, affording a valuable buffer against Habsburg incursions from northern Italy. French dominance was confirmed as Ferdinand surrendered Habsburg rights in Upper and Lower Alsace. France gained 'full sovereignty' over ten Imperial cities (including Münster and Landau) and most of the Rhineland between the Palatinate and the Swiss Confederation, as this summary map shows:

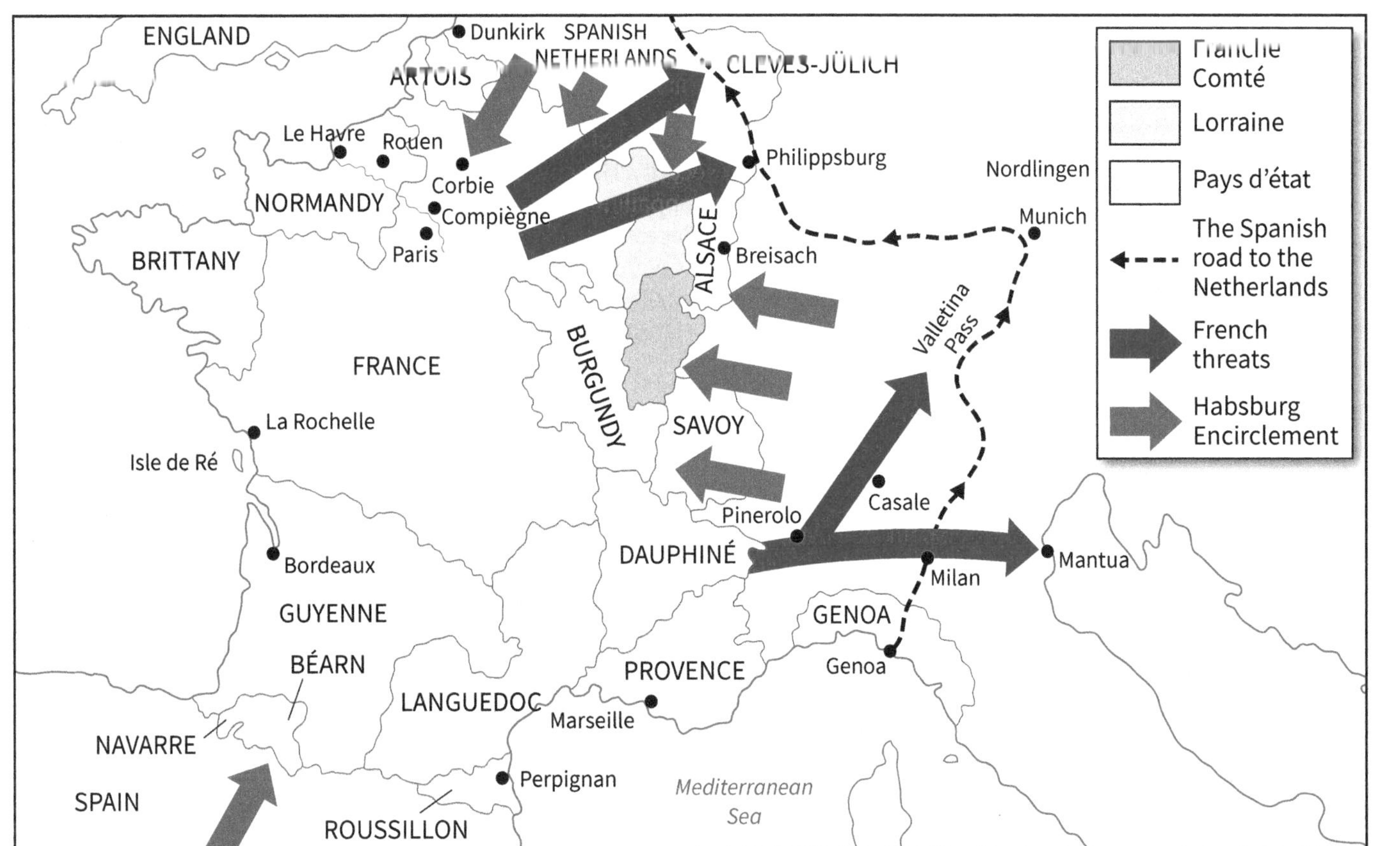

Figure 1.9: France's gains at the 1648 Treaty of Westphalia and 1659 Treaty of Pyrenees

Westphalia also significantly weakened Habsburg power by strengthening France's allies:

- Brandenburg gained Minden and Halberstadt
- Sweden effectively controlled almost the entire German coastline
- German elector princes and imperial cities were granted independence.

France now had established itself as the defender of its allies' rights and independence against Habsburg imperial power. This was a good outcome. Much had been achieved, but neither quickly nor in full.

Arguably, Mazarin's gains were too little too late. Mazarin was slow to prioritise and conclude peace. In 1646, he preferred a campaign against Spain in Italy, consuming sizeable resources that could have been deployed elsewhere. France's seizure of Piombino was of scant value to its bankrupt treasury and oppressed taxpayers. Mazarin further delayed peace with Spain by refusing to accept Philip as king of Portugal and not initiating talks with Spain's ambassador.

He also bungled the peace negotiations. Delusions of grandeur seem to have played a part. So too did Mazarin's desperation for peace, exacerbated by mounting internal disorder. Victory at Rocroi made him believe France could seize the Spanish Netherlands. Mazarin surreptitiously suggested this to Spain behind his Dutch allies' back, displaying a lack of tact and self-control. When his Dutch allies learned of this, they unilaterally concluded a separate peace in January 1648. This emboldened Spain in future negotiations.

Richard Wilkinson correctly calls Westphalia a 'flawed achievement'.[21]

Mazarin had secured neither of Richelieu's aims:

- ending the war with Spain
- pacifying Lorraine, which remained at war with France.

Subsequently, France's control of Alsace was precarious and inadequate, as was its north-eastern border security. Habsburg control of fortress capital city Strasbourg remained. Westphalia's appallingly vague terms left ten Alsace towns and local nobles able to retain their 'privileges' regarding the Empire, providing that these privileges did not weaken France's sovereignty. French dominance and border clarification was incomplete. When Westphalia and Mazarin were widely criticised, the point was being missed. War had been prolonged by incompetence, not intention.

With the Frondes' onset, Spain had renewed optimism that a fight could force a French surrender. In 1648, France was ruing missed opportunities, unable either to defeat Spain or force a Spanish surrender. Cue a Spanish fightback.

Between 1648–53, there was little prospect of France emerging supreme against Spain, at least on its own. The Frondes deprived Mazarin of his two best war generals, Turenne and Condé. It also provided a window of opportunity for a frustrating and humiliating Spanish fightback. Driven out of Catalonia, French armies also surrendered the Italian fortresses of Casale and Montferrato, along with Gravelines and Dunkirk in Flanders.

Dunkirk was hopelessly defended, with no army within 50 miles. Of the eight French ships that engaged an Anglo-Spanish force at Dunkirk in 1652, seven were sunk or captured. When Condé led a Spanish force which besieged Rocroi for ten days in 1653 and a joint Spanish-Lorraine attack on Arras in 1654, the trend of a defensive French fighting capacity was well and truly established.

At this moment of crisis, in 1652, France's greatest general Turenne was reconciled to the crown and government, because:

- He had married. This put an end to the power the Duchesse de Longueville held over him (he had previously been captivated by her).
- Mazarin's exile and Anne's concessions had reassured him.

Turenne's return as commander of the King's men in 1652 was pivotal to France gaining the upper hand in the war. With Turenne in command, French forces:

- captured Sainte-Menehould and Monzon in 1653
- drove Condé's army back from Arras
- captured Quesnoy and Stenay
- defeated Condé at Landrecies in 1655.

On the other hand, Turenne was defeated at Valenciennes in 1656. This strengthened Spanish morale and reluctance to compromise with French peace demands, thereby prolonging the war.

Turenne left Spain on the back foot, but undefeated. Evolution, not revolution, therefore characterised the rise of French power until 1658. A pivotal part was played by the end of civil war in France and its continuation in Catalonia, Portugal and Milan. Mazarin's reflective and skilful diplomacy also played a key part. After hearing that Spain sought military support from Cromwell, Mazarin immediately set about enticing him to aid France instead. He persuaded Henrietta Maria, Charles II and their court to leave France in 1654 and signed the Treaty of Westminster in November 1655. This wooed Cromwell by ending mutual trade embargos and French attacks on English ships. Mazarin also promised not to give refuge to any Cromwell enemy in France and to expel James, Duke of York.

Collaboration with an economic rival seemed odd, as did neglecting the dynastic rights of Louis XIV's aunt Henrietta Maria and her Stuart children. But it proved an undoubted masterstroke. It offered Mazarin a guarantee against exiled Frondeurs seeking asylum in England and above all, an opportunity for a full-blown military alliance to defeat Spain. The knockout blow duly arrived in 1658, when 6,500 well equipped English troops helped Turenne to rout the Spanish at the Battle of the Dunes. An English fleet also helped to recapture Dunkirk, thereby ending Spanish control of the English Channel and the North Sea. Now there was no stopping Turenne, who captured Gravelines, Ypres, Menin and Furnes in Flanders. Outnumbered, humiliated and bankrupt, Philip IV of Spain would now have to accept a punishing peace treaty.

Repugnant though Mazarin's alliance with Protestant Republican England may have seemed, it undoubtedly proved the right move at the right time.

Diplomatically, if not domestically, Mazarin was very successful in increasing French power. He did fail to encourage revolt in Naples and to secure the support of German electors for Louis to succeed Ferdinand as Emperor after his death in 1657. Instead, his son Leopold was anointed as Holy Roman Emperor. But he had notable successes. By playing on German princes' fears of renewed Habsburg imperial ambitions after Leopold's succession, he created the **League of German Princes** in 1658. This afforded France the right to 'protect' long stretches of the Rhineland, thereby strengthening its border and opportunity for pre-emptive military action. The peace settlement he achieved a year later eclipsed everything achieved so far and surpassed all expectations.

The Treaty of the Pyrenees, 1659

Mazarin failed to secure German electors' support for Louis to succeed Ferdinand as Emperor after his death in 1657. Instead, Ferdinand's son Leopold was chosen. But diplomatically, Mazarin was very successful in increasing French power. The League of German Princes afforded France:

- 'protection' of long stretches of the Rhineland
- strengthened border security
- opportunities for launching pre-emptive military strikes against the Habsburgs.

The Treaty of the Pyrenees was signed in November 1659. This confirmed all French gains at Westphalia and French supremacy over Spain. France:

- gained Roussillon and Cerdagne in the south
- subsequently established a sovereign council and control in Roussillon
- gained all of Artois (except Aire and St Omer), Gravelines, Landrecies, Le Quesnoy, Avesnes and Thionville in the north
- controlled Luxembourg by gaining Montmédy
- effectively controlled Lorraine; this was to be returned to Duke Charles IV as France's defortified satellite state
- annexed Barrois in Lorraine entirely, gaining rights of military access, and quartering and provisioning of troops
- persuaded Philip IV to cede Jülich to the Duke of Neuburg, a French ally.

These gains shattered Habsburg prestige and exposed the Emperor's German and Austrian territories to further attack, along with the Spanish Netherlands and Spain itself.

Here was a significantly better settlement for France than Westphalia, secured by crushing victories such as Dunes (1658) and its aftermath and skilful diplomacy. Arguably, this justified the continuation of war. Louis also received a trump card by gaining Spanish consent to marry Maria Theresa. As the only surviving child of Philip IV's first marriage, there being no male heir, she afforded an opportunity for Louis to gain the Spanish inheritance after Philip IV's death. This included:

- Spain's Italian lands, including Milan, Naples, Genoa, Sardinia and Sicily
- the Spanish Netherlands and land in Flanders
- the Spanish Indies
- Mexico, Central America and all South America except Brazil
- the Canaries and garrisons of Oran and Cueta (in modern-day Algeria and Morocco respectively) in Africa.

Mazarin elicited Philip IV's consent with a cunning theatrical ruse. By broadcasting Louis' intended betrothal to the Duke of Savoy's daughter Marguerite and sending France's court to Lyon to finalise terms, he horrified Philip who promptly consented to Louis marrying Maria Theresa.

Mazarin was also shrewd enough to ensure that French gains were, in Geoffrey Treasure's words 'substantial, but not provocatively excessive'.[22]

Louis conditionally renounced all claims to Spain's throne for a 500,000 gold-**écu** dowry payment. This seemed unlikely to be paid given the woeful state of Spanish finances (see Chapter 3, France and Spain). So it seemed likely that Maria Theresa's claims, and those of her children with Louis, would stand, thereby affording the Sun King an opportunity to seize the vast Spanish Empire.

French sensitivity to European opinion and the balance of power was also reflected in handing back:

- Dunkirk and Mardyke to England
- Barrois to Lorraine and affirming its independence in the 1661 Treaty of Vincennes, in response to the Duke of Lorraine's refusal to accept the treaty; Mazarin gained villages providing a French military corridor into Germany, solving the problem of Lorraine by removing its territorial integrity.

Mazarin also:

- pardoned traitor Condé and returned all his lands to him
- abandoned France's claim to Catalonia and support for her Portuguese allies, for now at least.

Ultimately, Mazarin showed the finesse in foreign affairs that he had lacked in domestic ones. David Maland accurately describes the Peace of the Pyrenees as 'the greatest moment in French history over the past hundred years'.[23] France certainly had never had such an advantageous international position, or a better level of national security and opportunities for future expansion. No wonder that part of an inscription above the arch erected above the Porte Saint-Antoine for Louis' formal entry to Paris with his new bride, Maria Theresa praised the peace 'gained by the diligent aid of Jules Mazarin'.[24]

ACTIVITY 1.14

Look up and define:

- Treaty of Westphalia
- Treaty of Westminster
- Battle of Dunes
- Treaty of the Pyrenees
- Maria Theresa
- League of German Princes
- Treaty of Vincennes.

ACTIVITY 1.15

Create a timeline of 1643–1661 and add notes drawing attention to French military and diplomatic successes.

The condition of France at the accession of Louis XIV in 1661

Figure 1.10: Louis XIV literally saw and paraded himself as Apollo in ballets, showing his belief that his influence was universal and that he had no need for a First Minister

Whether Mazarin's foreign policy gains merited the strain upon France is debateable. Mazarin had left Louis a strong but mixed hand. France in 1661 was beset with inherent opportunities and weaknesses:

- politically, the preconditions existed for Louis confidently to assert his personal authority in 1661, but barriers and challenges remained
- economically, France was stagnating
- socially, the essential bonds of interdependence between Crown and elites were strengthened, but huge gaps existed between rich and poor, threatening disorder.

Let's examine these in turn.

Politics

Louis was mentally conditioned to rule by himself immediately after Mazarin died. He was baptised Louis Dieudonné (Louis the God-given) after his parents' 23 years of childless marriage and four miscarriages. Jean Bodin's sixteenth-century Divine Right theory enhanced his 'God-given' status, stating that:

- sovereigns were God's custodians
- held all legitimate power
- could never be actively resisted or limited by human laws.

Such beliefs inevitably gave Louis great confidence in his personal authority and mandate for asserting it, especially in defence of French Catholicism.

Vindication of Louis' divine supremacy also came from his coming-of-age ceremony in September 1651. Louis displayed himself ostentatiously to Parisians as a living embodiment of Apollo (the Greek sun God, whose influence was universal).

Every aspect of Louis' five-hour coronation ceremony in June 1654 was stage-managed to promote Louis' divine legitimacy:

What happened:	**What it meant:**
Receiving **Charlemagne**'s crown	Louis' lineage was ancient and his legitimacy as king beyond question
Holding a sceptre and jewelled sword of state	Louis held all political and military power
Being acclaimed by 2,000 nobles	France was unified under Louis' single sovereign authority
Being anointed by oil from the sacred phial of **St Clovis** (reputedly sent from heaven)	God had, without question, appointed and blessed Louis as king
Louis' ceremonial touching of scrofula (a form of tuberculosis) sufferers stating: 'the king touches you, may God cure you.'[25]	Louis was God's deputy and embodiment on earth.

Table 1.3: Louis' coronation ceremony and its significance

The Frondes also developed Louis' readiness for personal rule. The rebels' loyalty to Louis justified this. Mazarin had taught Louis much about engendering noble compliance through the carrot of compromise, bribery and patronage. Such steps included:

- pardoning almost all Frondeurs
- his political ploy with Gaston to arrest Condé

- offering 530,000 livres, a dukedom and complete amnesty to secure the Comte du Daugnon's allegiance and control of vital ports in the southwest
- marrying his nieces to Louis de Bourbon and Conti.

Louis' grounding for kingship also involved:

- being instructed in government procedures by Mazarin and Anne
- overseeing the Council of State from 1649
- ordering Gondi's arrest – on his own authority – in December 1652
- daily examination of government matters with Mazarin during 1653–55
- confidently rebuking the Paris Parlement in April 1655 for ignoring his lit de justice to register 14 fiscal edicts
- gaining insight into military affairs by observing Turenne's victories at Monzon and Dunes
- direct military intervention with Mazarin to subjugate Marseille to royal authority in January 1660.

By sending 6,000 soldiers to Marseille, Louis curtailed challenges to new fiscal charges and royal authority and removed opportunities for resistance. By personally entering Marseilles and prohibiting its elites from making administrative appointments without royal governor approval, Louis and Mazarin firmly placed it under royal control. Politically astute and confident 'beyond his years'[26], Louis had no need for a Chief Minister after Mazarin's death. He would be his own man and king.

However, the political situation in 1661 was not at all suited to confrontational rule. Political 'give and take' was clearly required:

- Divine right theory categorically rejected any form of tyrannical rule. It emphasized two things as being above the King's will: God's judgement and fundamental laws (such as Succession Law). This precluded anyone other than a surviving male heir from succeeding Louis.
- Louis therefore had to respect existing laws and the authority of sovereign courts
- The Frondes highlighted the futility of a coercive approach towards the Paris Parlement.
- The deaths of royalist Parlementaires Talon in 1652, and de Mesme in 1650 had weakened the crown's influence in the Paris Parlement
- Sovereign courts had successfully obstructed proposals to restore intendants and impose new taxes during 1653–4 and 1656.

Mazarin had already shown the value of coexistence rather than coercion by:

- reducing royal interventions in **judicial** appointments and processes
- accepting Parlement's right and scope for remonstrance after lits de justice in 1652 and 1655
- scaling back new intendant appointments, thereby halting the trend towards conciliar justice
- increasing backhand financier payments (totalling 67% and 79% of secret payments in 1654 and 1657 respectively).

By 1661, the crown and Parlement had realised they needed not to trespass on one another's territory. A similar situation emerged with other vested interests. Paid well above 5% interest, rentiers allowed war finance borrowing on a staggering scale:

Year:	**Sum borrowed:**
1655	32.8 million
1656	78.6 million
1657	74.7 million.

Table 1.4: Increases in borrowing to finance the war effort

Proliferating **venal** office sales – totalling 60,000 in 1661 – netted short term popularity and cash, but undermined royal control of taxation. So too did reliance upon tax farms; by 1658, only 11% of taxes actually reached the treasury. Louis' authority, then, had well-defined limits. The crown's security rested upon consensus, not conflict.

Economy

With a 451 million debt, France's finances were in serious disarray in 1661, as was its pre-industrial economy. This was predominantly based around agriculture, not large industries. It was also neglected badly and damaged by royal policies, where they existed. Richelieu's strategy was to found French colonies and stimulate communications and French naval production. He *attempted* 'constructive' economic reforms, including:

- *promoting road and canal building and trying to make rivers navigable* – by completing the important Seine-Loire link in 1642 and reducing most **péages** (road and river **tolls**)
- *founding France's navy* – garrisons at Toulon and La Rochelle protected pirate raids on French ships
- *stimulating ship building, creating thousands of jobs* – from no naval vessels in 1626, France had 63 ocean-worthy warships from Atlantic ports by 1642 and a 22-galley Mediterranean fleet.
- *establishing French colonies* – Richelieu founded New France (modern day Nova Scotia), French Baltic merchant colonies and thriving French slave profiteering and sugar manufacture in the Caribbean, with over 7,000 French colonists established on Martinique, St Kitts and Guadeloupe.

Far from being wonderfully transformed, however, France's economy was woefully inadequate, especially in infrastructure and opportunities for prosperity. Agriculture – involving 85% of the population – remained backward, with inadequate use of manure, insufficient scientific breeding and ineffective ploughs. Communication was equally inadequate. Serious barriers to merchant urban trade and wealth remained. Bad roads and bandit-infested districts like Périgord frequently forced merchants to make 100-mile detours. Internal trade remained prohibitively costly and time consuming. Transporting a bale of cloth from Rouen to Lyon took a month; travelling between Paris and Bordeaux two weeks. Colonial enterprise was extremely limited, with just 200 French 'New France' and Quebec colonists by 1642. Constantly threatened by **Native Americans**, bad weather, wild animals and inadequate financial support, French colonists struggled to compete with settlers from Britain.

Richelieu's excessive regulations aimed at increasing quality and production, but also hindered prosperity. Inspectors interfered with iron and beer production and master craftsmen could not produce without a permit, thereby stifling initiative.

Various regions suffered economic devastation from war: Picardy, Champagne, Île-de-France, Artois, Anjou and Bordeaux. Sporadic troop incursions brought arson, rape and robbery.

Mazarin's policies further harmed trade. By placing prohibitive duties on English textiles in 1654, Finance Superintendant Nicholas Fouquet encouraged English exclusion and confiscation of French wine, thereby damaging its biggest export market. Merchants were united in hostility to royal policy. Complaints included 'intolerable losses for Guyenne and the entire Loire region'. Parisian tradesmen also bemoaned foreign powers 'forbidding entry of our merchandise or imposing new duties on it; in either event the consequence is only loss of revenue for his Majesty and lack of employment for his subjects.'[27]

Mazarin's failure to quickly conclude war exposed the fragility of French naval protection for merchant textile interests in Rouen, Saint-Malo and Atlantic ports. These were severely damaged in 1656–7 when French ships covertly exporting to

Spanish America were captured or destroyed. By 1661, production costs and foreign imports had soared. Cloth, linen, leather, paper and sugar trade and manufacture in Rouen and across Normandy had collapsed.

Like an ailing football team of underachieving prima donna show ponies, France's economy in 1661 was misfiring badly and performing poorly compared to its competitors. It certainly was not producing the goods, literally:

- French mines and factories produced only a third of England's, even though France's population was two thirds higher at 20 million
- Industrial production and overseas trade lagged behind the Dutch Republic.

Key terms

Estates: the three social groups of French society: the clergy (First Estate) the nobility (Second estate) and the bourgeoisie and peasantry (Third estate).

Society

The structure of French society in 1661 was based around its system of '**Estates**':

Within this system, various tensions existed, not least between the **noblesse de robe** (**robe nobility**) and the **noblesse d'épée** (sword nobility). Sword nobles and **officiers** resented the ennoblement of robe nobles through increasing administrative office sales. These undermined the prestige and value of their own investments and the notion that military or feudal service was the benchmark of noble status.

Tensions also existed between the 'estates'. The tax system exempted those who could afford the most:

- the **First Estate** (clergy)
- the **second estate** (nobility)
- the **Third Estate bourgeoisie** (judicial, town council and financial administration office buyers).

It thus disproportionately hit those least able to pay, the **peasantry**. This group made up about 75% of the population. Of them, about 75% were subsistence farmers working poor land. Agricultural backwardness meant that they could not meet the rises in taxation. The **tithe** (a 10% tax of income paid to the church) was a further burden. The near doubling of taxes since 1635 intolerably strained peasant income. By 1661, the taxation burden reached its highest point, triggering an upsurge in disorder and rebellion.

Protest against mounting sales taxes and coercive collection methods saw municipal-council chambers invaded in Angers in 1656. Tax collectors were lynched in Guyenne 1655–6, as shown by a Council of Finance decree from May 1656:

'For several years frequent rebellions and uprisings have arisen in several towns and parishes of the election of Bordeaux ... the inhabitants have not imposed the taxes of 1655 nor the taxes for the present year 1656 ... They have attacked and assaulted the **bailiffs** and fusiliers sent to coerce payment from them, and have killed several of them.'[28]

Royal troops were slow to quell the **Sabotier rebellion** in 1658. Rebellions continued around Gien, Montargis and Clamecy within the généralité of Orléans, making tax collection 'impossible'[29]

So widespread was the Anjou and Normandy 1658 anti-tax movement that it attracted Condé's backing and Colbert feared that 'a league of lesser nobles might gain all the provinces of the realm'[30]

Aristocratic connivance in revolt was so habitual that nobles revolted in nine of 13 provinces on the 1650s. The lack of order and control over provincial society was also reflected in the relative immunity from taxation of pays d'états; while covering a third

Key terms

A **dynasty** is a family that holds on to a measure of power over several generations. '**Dynastic ambitions**' are thus the ambitions to increase power, retain power and pass power to the next generation. This was often achieved through marriages with other dynasties.

ACTIVITY 1.16

Look up and summarise:

- Péages
- First estate
- Second estate
- Third estate
- Bourgeoisie
- Princes of the blood.

ACTIVITY 1.17

Write short biographical notes on Jean Bodin.

of France, they only contributed a tenth of royal income. By 1661, intendants reported the need to tackle the grossly disproportionate tax burden to Colbert:

'Less than half of the land in the kingdom is liable to the taille; the nobles who own the greater part pay nothing; the citizens of several towns who own land in the surrounding countryside are exempt by privilege, office, or favour; only the miserable peasant has to pay.'[31]

Increasing social division was also exacerbated by proliferating secret payments, rentes and office sales. These afforded tax exemption, salaries, pensions and embezzlement opportunities. In 1661, about 37% of taxes paid reached the Treasury. Prospects for self-enrichment also abounded for tax farmers, who increasingly collected royal taxes and siphoned off as much as 70%. Over 66% of tax-farm revenue was swallowed up through spiralling collection costs, pensions and secret payments to rentiers. By 1661, interest payments on royal debt reached 27 million. Social division was further reflected politically. Unlike the Third **estate**, the elites wielded power over judicial affairs and taxation, especially in the provincial estates.

Mazarin's determination to fund the war and avoid further Frondes saw conciliation, not confrontation, of vested interests. He cultivated a reciprocal relationship with the nobles known as princes of the blood. Most Frondeurs were allowed to return to their estates and pursue a lifestyle reflecting their lifestyle and **dynastic** ambitions. For Turenne (in 1650) and Condé (in 1660), this meant returning with a full pardon as generals. With his reputation restored, Mazarin was happy to be embraced as Louis XIV's chief subordinate and exemplify the new noble ideal of courtier gentleman. Having built bridges and renewed bonds of interdependence with his most natural supporters, Louis XIV was well placed for personal rule in 1661.

Timeline

1610–1643	Louis XIII king of France
1615	Louis XIII married Anne of Austria
1624–1642	Armand Jean du Plessis de Richelieu French Chief Minister of France
1626–1629	Huguenot revolts
1629	Edict of Grace (or 'of Alès')
1635	Richelieu took France into the Thirty Years War
1638	Birth of Louis
1635	Académie Française
1640	Cornelius Jansen's Augustinus published
1640	Royal printing press founded
1641	Paris Parlement forced to register an edict preventing it from discussing state affairs without royal permission
1642	Seine-Loire link completed
1643	Louis XIII died
1643	Duc D'Enghien's victory over Spain at Rocroi
1643	Patricelli D'Hémery became finance minister

1643	Cours des Aides ordered to register intendants' new fiscal powers
1643	Condé's victory at Rocroi
1644	Condé's defeat of Bavaria at Freiburg
1644	Gravelines' surrender
1644	Toisé introduced
1644	Toisé collection resumed amid difficulties
1645	Edict taxing royal domains; Molé and Talon denounced royal tyranny; tax suspended
1648	Conflict with Paris Parlement regarding alienated royal domain tax
1648	Anne helped Louis XIV hold a lit de justice in the Paris Parlement in January
1648	Magistrate Pierre Broussel assumed new powers over taxation
1648–53	The Frondes
1649	Peace of Rueil
1649	Mazarin, Anne and court fled Paris for Saint-Germain
1652	Gondi nominated as a Cardinal (took the title Cardinal de Retz)
1650	Mazarin arrested Condé; Conti and Longueville: 'princes of the blood'
1651	Mazarin left France in February
1651	Louis' coming-of-age ceremony in September
1651	Louis ended his minority and recalled Mazarin in September
1651	Condé committed treason by accepting Spanish military and financial assistance
1652	Battle of Faubourg Saint-Antoine
1652–1653	Mazarin's chosen second exile
1654	Louis' coronation in June
1654	Queen Henrietta Maria and Charles II of England and Scotland left France
1655	Treaty of Westminster
1656	Turenne was defeated at Valenciennes
1657	Emperor Ferdinand's death; Leopold elected
1658	Battle of the Dunes
1658	League of German Princes
1659	The Treaty of the Pyrenees
1661	Treaty of Vincennes
1661	Jules Mazarin's death
1661	Louis XIV took personal control of affairs

Practice essay questions

1. How far had Mazarin's foreign policy been successful by 1661?
2. 'Mazarin handled opposition poorly in the years 1643–53.' Explain why you agree or disagree.
3. 'Inept royal financial policy was the biggest reason for the Frondes between 1648 and 1653.' Explain why you agree or disagree.
4. 'Louis XIV was extremely well placed to extend his political authority by 1661.' Explain why you agree or disagree with this view.
5. 'Economic backwardness was by far the biggest problem Louis XIV inherited in 1661.' Explain why you agree or disagree with this view.
6. 'The Treaty of Westphalia failed to achieve French ambitions.' Explain why you agree or disagree.
7. With reference to these sources and your understanding of the historical context, which of these two sources is the more valuable in explaining Fouquet's contribution as finance minister between 1654 and 1661?

Extract A

Nicolas Fouquet's letter to his fellow minister and adviser to Louis XIV, Le

Tellier, undated (after his arrest) explaining his defence and points to be made to the King.

'... All those who during the minority and during the wars carried arms against his Majesty, excited troubles on his state, wished to remove his crown, assisted in the councils of factious individuals ... all such individuals are left in peace, enjoying their wealth, their offices ... Monsieur Le Tellier well knows that at the end of 1654, Servien and even the Cardinal himself had run out of money and the entire kingdom was on the edge of disaster. At this point, I took over Servien's responsibilities and through my zeal and application – but what is more through my own resources and those of my friends – I restored the state finances and kept them going through crisis after crisis over a period of seven years, so that we not only had all we needed but also prevailed over our enemies. I may have done some blameworthy things, but I did what I had to do since it was the only way to avert disaster'.

Source : Fouquet's letter to Le Tellier, cited and translated by Adolphe Cheruel, *Mémoires sur la vie publique et privée de Fouquet, Surintendant des Finances* (2 vols., Paris, 1862), vol. 2, pp. 262–70

Extract B

At least some five years afterwards, Louis XIV, helped by his ministers, wrote about Fouquet's arrest in a private memoir intended to advise the Dauphin about government.

It might seem strange that I still employed Fouquet once I knew of his thefts, but I knew he was intelligent and very knowledgeable, which made me think that, provided he avowed his past faults and promised to correct them, he might serve me well. I therefore placed Colbert beside him as controller but he could not stop his excessive expenditure in fortifying and beautifying his palaces, forming secret factions against me and putting in the hands of his friends important sources of income which he had gained at my expense, hoping to pay himself back when he became the chief minister. All of France, convinced like me of the Surintendant's misconduct, applauded his arrest.

Source : Extract from Louis' 'Mémoires', adapted translations from J. Longnon, ed., *Mémoires de Louis XIV* (Paris, 1927)

Chapter summary

You should now understand the context in which Louis XIV came to the throne as a child, including the problems bequeathed to him by his father, and the influence of Richelieu and Mazarin. You will also have grasped how France was ruled, and by whom, during his minority. From reading this chapter, you will:

- know the key features of Richelieu's and Louis XIII's legacy in 1643
- assess that legacy's relative strengths and weaknesses
- understand the roles of Anne of Austria and Mazarin
- understand why opposition and unrest arose during Louis XIV's minority
- understand the reasons for, main events and results of, the Frondes
- judge how far French power rose against the Habsburgs from 1643 and after the treaties of Westphalia and Pyrenees
- assess France's political, economic and social condition upon Louis XIV's accession in 1661.

End notes

1 Treasure G. *Mazarin: The Crisis of Absolutism in France.* London: Routledge; 1997.

2 Cited by Knecht R. Cardinal Richelieu: Hero or Villain? *History Today.* 2003; Vol. 53.3.

3 Council of State Decree (13 June, 1643). Cited by Bonney R. *Society and Government in France under Richelieu and Mazarin, 1624-61.* New York: Palgrave Macmillan; 1988.

4 Cited by Treasure G. *Mazarin: The Crisis of Absolutism in France.* London: Routledge; 1997. p.82

5 Kleinman R. *Anne of Austria, Queen of France, 1601–1666.* Columbus: Ohio State University Press; 1988. p. 223–4.

6 Ibid. p. 143.

7 Hanley S. *The "Lit De Justice" of the Kings of France: Constitutional Ideology in Legend, Ritual, and Discourse.* Princeton: Princeton University Press; 2014. p. 310.

8 Ibid. p. 310.

9 Treasure G. *Mazarin: The Crisis of Absolutism in France.* London: Routledge; 1997. p. 63.

10 Moote A. *The Revolt of the Judges: The Parlement of Paris and the Fronde.* Princeton: Princeton University Press; 2015. p. 66.

11 Treasure G. *Louis XIV.* Harlow: Longman; 2001. p. 5.

12 Ibid. p. 5.

13 Treasure G. *Mazarin: The Crisis of Absolutism in France.* London: Routledge; 1997. p. 105.

14 Wilkinson R. *France and the Cardinals 1610–1661.* London: Hodder & Stoughton; 1995. p. 104.

15 Bonney R. *Society and Government in France under Richelieu and Mazarin, 1624-61.* New York: Palgrave Macmillan; 1988. p. 120–1.

16 Ibid. p. 124.

17 Ibid. p. 122–3.

18 Treasure G. *Mazarin: The Crisis of Absolutism in France.* London: Routledge; 1997. p. 142.

19 Cited by Bonney R. *Society and Government in France under Richelieu and Mazarin, 1624-61.* New York: Palgrave Macmillan; 1988. p. 178.

20 Wilkinson R. *France and the Cardinals 1610–1661.* London: Hodder & Stoughton; 1995. p. 102.

21 Ibid. p. 89.

22 Treasure G. *Mazarin: The Crisis of Absolutism in France.* London: Routledge; 1997. p. 259.

23 Maland D. *Europe in the Seventeenth Century.* London: Macmillan Education; 1986. p. 205–6.

24 Treasure G. *Louis XIV.* Harlow: Longman; 2001. p. 150.

25 Treasure G. *Mazarin: The Crisis of Absolutism in France.* London: Routledge; 1997. p. 206; Treasure G. *Louis XIV.* Harlow: Longman; 2001. p. 19–20.

26 Treasure G. *Louis XIV.* Harlow: Longman; 2001. p. 15.

27 Rothkrug L. *Opposition to Louis XIV: The Political and Social Origins of the French Enlightenment.* Princeton: Princeton University Press; 1965. p. 184–6.

28 Bonney R. *Society and Government in France under Richelieu and Mazarin, 1624-61.* New York: Palgrave Macmillan; 1988. p. 232.

29 Ibid. p. 237.

30 Treasure G. *Mazarin: The Crisis of Absolutism in France.* London: Routledge; 1997. p. 214.

31 Maland D. *Europe in the Seventeenth Century.* London: Macmillan Education; 1983. p. 313.

2 The establishment of absolutism at home, 1661–1685

In this chapter, we will look into:

- Louis XIV and Divine Right: personality and aims; the restoration of order; the centralisation of royal authority; the role of Versailles
- Louis XIV and patronage of art, culture and science: the Académie Française; the Academy of Sciences; the role of Colbert
- finance and the economy: the reforms of Colbert; taxation; trade and communications within France; mercantilism; overseas trade and colonisation
- Louis XIV and the Church: disputes with the papacy; persecution of Jansenists; policies towards Huguenots and the Revocation Edict of 1685.

Louis XIV and Divine Right

In 17th-century Europe, **absolutism** was the constant pursuit of, and sometimes struggle for, royal freedom of action. In practice, it was a marriage of convenience between the King and his most privileged subjects, allowing royal authority's extension within conservative limits.

Since the late 16th century, French Divine Right theorists Jean Bodin, Charles Loyseau and André Duchesne claimed that kings were free from institutional checks upon their power and defined laws because they:

Key terms

Absolutism: political theory (and sometimes practice) whereby a king held unrestrained power.

- held power directly from God and only answered to Him
- legitimately asserted absolutist royal authority as the only way to avoid disorder
- held supreme sovereign authority above parlements, estates, customary and fundamental law
- could impose laws on all subjects regardless of their agreement.

Jacques-Bénigne Bossuet (the **Dauphin**'s personal tutor from 1670) further developed the sacrosanct nature of royal authority, describing Louis as God's earthly representative:

'God has the kings anointed by his prophets … Royal authority is sacred … God established kings as his ministers, and reigns through them over nations … All power comes from God … Princes therefore act as ministers of God, and his lieutenants on earth. It is through them that he exercises his rule … The royal throne is not the throne of a man, but the throne of God himself.'[1]

The 'dauphin' was the title of the French king's heir. The title was held by four different people during Louis XIV's reign:

- the eldest son Louis (dubbed the 'Grand Dauphin' after the birth of his son)
- Louis Duke of Burgundy the 'Petit Dauphin'
- Louis Duke of Brittany, oldest son of the Petit Dauphin
- Louis the 'bien aimé' who became Dauphin when his brother died, and lived to become Louis XV.

However, Divine Right also limited royal authority by emphasising that:

- Succession Law only allowed a male legitimate heir to succeed as king.
- Kings were subject to God's judgement.
- Customary natural and fundamental laws (such as succession laws) were above the king's will
- Monarchs should only do just and praiseworthy deeds.

Royal might was divinely right, but with restrictions. Bossuet categorically rejected arbitrary power, stating that kings must respect customary laws, institutions and private property.

Louis' absolutism would therefore be extended through consensus, not conflict.

ACTIVITY 2.1

Create a mind map for the concept of Divine Right using the information above and further research. Draw attention to the religious and political significance and give examples of it in practice.

Louis' aims and personality

Nicknamed Dieudonné (God given) and described as Le Roi Soleil (Sun King), Louis unsurprisingly saw himself as France's salvation, with universal influence and control. His self-confessed dominating passion was projecting his kingdom's greatness and his own. He may not actually have said 'l'état c'est moi' (I am the state), as often claimed, but he certainly wanted to:

- eradicate all sources of disorder and schism
- be the centre of a harmonious and ordered universe
- personally control and centralise government
- extend his authority over ministers, handle councils and parlements as tame royal servants
- restore royal financial order
- eliminate heresy (this was his coronation oath).

However, Louis thought conservatively, not confrontationally. He intended to:

- recognise his conformist Christian subjects' rights and status
- pick his battles carefully (e.g. with finance minister Fouquet)
- encourage compliance from the elites.

These ambitions required adept use and manipulation of patronage. Louis XIV's Mémoires, written for the Dauphin's instruction and drafted in the 1660s from notes he dictated, accurately record his core beliefs and personal commitment to consensual government:

'My son, we must consider the good of our subjects far more than our own. They are almost part of us, for we are the head of a body of which they are the members. It is only for their advantage that we must give them laws, and we should only use this power which we have over them to work more effectively for their happiness. It is wonderful to deserve from them the title father along with that of master, and if the one belongs to us by right of our birth, the other must be the sweetest object of our ambition.'[2]

Vested interests (people with something to lose in case of any changes) were therefore to be appeased, not antagonised. As benevolent head of an ordered and conformist society, Louis coveted glory, fame and honour. Anything else detracted from his role as God's custodian and defender of French Catholicism, and from his quest for universal influence.

Louis liked acting impulsively and making war and love. Wars spanned 36 of the 54 years of his personal rule. He had three openly acknowledged mistresses, including Louise de la Vallière, Madame de Montespan and Madame de Maintenon. Historian Antonia Fraser stated that Louis 'made love three times a day'.[3] According to Lisa Hilton: 'He would quite often, if his mistress was too slow in taking her dress off, have a turn with her lady's maid whilst he was waiting.'[4]

Figure 2.1: Uma Thurman as Madame de Montespan in the film *Vatel* (2000)

Louis wished to atone for his sins after committing double adultery with Madame de Montespan in the 1660s. Publically, he was very pious. He rebuked his sister-in-law Liselotte for bawdy comments about her servants' lovers and the Dauphin. English philosopher John Locke, who travelled extensively in France 1674-9, praised the king's religious devotion.

Louis' self-confidence and strong-mindedness were also remarkable. He devoted six to nine hours daily to government business. Courtier and autobiographer Saint-Simon claimed Louis was easily flattered and manipulated. However, Primi Visconti, count of Saint-Mayol, who observed the court from 1673–83, begged to differ:

ACTIVITY 2.2

1 How convincing is Primi Visconti's observation of Louis' personality as king?

2 Imagine you are a courtier writing a secret diary. Sum up the main aspects of Louis' aims and personality.

'...no prince was ever less dominated ... he wants to know everything from his ministers about affairs of state ... in short, in any given day, there are very few events about which he is not well informed ... His life is very regulated.'[5]

To our modern eyes, Louis may seem egocentric and vain, commissioning over 300 portraits of his likeness and 500 tapestries. He loved projecting ***gloire*** (glory) through performance, appearing in 9 ballets as Apollo by 1659. Craving attention at all times, he saw himself as master of his ministerial government, kingdom and court and leading actor in a continuing play. The business of being king involved role play (see The role of Versailles in this chapter).

The restoration of order

Ezéchiel Spanheim (envoy to several German princes 1666, 1668 and 1678-87) observed Louis' compulsive obsession with orderliness and solemnity at court:

'He likes order, deference and sobriety ... [and] as a result has a well-regulated Court and submissive courtiers ... His conduct is as regular and uniform in amusements as in public affairs.'[6]

From 1661, Louis set about restoring the natural order of strong personal royal rule without a Chief Minister. This involved taking three principal measures:

- actively leading conciliar royal government
- disgracing finance minister Nicolas Fouquet
- curtailing the parlements' powers.

Upon Mazarin's death, Louis immediately summoned his experienced and talented ministerial team of Le Tellier, Séguier, Lionne and Fouquet to tell them that none of them would be Mazarin's successor:

'It is now time that I govern them myself. You will assist me with your counsels when I ask for them. Outside of the regular business of justice ... I request and order you to seal no orders except by my command, or after having discussed them with me, or at least not until a secretary brings them to you on my behalf. And you Messieurs of state, I order you not to sign anything, not even a passport, without my command; to render account to me personally each day and favour no one.'[7]

When asked by the Archbishop of Paris and ministers to whom they should report for instructions, Louis succinctly replied 'A moi' (to me). Strong personal rule was Louis' antidote to the disorders he had witnessed during his minority and Frondes.

Louis also engendered ministerial compliance by publically disgracing and dismissing the ambitious finance minister Fouquet. Fouquet had mocked the idea of Louis being his own first minister, shown undue interest in Louise de la Vallière and ostentatiously displayed his wealth upon Louis' visit to his château of Vaux-le-Vicomte in 1661. The motto on his coat of arms was *Quo non ascendam* (meaning 'To what heights can I not rise?'). Fouquet therefore seemed an upstart and rival in Louis' quest for unrivalled *gloire*. Within three weeks, he was arrested and accused of embezzlement and, more absurdly, of fortifying Belle-Isle to defy Louis.

Fouquet's imprisonment served two purposes:

- It served as a warning to other ministers.
- It gave Louis the chance to personally control finance until 1665 when he promoted Jean-Baptiste Colbert as **Controlleur-Général**.

Colbert ousted Chancellor Séguier, reducing the legal profession's conciliar influence. As Louis' key figure in government, Colbert acted as a willing careerist puppet, controlling finance, law and judicial administration. He focused upon restoring order to royal finances, as we will see later in this chapter.

Louis succeeded in limiting the parlements' powers by:

- making royal council decrees superior to those of the parlements in 1661 and 1665
- reducing the capital value of offices and Parlement's capacity to discuss edicts: 'I ordered Lamoignan to assemble Parlement and tell the councillors that I no longer wanted them to discuss edicts verified in my presence, and to see if any among them dared to disobey them ... I desired to use this event as a shining example of the submission of this court and of my severity to punish them. I received total witness of the total restoration of royal authority.'[8]

This account by Albert Hemscher accurately reflects Parlement's docility by 1665. With office values five times those of 1638, the paulette extended and ongoing opportunities to accrue unofficial fees, judicial officiers saw no serious threat to their status and investments. Approval for Louis' anti-papal religious policy also dissuaded opposition. Louis exploited this apathy, revoking judgements adverse to royal policy and removing Parlement's right of remonstrance in 1673. Subsequently, Parlement could no longer discuss laws before they had been passed. With Parlement silenced, order seemed restored.

Centralisation of government

Louis' absolutism was also apparent in his centralised system of conciliar government. He tightly controlled his **Conseil d'en haut** (or ministerial council of state, the main council). This was deliberately small and easily convened. Three loyal ministers (Lionne, Le Tellier and Colbert) all owed their political power to Louis and met him in an advisory capacity thrice weekly. Crucially, participation from any royal family or princes of the blood was prohibited. Louis made ministerial power a select privilege, limiting the number of ministers to just 16 in 1661–1715. He alone decided policy.

The same applied to his new Finance Council and **Conseil des depêches**. This met twice weekly, dealt with domestic affairs and allowed Louis to invite princes of the blood as he chose, thereby presenting a façade of consultation. Louis boasted that 'the right of deliberation and resolution belongs to the head alone'[9] and that his ministers merely executed his orders.

Saint-Simon claimed Louis' ministerial choices were made from vanity, yet he chose talented and experienced men, including Michel Le Tellier (war minister, replaced by son Louvois in 1677) and Jean-Baptiste Colbert (finance, economy, law and arts). The king claimed in his memoirs to have kept them on a tight rein:

'I commanded the four secretaries of state to sign nothing in future without discussing it with me, and the same for the surintendant. As to the persons who were to help me with my work ... in order to concentrate the whole authority of a master more fully in myself ... I resolved to enter into details with a minister when they would least expect it.'[10]

This seems fairly apt. The king had the power to overrule Colbert together with other ministers and any government committees whenever he chose. Colbert was powerful, but Louis was in control; he rebuked Colbert when in 1671 he once questioned royal policy. Colbert advised his son, Seignelay:

'Never as long as you live send out anything in the king's name without his express approval'.[11]

Jean-Baptiste Colbert was born into a merchant family and had been:

- a secret agent of Mazarin during the Frondes
- recommended by Mazarin.

Colbert worked tirelessly until his death in 1683. Within the sphere of royal patronage of arts, culture and science, he was the perfect royal servant, often working fifteen-hour days, creating and actively collaborating with a network of Académies and servile royal cultural propagandists to produce symbols of Louis' magnificence as king.

Beyond Paris, however, Louis' power had clear bounds. Colbert's failure to standardise and control legal procedures highlighted the limits of Louis' judicial control. New legal codes aimed to streamline procedures for:

- civil law (1667)
- criminal law (1670)
- maritime law (1672)
- commercial law (1673).

They were never uniformly enforced; inadequate communications in the provinces and numbers of intendants (and those capable of resisting bribes) meant that provincial magistrates passively resisted royal edicts. So too did intendant corruption. To relieve the load on the central courts and placate the local elites, Louis tolerated some 70,000 separate tribunal courts alongside the lower levels of the judicial system; these were notoriously corrupt and inefficient. Royal edicts were frequently ignored by private judicial assemblies in pays d'états including Orange, Burgundy and Clermontois. Evasions of royal directives continued unabated, costing the crown considerable revenue.

Colbert relied upon hand-picked intendants (lawyers with administrative experience) to regularly report on all affairs in provinces and towns. Intendants surveyed roads and rivers, supervised tax collection, parlements, police work, army billeting and conscription and religious conversions.

But Louis simply lacked the administrative infrastructure to remove institutional checks upon his provincial authority. Poor communications invited increasing conditions for deviance and dishonesty. Intendants were neither uniformly dispatched nor could they be depended upon to reliably inform Louis or enable him to assert his writ in the provinces. Only 33 intendants existed in 1673. Béarn had no intendant until 1682. Overworked and understaffed, intendants often entrusted their activities to totally unsuitable sub-delegates. Consequently, reports were often superficial, surveys rushed and royal edicts ignored.

Quality, then, varied as much as quantity, thereby frustrating royal provincial authority. Here Louis had to accept negotiation, compromise and diminishing returns as the norm. While some intendants made roads and improved postal systems, intendants in Aix, Provence and Montauban succumbed to bribes and falsified reports.

Beyond Paris, therefore, serious limitations remained upon Louis XIV's power. Absolutism remained a largely frustrated ideal.

ACTIVITY 2.3

1. Prepare an essay or presentation on: How successful was Louis in restoring order and centralising government from 1661–85?
2. How convincing are the sources in this section as evidence about Louis' success in restoring order and centralising government?

The role of Versailles

What Louis could not fulfil in the provinces, he fabricated at court. Constructing the Versailles palace (on the site of Louis XIII's hunting lodge) created a magnificent stage for acting out greatness and control over nature and a tamed aristocracy.

Versailles' key developments over the years included:

- a garden enlargement to maximise theatrical space for spectacular fêtes (1661)
- a radical artistic and architectural transformation to impress and overwhelm (1668)
- making the palace into Louis' permanent royal residence and seat of government (1682).

Landscape gardener André Le Nôtre 'exemplified the victory of rule over disorder' by draining the marshland and transforming it into a classically formal pattern with:

- symmetrical lawns and paths
- stately avenues, terraces and clipped yews
- 300 sculptures
- an orangery
- a 1,500 metre Grand Canal
- flower beds (changed daily, so they shone with colour all year round).

Versailles generated awe and wonder. Its 1,400 fountains:

- reflected the sky, showing Louis' union of heaven and earth
- reinforced Louis' 'Sun King' universal influence. The Apollo fountain (1671) depicted the sun god on his chariot. The Dragon fountain represented Apollo killing a python.
- showed Louis' control of nature, being supplied with Seine river-water from three miles away by using the 221 pump machine of Marly (built 1681-88).

Architect Louis le Vau further augmented Louis' *gloire* by:

- creating a three-sided courtyard to astound and overwhelm visitors
- adopting an Italian-style invisible roof, hidden by a balustrade adorned with trophies
- building a menagerie and seven royal apartments named after the planets, appealing to Louis' desire for universal influence.

Le Vau also started the glorious Ambassadors' Staircase, built to celebrate Louis' triumphal return from wars and for ceremonial audiences. Completed by Hardouin-Mansart (architect from 1675), the staircase depicted trophies, chariots, and courtiers admiring Louis' stately possessions. Its frescoed ceiling, showing peoples of four continents as subject to Louis' power, astounded foreign dignitaries. Versailles perfectly satisfied Louis' quest for *gloire* and positive representational culture in his *Hall of Mirrors* (completed in 1684). With 357 mirrors, 17 glass doors and thousands of crystal candles on chandeliers, the great hall offered the perfect backdrop for reflecting and illuminating Louis. Mansart also:

- imposed a uniform façade on Versailles' garden side
- increased its total length to 550 metres.

This created a vision of discipline, order and harmony.

Figure 2.2: The Hall of Mirrors at Versailles

On this vast stage, Louis basked in public spectacle virtually all of his waking life. Six successive parties of over one hundred people observed the ***petit lever*** (his morning wake up). A select few of highest rank saw Louis leave his bed, while less favoured courtiers watched him complete dressing and put on his wig. Processions formed to see Louis traverse the Hall of Mirrors to take mass; while he worshipped God, courtiers worshipped him. Courtiers also observed Louis formally dining (**grand couvert**) and vied for involvement in his **petit coucher** (attending him to bed). Louis was occupying centre stage, literally, as his servile courtiers' master.

On the surface, Versailles appeared to tame the nobility, reducing powerful individuals to a dependency upon courting Louis' favour by attending to his every need. Competition for proximity to the king was fierce and rituals enticed former rebels. Louis was helped into his dressing gown by the Duc de Bouillon (whose father had rebelled), while ex-Frondeur Duc de la Rochefoucauld pulled on his breeches. Louis dominated patronage, refusing to give offices to the outspoken Fréjus bishop, Joseph Zongo Ondedei, and transferring court absentee the Duc de Longueville's governorship to trusted courtier Duc de Montausier.

In reality, however, Versailles only allowed very limited domination over the elites, housing just 5% of French nobles, due to its prohibitively high expense.

Versailles massaged Louis' ego, engendering sycophancy and ambition. Louis' domination of patronage enabled him to reward informants who helped to increase royal tax revenue, including noblewomen Louise Valençay and Lucrèce Bouhier. Comte d'Armagnac received 10,000 livres in 1685 for denouncing embezzler de Bruyn.

Saint-Simon, who sometimes held a candlestick at the *coucher*, complained:

'Versailles is the gloomiest and most unpleasant of all places ... the air is bad ... Without following any general design, he built the beautiful and ... ugly, all jumbled together. ... I might never finish talking about the monstrous defects of a palace so immense and so costly, with its trappings.'[12]

Nevertheless, Versailles considerably benefited France (Louis), becoming envied across Europe and a magnificent illusion of his divine *gloire*.

ACTIVITY 2.4

1. Make notes on Versailles or create either a tourist guide or courtier diary. This must include the political significance and purpose of the gardens, architecture, timetabling of Louis' life at Versailles and his use of patronage. Use the information above and wider research.
2. How convincing is Saint-Simon's view on the effects of Versailles?

Louis XIV and patronage of art, culture and science

Louis' quest for grandeur and conformity meant placing the arts, culture and science under his control. By patronising artists, writers and scientists whose work focused purely upon celebrating his actions as state achievements, Louis hoped to win hearts and minds, legitimise his regime and constantly renew and repackage his charisma through state 'sanctioned **iconography**'[13] (royal propaganda using positive visual images of the Sun King).

Académie Française

The Académie Française had been established in 1635 to standardise literary work and promote pro-royal establishment culture. Under Louis XIV, it actively promoted **positive representational culture**; from 1671, it held prize competitions for the best **panegyric** (published writing or speech praising the king), such as Jacques La Beaune's 1684 tribute to 'the most munificent Louis the Great, father and patron of the liberal arts'.[14] The Académie Française gave a medal to Madeleine de Scudéry for her essay on Louis' *gloire*. Founding Académie member, poet and critic Jean Chapelain advised the government on the literary glorification of the king and drew up a long report for the uses of the arts 'for preserving the king's enterprises'.[15] This perfectly suited Colbert's plan to make Louis dominant as patron of the arts. Chapelain and fellow Académie Française members Amable Bourzeis, Jacques Cassagnes and François Charpentier formed a committee called the 'petite Académie' to compose descriptions for medals and tapestries and supervise the creation of Louis' image as well as promote it. It also developed a 'department of glory' and celebrated Louis' every action and achievement – perceived or real – as king.

Chapelain proposed to Colbert a plan to patronise art and culture and incentivise propaganda, recruiting 90 writers, including 18 historians. This included a huge campaign of medallic propaganda. The Petite Académie project-managed some 70 medals in the 1660s, 67 in the 1670s and 49 in the 1680s. Medals depicted Louis as a supreme and selfless monarch who provided 'assiduity at his councils' despite illness and 'Order and Happiness' after 'chaos had ruled everywhere'. Inscriptions largely resonated a triumphalist theme, including the capture of Lille and Franche-Comté during the 1667-8 War of Devolution. Louis was depicted at the epicentre of his reign's achievements, heroically commanding victory in the trenches of Douai (1667), as 'the great' (1671), capturing Luxembourg (1684) and 'extinguishing heresy' after the 1685 **Edict of Fontainebleau**.

Winning literate hearts and minds was another priority for the Petite Académie. Chapelain told Italian poet Graziani that:

'His Majesty makes gifts to people of merit for no other motive than acting in a royal manner in every way and absolutely not in order to be praised.'[16]

Chapelain's own actions spoke louder than his words. He produced triumphalist sonnets that featured Louis' invasions of Flanders and 1673 siege of Maastricht. He recruited a coterie of willing propagandists, including Charles Perrault and Jean Racine (Académie Française members from 1672). Dramatist-historiographer Racine described Louis as Alexander the Great and:

'no less an excellent captain than a great statesman ... Revered by his subjects, feared by his enemies, admired by the whole world.'[17]

He also avidly manufactured the consent for and jubilation of the Dutch War. Racine accused Holland of 'allying herself with the enemies of France, oppressing the Catholics, competing with French trade and boasting that by herself she had set limits on the king's conquests'.[18]

This theme was echoed in the **Gazette de France** newspaper which reported the 'glorious action of this marvellous monarch' with allegorical headlines such as 'See how Victory and Glory take pleasure heaping their crowns on such a great-souled monarch.'[19]

Playwright Pierre Corneille compared Louis to Caesar and claimed that Louis only had to appear and his enemies' walls would collapse. Louis was compared to Atlas and Hercules by Académie Française scholar Charles Cotin and to Apollo and Neptune in Molière's plays. Versailles diplomat Ezéchiel Spanheim aptly noted that Louis was eulogised as:

'the sole author and inspiration of all the successes of his reign, attributing them entirely to his wisdom, prudence, courage and direction.'[20]

Louis' *gloire* was a multi-media project in which he took a central role. His appointment as Académie Française President in 1672 enshrined his status as patron and hero, as did his performance in stunning fêtes such as the 1664 'Pleasures of the Enchanted Island'. This combined fireworks, equestrian parades, opera, comedy, theatre, ballet and fantasy (Apollo's chariot, an astonishing floating whale and Louis as hero 'Roger' escaping from sorceress Alcine's captivity). Subsequent festivities followed the 1668 peace of Aix and 1674 capture of Franche-Comté, thereby showcasing Louis' domination of enemies and nature.

Key terms

Gazette de France: a newpaper which was produced twice a week and devoted substantial coverage to the king's actions. So too did the monthly *Mercure Galant.*

Academy of Sciences

Louis had no personal interest in science other than to further his own image as a 'magnificent patron of learning'.[21] He was supposedly captivated by a 'burning mirror' demonstration and an elephant dissection, but his creation of the **Academy of Sciences** in 1666 was, as with many other aspects of his reign, more concerned with perception than reality. Louis' motive was to have a government advisory body on scientific matters, above all to reinforce his cultivated image and perceived academic acumen. To this end, Sébastien Le Clerc portrayed a fictitious visit of Louis to the Academy in 1670. This was invaluable propaganda for Louis. At a time when state patronage of science was uncommon, Louis was publically associated with scientific research; this supported the notion of his control of nature.

Royal patronage funded pensions to at least 16 scientists. 50% of these worked in astronomy or mathematics, with the rest in chemistry, botany or anatomy. It also fundcd:

- Claude Perrault's astronomical observatory in 1672
- a laboratory within the royal library, dissections (including one of a crocodile) and a menagerie of exotic animals for this purpose
- an annual 9,000-livre pension to lure Italian astronomer Gian-Domenico Cassini from Bologna to Paris in 1669. Cassini discovered Jupiter's Great Red Spot and speed rotation. He became director of the observatory, discovered Saturn's four satellites and made the first accurate measurement of earth's distance from the sun.
- lavish, extensively illustrated volumes such as the *Natural History of Animals* (1671 and 1676) and *Natural History of Plants* (1676 and 1679)
- France's first scientific journal, the '*Journal des Savants*'. First appearing in 1665, this aimed to publicise Robert Hooke's *Micrographia*, a book about what can be seen using a lens, and share news of discoveries in physics, chemistry, mechanical and mathematical inventions, celestial and meteorological observations and anatomical discoveries.

The Academy of Sciences focused upon 'modern' rather than classical science and emphasised experimental and collaborative learning. Unlike other académies, it received no formal regulations or structure, but it was still carefully controlled. Its head was Colbert's former librarian Pierre Carcavy, while the *Journal des Savants* was closely monitored by a handpicked original editorial team. This included Chapelain's friend Denis de Sallo, fellow petite academian Bourzeis and Jean Gallois (former tutor to Colbert's children). Science was to serve the state. In 1668, Colbert tasked astronomer Academy members Jean Picard and Gilles de Roberval to make an exact map of France; without this, intendants could have no reliable grasp of French geography. Picard surveyed an 80-mile stretch of open country north of Paris and made more accurate calculations of the longitude and latitude of major cities. This enabled publication of a new atlas in 1684 which eradicated many serious errors in existing maps. Colbert also recruited Dutch mathematician-inventor Christiaan Huygens to assist with navigational problems for his navy. Huygens was instructed to perfect a pendulum clock capable of keeping accurate time aboard ships to help determine accurate longitudes at sea. Ultimately, this failed, as Jean Richer discovered during a 1668 Atlantic fleet tour and follow-up voyage to Acadia. Colbert also instructed Philippe de la Hire to engineer a water supply to Versailles in 1683-4, but this too failed to fully deliver the goods.

However, the Academy of Science perfectly fitted Louis' love of servility. Where it sometimes fell short in practicalities, it more than made up for in perception; each utilitarian breakthrough it reportedly made further bolstered Louis' *gloire* as patron.

Role of Colbert

Colbert's significance lay in making both arts and science contribute to Louis' grandeur and delegated concrete proposals to specialists such as Chapelain, Perrault and Charles Le Brun. Colbert took a leading role in increasing the royal collection of medals paintings, manuscripts and statues. He centralised engraving in 1667. In addition, he incentivised positive representational culture and played an active role in recruitment. He invited, subsidised and supervised the latest artists and cutting-edge scientists, including Racine, Cassini and Huygens. He also bureaucratised the arts and intervened as censor.

Colbert was the perfect royal servant for Louis XIV, dedicating hours to manufacturing the king's cultivated image. He gave Académie Française members fixed working hours and a pendulum clock to instil a precise sense of time, thereby matching Louis' desire for regulation. He also actively ensured that all projects met his own exacting standards to promote Louis' *gloire* by:

- meeting the five Petite Académie members at home every Tuesday and Friday to discuss inscriptions and engravings for public monuments and medals
- editing and proofreading texts before publication; even festival descriptions by Perrault and official royal historian André Félibien were amended
- dissuading Louis from backing Gianlorenzo Bernini's plans to develop the Louvre (after he clashed with the Petite Académie over the supremacy of Italian above French architecture)
- launching a plan to erect monuments to Louis' greatness - tombs, obelisks (such as Charles Perrault's 1666 stone pillar glorifying Louis) and triumphal arches (including the Porte Martin in Paris which was inscribed 'to Louis the Great')
- establishing Académies (organisations of hired writers and artists who mostly worked for the glorification of Louis). This included the Academy of Opera in 1669, Lully's Royal Academy of Music in 1671 and Academy of Dance in 1672 and the Academy of Architecture in 1671
- directing the Academy of Painting and Sculpture from 1661; within two years, it was holding competitions for the finest statue or painting of Louis' 'heroic actions'. Colbert also enlisted Henri Testelin to portray Louis as '*Protector of the Academy of Painting and Sculpture*', thereby reinforcing his image as patron of the arts. He also appointed Le Brun as Academy director to give artists a strict formal education and make French art and culture a paradigm of unrivalled excellence
- subsidising the manufacturing of Louis XIV's *gloire*. This included opening the Gobelins state factory in 1663 with 200 workers to produce royal palace furnishing and over 300 portraits and 500 tapestries of Louis' achievements, with Louis depicted as Alexander the Great, Apollo, Jupiter, Neptune or Hercules
- funding Chapelain's recruitment drive for the arts, offering 100,000 livres in annual pensions to writers and generous salaries to artists to glorify Louis, including Swiss painter Joseph Werner (1662), Flemish engraver Gérard Edelinck (1666) and sculptor Martin van den Bogaert
- financing Academy of Science recruitment, equipment, laboratory research and volume publications. He also consulted it regarding navigation, machine inventions, military and civil engineering projects, e.g. supplying Versailles.

Colbert was a great talent spotter. By employing Charles Le Brun as official painter to the king, he took Louis' iconographic appeal to another level in the interior decoration at Versailles. Le Brun's Grande Gallerie decoration was inscribed 'The pre-eminence of France recognised by Spain' and focused entirely upon the 'history of the king's actions'. His vast Hall of Mirrors ceiling masterpiece '*The King Governs For Himself*' pictured Louis holding a rudder and being guided to glory by Minerva (goddess of wisdom) and Neptune (god of the sea). Nine other large paintings celebrated Louis' Dutch War conquests in 1672–9. France's defeated enemies, identified by Spanish and Habsburg coats of arms, appeared as a python, a hydra (a multi-headed serpent to infer evil) and a woman tearing at her clothes. Colbert's Petite Académie provided inscriptions for each painting and descriptions for the *Mercure Galant* newspaper. This ensured that Louis' celebrated narrative reached a wider audience and would be interpreted in the way the king required.

Colbert also strove to repress **dissident** voices. He increased royal surveillance of Parisian printing by establishing the Conseil de Police in 1666–7, headed by Gabriel Nicolas de la Reynie. This empowered 48 commissioners to patrol and regularly report on printing. It also only allowed 30 printers and booksellers to operate within guilds, thereby subjecting them to tight regulations and royal inspections. Nevertheless, the problem of clandestine literature still remained.

ACTIVITY 2.5

Create a two-column table. In the left-hand column list reasons to think that Louis took into account the needs of France when he acted as a patron to the arts and sciences. In the right-hand column list reasons to think that his patronage was merely an exercise in appearances. Review the evidence you've gathered: what is your own view?

Overall, the fusion of the Académie Française and Academy of Sciences under Colbert's patronage significantly increased the positive representational culture at Louis' disposal and channels for its projection and dissemination. It also perfectly matched Louis' concept of monarchy, affording deference, order and *gloire*. For this reason, royal patronage of art, culture and science greatly boosted the symbol of Louis' absolutist control within France.

Finance and the economy

The reforms of Colbert

After Fouquet's disgrace, Colbert assumed increasing control as royal finance '**Surintendant**' until 1665 and **Controlleur-Général** until his death in 1683. His primary goal was maximising revenue for financing Louis' wars and *gloire*:

'It is simply, and solely, the abundance of money within a state which makes the difference in its grandeur and power.'[22]

With direct taxation at its highest possible point in 1661, Colbert strove to improve rather than overhaul a grotesquely wasteful and uneven collection system:

- over two thirds of taille (the main direct tax) and tax farm revenue was lost
- France's poorer people paid the most taille, while the rich – the clergy and nobility, including 40,000 officiers – were exempted
- despite constituting a third of France, pays d'états paid a tenth of all taxes.

With royal debts 451–700 million livres and 27 million livres paid annually on loans (some at 20% interest), Colbert aimed to reduce royal debts and dependency upon fat cat financiers:

'We recognise that the disorders and malpractices which have marred the running of finances for many years past are responsible for all the evils with which our subjects have been burdened, and have caused extraordinary surcharges which have been unavoidably laid upon them as a means of defraying the state.'[23]

Colbert knew that financial solvency required a thriving French economy. Taxation could only fill royal coffers if trade and industrial production generated sufficient wealth. Colbert described commercial companies as 'armies of the king' and industries as 'his reserves'. Paying scant attention to agriculture and food production, Colbert prioritised maximising French commercial activity at Dutch and English expense by:

- kick-starting domestic trade and industry
- stimulating overseas trade and exports
- improving communications
- attracting skilled immigrants
- protecting national industries through tariffs and regulations
- developing a navy to protect colonial trade.

Colbert reined in loan expenditure. His **Chambre de Justice** exploited Fouquet's disgrace and concerns of corruption to fine 500 financiers 156 million livres by 1665.

50% of rentes were repudiated and others rescheduled at their 1639 (lower interest) figure. From 27 million livres in 1661, interest payments were just 8 million by 1683; royal rentier debt fell by about 60%.

However, Colbert's action was ephemeral. Impassioned opposition to 'injustices' by the Chambre de justice led to its cessation in 1669. Colbert also reneged on rente repudiation during the Dutch War (1672–9). That conflict consumed 66% of expenditure, prompting loans of 7% and 10% – a clear break of Colbert's self-imposed 5% limit from 1665.

Taxation

Colbert reduced direct taxation from 60% to 40% of revenue, and net taille yield from 42 million livres to 35 million livres. He also *appeared* to improve efficiency. Intendants supervised collection, reported regularly and tackled embezzlement and underpayment. Colbert's figures suggest considerable success. While 52% of taxation revenue was lost in 1661, the loss amounted to just 20% in 1683. Taille yields in **pays d'élection** were 6 million livres higher in 1676–78 than in 1672.

Colbert also increased indirect tax (**aides**) yields by 250% in 1661–75 and by 74% by 1683. Colbert's united tax-farm syndicate in 1668 also apparently increased profitability, as did royal estate surveys and instructions for improving their management; this quadrupled yields by 1672. In 1681, the syndicate was sold for an annual sum of 56,670,000 livres.

Colbert's financial summary 1662–1680 appeared successful, with a surplus during the 1660s and the three years of the Dutch War.

However, direct taxation remained inequitable and inefficient:

- Between 1662 and 1683, taille yields in the pays d'états were on average 94% lower than in the pays d'élections.
- The taille yielded an average of 2.1 million livres from the pays d'états in 1662–83 compared to 36.5 million from the pays d'élection.
- 30% of taxes remained lost.
- In 1673, Languedoc's estate merely collected 41% of the money it had pledged in taxation.
- Direct tax avoidance by the rich remained unchallenged.

Colbert's 'grand enquiry' uncovered 1,000 'false nobles' in Provence – people with bogus titles claiming exemption. But this was abandoned in 1670, as were plans to make a property tax (taille réelle) universal after officials failed to provide a national survey and census. Proliferating office sales – numbering 60,000 by 1683 – further increased exemptions, Third Estate tax burdens and corruption opportunities. Louis XIV made the clergy's **don gratuit** non-negotiable from 1672, but mounting opposition to 'oppressive' royal taxation entrenched Colbert's unwillingness to challenge elite tax exemption.

Colbert failed to alleviate peasant tax burdens. He significantly increased indirect taxes (aides) on salt (gabelle), drink and tobacco. This caused serious revolt in Bordeaux in 1674 and Brittany in 1675–6, requiring 10,000 troops to restore order.

Colbert's financial and economic policies arguably did more harm than good, except when measured by the yardstick of the king's *gloire*. Colbert funded Louis XIV's wars and positive representational culture, but failed in his goal of balancing the books. 1670 saw no war, but there was still debt. In 1679, the **deficit** was more than double that of 1672 and it doubled again, reaching 4.5 million livres in 1680.

From 1681–83, Colbert allegedly reduced debts by 67%, increased royal tax-farm revenues by 75% and achieved 79% net revenue from gross. But his successor Le Pelletier found major discrepancies in his figures. Facing rising expenditure and debt, he had to allow still more selling of offices, thereby exacerbating France's grossly uneven and inefficient taxation system.

Trade and communications within France

Colbert aimed to stimulate trade by promising:

'…help with everything that concerns their (merchants) trading … To examine all … tariffs on goods entering and leaving the realm … To repair … public highways and to continue removing the tolls levied on river routes … To study carefully possible communications between the various seas.'[24]

In summary, Colbert's policies included:

- dividing France into three free-trade areas – central provinces, outlying provinces and Alsace
- eradicating the tolls and tariffs that inhibited internal trade
- discouraging foreign competition, with heavy tariffs on English and Dutch imports in 1664 (increased further in 1667)
- incentivising commercial and communications investment by offering gifts, lucrative pensions, tax breaks and titles of nobility
- modernising French roads and rivers to increase commercial profitability.

Colbert had limited success in standardising French péages (tolls). His five Great Farms achieved uniform toll rates in northern provinces, which were more amenable to royal intervention. Colbert spent 600,000 livres on improving roads and subjected peasants to the **corvée** (a month's forced labour on highway maintenance). This allowed completion of France's first paved road between Paris and Orléans. Colbert also persuaded local millionaire Pierre-Paul Riquet and the Archbishop of Toulouse to invest in the Canal des deux Mers. Opened in 1681, this 170 mile waterway was an incredible civil engineering feat with more than 100 locks and three aqueducts. It boosted trade by accommodating barges of 200 tonnes from the Mediterranean to the Atlantic and reducing transport costs by 75%. Colbert also established a postal system with 800 post offices.

Figure 2.3: Colbert discussing plans with Louis XIV

However, Colbert's trade and communications initiatives had many failures. Private investment in transport remained inadequate. The Canal des deux Mers consumed a staggering 7.5 million livres of taxpayers' money at a time when many peasants faced starvation. Colbert's attempts to simplify import and export customs dues for the whole kingdom were obstructed by many profiteers of the old system.

He also failed to remove péages, which remained a dead weight on internal trade; the River Rhône kept the majority of its 40 toll stations. Bandit crime meant that transporting goods remained risky, even near Paris. So too did opposition to road improvement from many local authorities and landowners; they had a vested interest in bad roads as they were legally entitled to all spilt merchandise. Subsequently, the nobility continued in its apathy regarding internal trade. It remained too slow to be profitable. Wine could be four days in transit from Paris to Orléans. Bales of cloth took a month from Rouen to Lyon. Throughout the reign, Alsace could trade more profitably with German states than with France.

Colbert's own policies actually hindered trade. He retained **traites**, lucrative government taxes on internal goods, often levied more than once on single journey. This made many transactions unprofitable, while rising taxes stifled demand. Colbert also failed to standardise weights and measures. Entrenched opposition meant wide variations remained. 100 pounds in Lyon equalled 86 in Paris, while 100 in Paris equalled 120 in Toulouse, Avignon and Montpelier. Aside from the yardstick of fuelling Louis' *gloire*, Colbert's financial and economic policies did more harm than good.

Mercantilism

Colbert's **mercantilism** policy was economic warfare to increase French power at the expense of its rivals. He noted: 'Trade is the source of finance and finance is the vital nerve of war'.[25]

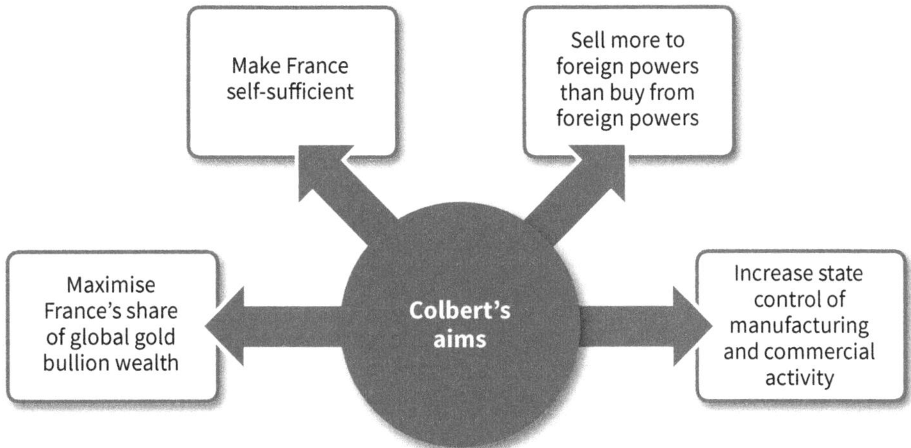

Figure 2.4: Colbert's mercantilist policy aims

Colbert established high-end domestic manufacturing companies. Arguably, these succeeded in revitalising French industry:

- His 1665 Abbeville Van Robais textile factory employed 400 artisans
- His Point-de-France Venetian-lace industry became established in several towns, including Reims and Auxerre.
- High end manufacturing was stimulated. Colbert's Beauvais, Chaillot and Gobelins tapestry goods rivalled imports, as did his 1667 Tourlaville mirror workshop.
- Quality lace-making from Auxerre sold abroad.
- 500,000 skilled fine cloth workers were employed in Languedoc's Carcassonne district.

Key terms

Mercantilism: the policy of protecting home industries through tariffs (import duties) on foreign goods and subsidies for home production.

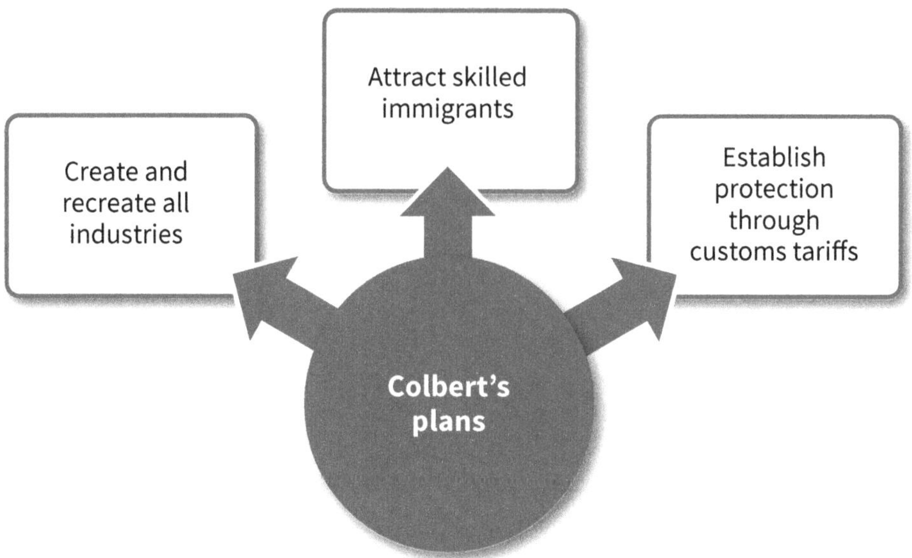

Figure 2.5: Colbert's policies for transforming France's economy

However, Colbert's showpiece industries were costly and impeded entrepreneurial development. Private industries only received 2.5% of the 20 million livres awarded Gobelins in annual subsidies. Funding to the royal Beauvais manufacturing business ceased completely during the Dutch War, 1672–79. Agriculture was neglected altogether and remained backward. Both Louis XIV's and the nobility largely eschewed industrial investment, as shown below:

Manufacturing sector:	Subsidy amount (livres):	Subsidy amount as % of gross domestic product 1665–85:
Mirrors 1667–83	284,725	0.01%
Soap 1665–85	400,000	0.02%
Subsidies for privileged royal companies manufacturing lace, glass, tapestry, metals and ships, 1665–85	16 million	1%

Table 2.1: Royal subsidies to manufacturing industries as a percentage of French GDP 1665–85

Colbert had some success attracting skilled immigrants, including Dutch tapestry makers and dyers, Italian silk workers, glassblowers and lace makers, Spanish leather workers and hatters, English miners, iron-founders and naval constructors. However, this was partly offset by the estimated 37% of skilled Huguenots who fled France 1661–79.

Colbert doubled and trebled import tariffs in 1667. However, this increased **inflation** and retaliatory French wine tariffs. It also negated tax yields, lasted for the entire Dutch War, depressed Brittany's trade and caused skilled worker and merchant emigration.

Colbert's obsessive pursuit of quality assurance involved excessive regulation and distrust of free enterprise. He insisted on minimum woollen thread counts and sizes from 1669 and made guild membership compulsory in 1673. Dijon saw twelve new guilds and Rennes nine. He also protected guild monopoly privileges through spies, intendant inspectors, punishments and prohibitions. He banned printed calico cloth production in 1683. Colbert published 150 decrees controlling industry 1664–83 and

248 articles' worth of fabric regulations for Amiens. These were widely ignored, as Colbert accepted:

'The King believes that to pressure the manufacturers of the realm to work in conformity with the ... regulations ... issued, it is important to induce fear in those who make defective fabric or those who accept it'.[26]

Contrary to royal policy, unregulated part-time spinning and weaving still thrived. Picardy's guild workers were outnumbered three to one. Artisans ignored Colbert's calico cloth ban. Colbert's 1680 ban of looms for fabrics except silk was overturned in 1684 following woollen and silk manufacturer opposition.

Colbert's inspectors raised standards and removed duties hindering Marseille's trade. This helped Languedoc textile merchants remove Dutch and English competition and eliminate precious metal coinage losses abroad. Overall, however, Colbert's obsessive mercantilism overestimated state power and underestimated the potential of French entrepreneurialism.

Overseas trade and colonisation

Colbert had some success in stimulating overseas trade, as evidenced by these achievements:

- Trade ships from Bordeaux and La Rochelle approximately tripled in number, 1660–83.
- There was a 93% increase in merchant ships over 300 tons carrying brandy, cloth and olive oil, 1664–84
- The number of individual merchants trading overseas doubled, 1664–1704.

Colbert openly encouraged overseas investment and established colonial trading companies to provide France with natural resources and manufacturing export markets:

- 1664: West Indies Company and East Indies Company
- 1670: Company of the North
- 1671: Levant Trading Company.

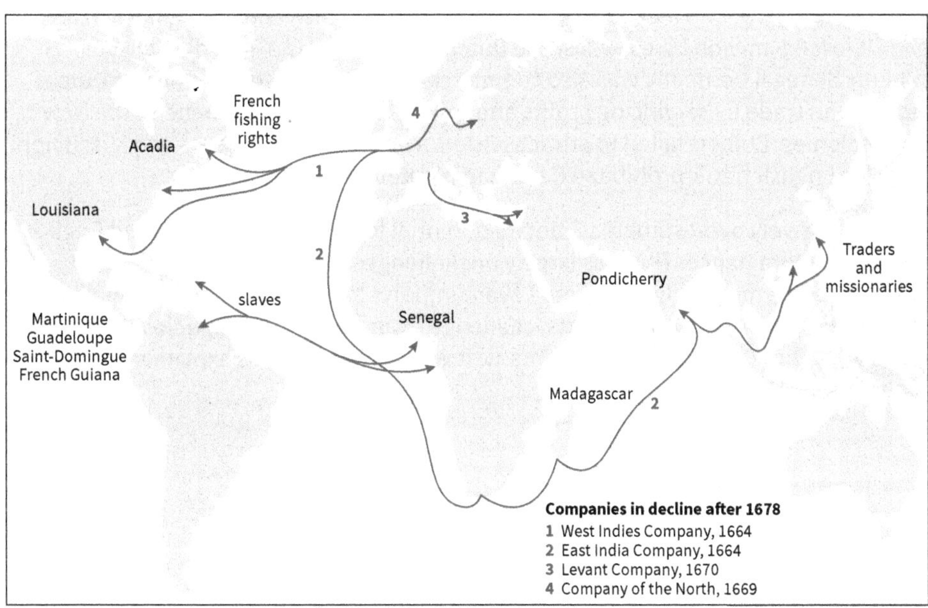

Figure 2.6: France's overseas trading companies established after 1661

These companies had some initial successes:

- Between 1674–72, West Indian company sugar production increased by 67%, with 29 processing refineries established in France.
- Lyon's Archbishop persuaded local merchants to invest 1 million livres in the East India Company. It established trading centres at Surinat and Pondicherry and gained entry into the spice market.
- French wine, textiles and West Indian sugar sustained a healthy Baltic trade before this was destroyed 1688–97.
- Canadian colonial intendant Jean Talon succeeded until 1672 in developing shipbuilding, West Indian trade, fishing industries, a brewery and commercial crops like flax and hemp.
- 800 single females aged 15–30, the 'King's daughters', helped to increase New France's population by 52% 1663–72.
- Adventurer Chevalier de la Salle reached the Gulf of Mexico in 1682 and called it Louisiana, thereby claiming for Louis XIV an empire that stretched across North America.

However, Colbert's success was again ephemeral and limited. Royal and noble indifference defeated his schemes, as did the Dutch War (1672–9). Colonial companies only received just 0.13% of domestic product 1665–85. By 1673, Canadian colonial funding and Talon's economic initiatives had collapsed. Noble and merchant apathy towards overseas investment was reinforced by:

- European economic depression 1660–85
- Colbert's radical rente reduction until 1669, which discouraged government based investment
- Dutch War funding - 7–10% interest rentes, renewed office sales and inheritance rights offered a far safer investment alternative.

Courtiers refused to subsidise the East Indies Company and warned Colbert in 1664:

'You have formed this great society of Indies ... However, many grumble and choose to seek fault with it; the officials, among others, complain that they are being forced to join ... it is a trap to impose the taille on the nobles and others ... exempt from it.'[27]

Excessive missionary expenditure, regulations and corruption left the East Indies Company bankrupt and incapable of challenging the English and Dutch. In eleven years, it lost 6.5 million livres, whilst the Dutch company paid a 40% dividend. Colbert's Senegal Company was also commercially unviable; it only undercut Dutch West African trade by sacrificing profits and thus also lacked investment. In the New World colonies, Colbert failed to attract settlers away from St Lawrence and Mississippi to run his English trade-prohibited Canadian plantations.

Colbert massively overestimated France's potential for challenging Dutch and English commercial dominance. This was largely unchallenged in Baltic timber and naval stores. Marseille merchants preferred Levant imports to exporting Carcassonne fine cloths. Colbert's bid to boost exports, challenge rivals and prevent **specie** from leaving France was a pipe dream by 1685. To many, it was a nightmare, as explained in the 'Challenges at Home' chapter.

ACTIVITY 2.6

Write a short essay on each of the following:

- What do you think were the key problems facing Colbert when he tried to reform the French tax system?
- What do you think were Colbert's economic successes?
- What do you think were Colbert's economic failures?
- 'Financial reform was Colbert's greatest achievement'. How far do you agree?

Louis XIV and the Church

Disputes with the papacy

Louis was inconsistent in exerting his authority over the **papacy**. He saw himself as God's custodian and the dominant regulator of the Catholic Church. Defying **papal** authority allowed Louis to display unlimited power and appealed to his **Gallican** supporters (those who favoured French ecclesiastical independence from Rome). These included:

- the Paris Parlement
- the **Sorbonne**
- most of the French Assembly of Clergy.

However, Louis was neither willing nor able totally to burn his bridges with Rome. His **Jesuit** advisers (Roman Catholics who favoured collaboration with the **Pope**) supported the doctrine of **papal infallibility** on spiritual matters and morals. Louis also needed papal support to crusade against the **Jansenists**, as explained later in this section. Separation from Rome, therefore, was as distasteful to Louis as submission. Pragmatic opportunism, not a predetermined plan, led Louis into multiple papal disputes 1661–85. These increased his absolutist freedom of action, but ultimately proved to be self-defeating.

In the 1660s, Louis initially adopted an overtly anti-papal position that he later abandoned. In 1662 papal Corsican guards in Rome fired shots at the coach of French ambassador Créquy, killing and wounding members of his entourage. Louis threatened to invade the papal state of Avignon until papal legate Cardinal Chigi publicly apologised in 1664. Pope Alexander VII consented to:

- erecting a monument in Rome marking the place of the brawl
- accepting the French embassy's diplomatic and legal immunity from papal police.

However, Louis did not, and could not, sustain extending his authority over the pope. When the **nuncio** warned in 1666 of a '**schism**' with Rome if Louis only consulted laymen on spiritual affairs, the king saw this as 'too horrible to repeat' and abandoned Colbert's proposed alterations to priests' legal ages. Louis also accepted the pope's lead by agreeing to the 1668 Peace of the Church, which gave Jansenists the right of respectful silence.

Pope:	Louis' break-up actions:	Louis' make-up actions:
Alexander VII 1655–67	1662 Belligerent response to the **Corsican guards incident** 1664 Forcing the pope into a humiliating apology	1665 Condemning the Sorbonne's censure of the doctrine of papal infallibility 1666 Abandoning Colbert's plan to alter the legal age for priests' ordination
Clement IX 1667–69		1668 Accepting Clement IX's 'Peace of the Church'
Clement X 1670–76	1673 and 1675 Extending the régale	1693 Withdrawing the régale
Innocent XI 1676–89	1682 The **Four Gallican Articles**	1685 Increasing persecution of Huguenots and removal of toleration.

Table 2.2: Louis XIV's confrontation and compromises with the Papacy up to 1685

Key terms

Gallicanism was a movement which favoured a strong independent French Catholic Church. This included ensuring the French king as well as the pope had power, authority and influence over the church within France.

Papal infallibility: a doctrine that proposed that popes were never wrong on matters of theology.

From 1673, Louis pursued overtly Gallican policies and a firm collision course with Rome.

The **régale** was the king's right from the 1516 **Concordat of Bologna** to collect revenue from empty dioceses in northern France. With income of 10,000–40,000 livres commonly at stake, vacant **sees** offered valuable revenue for Louis' ongoing Dutch war. In 1673 and 1675, Louis therefore extended the régale to all of France, including the southern provinces of Guyenne, Dauphiné and Provence.

This overt negation of papal influence within French ecclesiastical affairs was unopposed by Pope Clement X and keenly supported by the Paris Parlement and all French clergy, except two bishops – Pavillon of Alet and Caulet of Pamiers.

In 1676 they appealed to the new pope, Innocent XI. He was no pushover and strongly opposed Louis. When Louis deprived Pavillon and Caulet of their revenues and imprisoned their supporters, Innocent threatened Louis with **excommunication**.

Louis responded by calling the Assembly of Clergy to pass Bishop Bossuet's Four Gallican Articles in 1682. These articles:

- reaffirmed the French king's rights
- were willingly registered by the Paris Parlement
- were conciliatory by saying that popes led on faith issues
- gave Innocent XI the opportunity to take umbrage and major offence.

Louis underestimated Innocent's capacity for obstructionism. His actions ultimately backfired. Innocent XI refused to institute bishops whom Louis had nominated. 35 bishoprics were therefore left vacant. Louis' increased persecution of the Huguenots cut no ice. Disgusted at Louis' failure to help defend Christendom in Vienna from **Ottoman** Turkish attack in 1683, and French ambassadorial detention of papal police in 1684, Innocent retaliated further – as explained in the chapters 4 and 5 – snubbing a new French ambassador in 1687 and opposing Louis in the 1688 Cologne election. What had started as defiance of papal authority came back to thwart Louis diplomatically and reputationally.

Key terms

The Ottomans: the dynasty which governed a vast empire based in Turkey, but the term is often used to name the regime and empire itself. During this period it controlled coastal North Africa and much of the Middle East. In addition, its rule of most of southeast Europe made it a menacing neighbour for the Habsburg rulers of Austria and Hungary.

Persecution of Jansenists

Jansenism was a school of thought within Roman Catholicism popular with many Paris parlementaires and bishops. Emanating from Cornelius Jansen's 1640 book the *Augustinus*, it argued that:

- man was hopelessly sinful
- could only be saved by God's grace
- God predetermined who entered heaven.

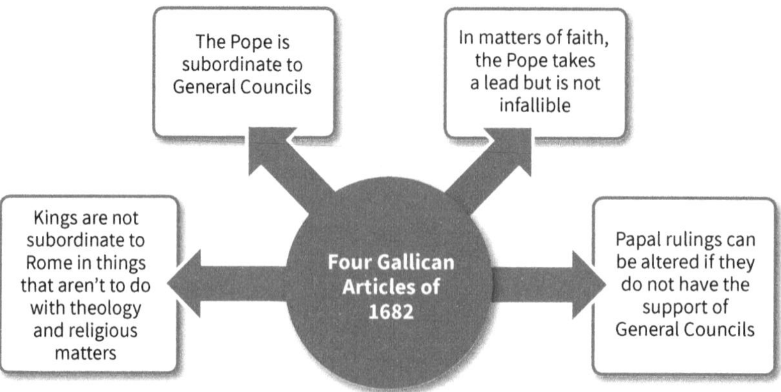

Figure 2.7: The Four Gallican Articles of 1682

This implied that the Catholic (especially Jesuit) emphasis on confession, penitence and atonement was irrelevant. Louis had pledged to eradicate heresy and saw Jansenism as an insurgent threat that needed tackling head on. Jansenist Saint-Cyran had actively opposed Richelieu's war against fellow-Catholic Habsburgs. Other Jansenists had been involved in the Frondes, including Gondi and Duchesses Chevreuse and Longueville. Jansenists remained an unresolved source of political disorder; Jansenists passively resisted **papal bulls** in 1653 and 1655 which condemned five Jansenist *Augustinus* propositions. Prominent Jansenist Antoine Arnauld claimed that although heretical, the propositions were not from Jansen's *Augustinus*. In 1656–7, Blaise Pascal's ***Lettres Provinciales*** satirically attacked Jesuit doctrine's supposed laxity. Jansensism continuingly offended the core beliefs of Louis' Jesuit confessors (Charles Paulin, Arnault 1645–70, La Chaise 1675–1709) and undermined Louis' personal priority in the 1660s – atoning for his promiscuity. Louis resolved to curb Jansenism for good.

Louis supported the pope's attempts to make all ecclesiastics sign a **formulary** unequivocally condemning Jansenist propositions. In 1661, Jesuit doctrines were imposed upon the Jansenist Port-Royal-des-Champs convent, its male leaders chased out and new novices forbidden. However, Port-Royal's nuns formulary, led by Arnauld's sisters Abbess Agnès Arnauld and Angélique de Saint Jean Arnauld, continued to question if the *Augustinus* contained the indicted propositions.

By 1664, Louis turned to his new Archbishop of Paris and former tutor Hardouin de Péréfixe to cajole the nuns into signing the formulary. When the nuns resolutely refused, Péréfixe exploded:

"Shut up! ...You are nothing but a stuck-up slip of a girl, a little goose, a know-nothing... You may be as pure as an angel but as proud as Lucifer. Off with you. Be off with you!"[28]

Further pressure was applied by accepting Alexander's 1665 bull *Regiminis apostolici*. This stated that the five propositions were in Jansen's book and heretical in the pope's understanding of them. Péréfixe gave all clerics just three months to accept this in writing or face excommunication. He also resorted to intimidation, sending 200 men armed with muskets and 20 police officers in eight wagons to Port-Royal to coerce compliance.

These measures backfired badly:

- 85% of the nuns refused to sign the formulary, as did the bishops of Alet, Angers, Pamiers and Beauvais, citing Gallican grounds.
- Angélique de Saint-Jean became a literary propagandist drama queen, after being exiled writing over 800 letters that depicted her as a human sacrifice and almost killed by the distress of what was occurring.
- Parlement refused to register the 1665 bull.

These factors combined with Gallicanism, and the positions of Madame Longueville and Arnauld, inspired opposition to Louis' increasingly **ultramonatist** policy.

With rising clerical factionalism and Louis' ally Pope Alexander's death in 1667, the Jesuits also faced mounting defamation from Antoine Arnauld:

"Those who force others, by whatever means, to embrace their lies, violate Christian humility and prudence ... break all laws to satisfy their vengeance and perpetrate abuses in Your Majesty's name."[29]

Key terms

Ultramonatanism was a concept popular with Jesuits which emphasised the pope's rights and power (over those of kings and general church councils) and collaboration with Rome.

Madame Longueville and Arnauld rallied every influence possible upon Pope Clement to intervene and reach a compromise. The 1668 'Peace of the Church':

- gave Jansenists the right of respectful silence as to whether Jansen had written the condemned propositions
- withdrew the formulary and armed guards
- permitted the nuns at Port-Royal to live and teach freely.

With the Dutch war imminent, this suited Louis. Arnauld's support for Huguenot persecution meant that Jansenist persecution was not yet needed. But Jansenism continuingly frustrated Louis XIV and functioned as a clandestine resistance movement.

This was evident by:

- Jansenist bishops Pavillon and Caulet's opposition to the régale
- Port-Royal's appointment in 1669, 1672, 1675 of former Frondeuse Madame Longueville's cousin, Marie du Forges, as abbess
- the growth of Jansenist literature from Port-Royal – alarmingly close to Versailles – urging anti-Jesuit and anti-formulary resistance.

Louis' Jesuit confessor from 1675, Père La Chaise, convinced Louis that the Jansenists' continuing refusal to submit implicitly challenged his divine sovereignty. He thus passed an edict suppressing Jansenism in Paris and Port-Royal in 1677.

With Abbess Saint-Jean ordered to reduce Port-Royal to only 50 women and seven of Port-Royal's defenders and patrons (including Madame Longueville, plus three of the Arnauld clan and De Retz) dead by 1679, Louis had renewed hope that Jansenism would die out. Antoine Arnauld had other ideas, bemoaning in two memoirs sent to Louis XIV in 1682–3 that 'the chicanery of the Jesuits' was 'unjust and unreasonable, and that God [was] offended it'.[30] By then, Louis had other priorities: Huguenots.

Policies towards Huguenots and the Revocation Edict of 1685

The 1598 **Edict of Nantes** allowed Huguenots:

- to legally coexist alongside Catholics
- freedom of worship and career
- the right to fortify certain towns.

Such privileges were sealed in yellow, rather than the green wax of a permanent edict and clashed with Louis' belief that his subjects should follow their king's religion. Louis' loathed heresy and cited his coronation oath as reason enough to extirpate it, no doubt alarmed at Huguenot Bonnesson's 1659 Sabotiers revolt (as described in Chapter 1). The Languedoc Estates and Toulouse parlement frequently petitioned him to curb Protestantism and Pierre Bernard's 1666 publication urged Louis to revoke the edict when necessary.

Louis' confessors advised that heretics were damned; conversions would be kind. Marshal Turenne's conversion in 1668 indicated that with suitable pressure, Huguenots could be restored to the Catholic fold.

Aim:	Actions:
Erode French Protestantism's religious basis	Dismantling 70% of Huguenot churches by the early 1680s Banning open air services Bribing Huguenots to convert, with cash payments from the 'treasury of conversion' created in 1676 Offering converts two years' immunity from taille
Undermining Protestant family life	Forbidding Catholic-Protestant intermarriage Requiring mixed-marriage children to be brought up as Catholics from 1680 Decreeing in 1681 that Huguenot children would be removed from families and placed in Catholic boarding schools Restricting Huguenot weddings, baptisms and funerals to immediate family only as witnesses, early mornings and late nights
Excluding Huguenots from professions and basic civil rights	Removing Huguenot lawyers, doctors, publishers, town officials and guild members Abolishing courts which protected Huguenot interests; subsequent lawsuits routinely ruled against Huguenots in Catholics' favour .

Table 2.3: Louis XIV's creeping persecution against the Huguenots and removal of their freedoms 1661–81

Figure 2.8: Image of a dragonnade conversion

Key terms

Dragonnades: government billeted French dragoon (cavalry) troops in Protestant homes. They were under instructions to make life as unpleasant as possible for their hosts to help end Protestantism in France.

The overtly discriminatory legislation was endured without rebellion. Huguenot population numbers reportedly fell by anywhere from 85% in 1661–79. Treasury conversion Chief Paul Pellison was applauded by Bishop Bossuet, Fénelon and even Arnauld for allegedly converting 50,000 Huguenots for 10 livres per head.

However, Louis' perception that Huguenotism was dying out by 1681 assumed a level of statistical reliability that was questionable in reality. Intendants vied for the highest conversion figures. Conversion offers of tax breaks, 6 livres for peasants and 3 000 livres for nobles, were unsustainable. Not all conversions were genuine. In Languedoc, conversions remained limited as too few priests spoke the local **Occitan** language.

Believing that Huguenotism was on the brink of extinction, Louis sanctioned a terror campaign to finish it off in 1681. Unless they converted, noncompliant Huguenots now faced rape, pillage, assault and vandalism of property by **dragonnades**. They also had to pay the costs of lodging troops and had their taille quadrupled.

Poitou intendant Marillac bragged that 30,000 Huguenots converted within 12 months. Subsequently, conversion through intimidation and coercion was applied to:

- Béarn and Languedoc (1683)
- Dauphiné and Provence (1685).

Again, reported success was accepted uncritically; Louvois reported these conversion figures in 1685:

Place:	Reported conversions 1685:
Dauphiné	30,000
Languedoc	25,000 in just 6 days
Montauban	34,000 in August.

Table 2.4: Reported conversion figures by dragonnades during 1685

Dragonnades supposedly prompted an estimated 75% of Huguenot conversions. However, they also attracted royal trepidation. Louvois publically distanced Louis from dragonnade use to avoid giving protestant enemies a propaganda gift. He therefore reprimanded Marillac and Limoges Intendant Pierre Le Bret for 'excessive zeal'. Intendant Nicolas Foucault was also challenged for sending one and a half dragonnade companies to force one woman to convert in Poitiers in October 1685, but Louvois remained committed to the dragonnades policy.

The sincerity of many 'conversions' was incredibly questionable. In 1683, Protestants resistance in Cévennes and Vivarais saw:

- assemblies convened
- 4,000 troops used to hunt down and hang 500–600 Protestants.

Nevertheless, the reported impact of conversion held sway over reality. With Colbert's death in 1683 went the one potential brake on anti-Huguenot policies. Louis' failure to help defend Vienna from Turkish attack (1683–4) left him desperate to act to restore papal favour and his international '**Most Christian King**' image. In October 1685, he revoked the Edict of Nantes in the Edict of Fontainebleau stating that:

'The best and greatest part of our subjects of Reformed Protestant Religion have embraced the Catholic faith.'[31]

Fontainebleau:

- completely banned outdoor Protestant worship
- exiled ministers who refused to conform within two weeks
- insisted that all Protestant children were baptised and educated as Catholic
- banned emigration
- condemned those attempting emigration to the galleys.

Both triumph and a tragedy in equal measure, this edict proved a mixed blessing, as explained in the Challenges at Home chapter.

Timeline

1516	Concordat of Bologna
1635	Académie Française established
1656–7	Blaise Pascal's *Lettres Provinciales* attacked Jesuit doctrines
1661	Work started on rebuilding Versailles
1661	Academy of Painting and Sculpture
1661	Jesuit doctrines were imposed upon the Port-Royal-des-Champs
1662	Louis' belligerent response to the Corsican-guards incident
1664	Pope apologised for Corsican-guards incident
1665	Sorbonne's censure of the doctrine of papal infallibility condemned
1665	Alexander's Bull *Regiminis apostolici*
1666	Colbert's plan to alter the legal age for priests' ordination abandoned
1666	Creation of the Academy of Sciences
1666–7	Conseil de Police established
1668	Peace of the Church
1669	Academy of Opéra
1671	Lully's Royal Academy of Music
1672	Academy of Dance
1671	Academy of Architecture
1677	Michel Le Tellier replaced by son Louvois
1682	The Four Gallican Articles
1683	Jean-Baptiste Colbert died
1685	Increasing persecution of Huguenots and removal of toleration
1685	Revocation of the Edict of Nantes
1715	Versailles building work completed

ACTIVITY 2.7

1. 'Louis succeeded in extending his authority over the papacy by 1685'. Explain why you agree or disagree with this view.
2. 'The success of anti-Huguenot persecution by 1679 was highly significant for Louis' decision to revoke the Edict of Nantes in 1685'. Explain why you agree or disagree with this view.

ACTIVITY 2.8

Prepare a class debate about Huguenots and Jansenists in Louis XIV's France. You should make preparatory notes on:

- Louis' reasons for persecuting each
- methods and stages of persecution
- results of persecution
- Did Jansenists pose a threat to Louis XIV?
- Did Huguenots pose a threat to Louis XIV?

Practice essay questions

1. 'Colbert's financial reforms were far more successful than his economic ones.' Explain why you agree or disagree with this view.
2. 'Colbert's contribution as a minister was highly significant to Louis' government in France.' Explain why you agree or disagree with this view.
3. 'Versailles was highly significant for extending Louis XIV's absolutism.' Explain why you agree or disagree with this view.
4. Gallicanism best explains Louis' religious policies between 1668 and 1682'. Explain why you agree or disagree with this view.
5. 'Louis only succeeded in persecuting the Huguenots between 1681–85.' Explain why you agree or disagree with this view.
6. With reference to these sources and your understanding of the historical context, which of these two sources is more valuable in explaining Louis' priorities in ruling France.

Extract A

'I was sufficiently master of myself…to hide from you the pain which I felt on hearing someone like you, on whom I have heaped much kindness, speak to me as you did…It is the memory of the services that you have given me, together with my friendship, which make me give this advice: profit from it and do not wish angering me again…I never wish to hear the subject mentioned again…I do not want a single complaint'.

Louis XIV to Colbert, 24 April 1671, cited by David Smith, ***Louis XIV***, Cambridge: Cambridge University Press; 1992, p.19–20.

Extract B

Louis de Rouvroy, the Duc de Saint-Simon (1675–1755) was a soldier, diplomat and courtier. In his memoirs, he reported on court life at Versailles and left a wonderfully detailed, gossipy account of strong personalities, ambition and rivalry, which was only published after his death.

'Glory was his passion, but he also liked order and regularity in all things, he was naturally prudent, moderate, and reserved; always master of his tongue and his emotions…. His Ministers, generals, mistresses, and courtiers soon found out his weak point, namely, his love of hearing his own praises. There was nothing he liked so much as flattery, or, to put it more plainly, adulation; the coarser and clumsier it was, the more he relished it'.

Saint-Simon *Memoirs*, http://www.louis-xiv.de/index.php?id=26

Chapter summary

At the end of this chapter, you should be able to:

- understand the concept of Divine Right and its relevance to the reign of Louis XIV
- assess Louis' character and his aims as king
- understand the extent to which Louis restored order, centralised royal authority and used Versailles
- understand Colbert's role in promoting Louis' patronage of culture
- know and assess Colbert's financial and economic reforms
- know, explain and assess Louis' religious policies.

End notes

1 Extracts from Bossuet's work on kingship. History.hanover.edu. 2016. Available from: https://history.hanover.edu/texts/bossuet.html

2 Cited in Smith D. *Louis XIV*. Cambridge: Cambridge University Press; 1992. p. 12.

3 *Versailles: The Dream of a King.* (2009). France: Les Films d'Ici.

4 *Versailles: The Dream of a King.* (2009). France: Les Films d'Ici.

5 Beik W. *Louis XIV and Absolutism*. London: Palgrave Macmillan; 2000. p. 59.

6 Smith D. *Louis XIV*. Cambridge: Cambridge University Press; 1992. p. 12. p.102–3

7 Wilkinson R. *France and the Cardinals 1610–1661*. London: Hodder & Stoughton; 1995. p.13–4.

8 Hamscher A. *The Parlement of Paris after the Fronde*. Pittsburgh: University of Pittsburgh Press; 1976. p.20–1.

9 Maland D. *Europe in the Seventeenth Century*. London: Macmillan Education; 1996. p. 287.

10 Treasure G. *Louis XIV*. Harlow: Longman; 2001. p. 9[illegible].

11 Cited by Maland D. *Europe in the Seventeenth Century*. London: Macmillan Education; 1983. p. 289.

12 Mémoires de Saint-Simon, Vol. XXVIII. Cited in Smith D. *Louis XIV*. Cambridge: Cambridge University Press; 1992. p. 104.

13 Höfer B. *Psychosomatic Disorders in Seventeenth Century French literature*. Farnham: Ashgate; 2009. p. 8.

14 Burke P. *The Fabrication of Louis XIV*. New Haven: Yale University Press; 1992. p. 23 & 25.

15 Ibid. p. 5, 22 & 50.

16 Ibid. p. 52.

17 Ibid. p. 76.

18 Ibid. p. 25 & 75–6.

19 Ibid. p. 76.

20 Ibid. p. 26; Brunel P. *Companion to Literary Myths*. London: Routledge; 1993. p. 749.

21 Burke P. *The Fabrication of Louis XIV*. New Haven: Yale University Press; 1992. p.126 & 130.

22 Treasure G. *Louis XIV*. Harlow: Longman; 2001. p. 113.

23 Royal Edict, November 1661. Cited by Mettam R. *Government and Society in Louis XIV's France*. London: Macmillan; 1977. p. 93–4.

24 Cited by Mettam R. *Government and Society in Louis XIV's France*. London: Macmillan; 1977. p. 175.

25 Smith G. Monopolies, Mercantilism, Illegal Buttons, and Saltpeter Men Libertarianism.org. 2012. Available from: http://www.libertarianism.org/publications/essays/excursions/monopolies-mercantilism-illegal-buttons-saltpeter-men

26 Horn J. *Economic Development in Early Modern France: The Privilege of Liberty, 1650–1820* (Cambridge Studies in Economic History - Second Series). Cambridge University Press; 2015. p. 40.

27 Cited by Mettam R. *Government and Society in Louis XIV's France*. London: Macmillan; 1977. p. 185.

28 Cited by Coon L, Haldane K, Sommer E. *That Gentle Strength: Historical Perspectives on Women in Christianity.* Charlottesville: University Press of Virginia; 1990. p. 185.

29 Cited by Strayer B. *Suffering Saints*. Brighton: Sussex Academic Press; 2012. p. 128.

30 Strayer B. *Suffering Saints: Jansenists and Convulsionnaires in France, 1640–1799.* Brighton: Sussex Academic Press; 2012. p. 142.

31 Treasure G. *Louis XIV*. Harlow: Longman; 2001. p. 226.

3 Louis XIV and Europe, 1661–1685

In this chapter, we will look into:

- the context of French foreign policy in 1661: Louis XIV's aims, the extent of French military resources; the Military Academy; the role of Louvois
- France and Spain: the decline of Spanish military power; the War of Devolution
- France and the Dutch Republic: relations between Louis XIV and Charles II of England; the Franco-Dutch War; the Peace of Nijmegen
- France and the policy of Réunions: the drive to annex 'lost' territories to France such as Luxembourg, Casale and Strasbourg; the Truce of Ratisbon.

The context of French foreign policy in 1661

Louis XIV's aims

Truth is always the first casualty of war. It is also often the first casualty of History. Some historians have categorised Louis' foreign-policy aims as aggressive and expansionist. One, David Starkey, has even compared him to Hitler. This view seems rather far-fetched and simplistic. Louis' invasions were not racially motivated and often pursued defensive objectives. Equally misleading are assertions that Louis' policy was purely defensive and dynastic, as he sometimes claimed. Louis often veiled his actions in blatant propaganda, casting his victims as aggressors. He struggled to see how his actions would be interpreted by others.

In reality, Louis' foreign policy was motivated by different aims at different times. He was too impulsive and pragmatic an individual to dogmatically pursue one foreign policy aim above all others. Rather, he had a series of interlinked aims. They also changed – before, during and after wars – and responded to different influences, sources, constantly changing circumstances and whatever goals suited him at the time.

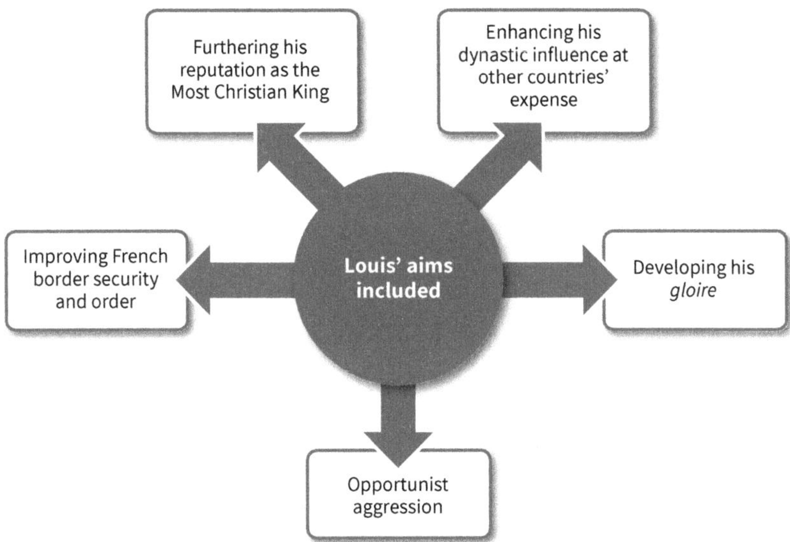

Figure 3.1: Louis' aims

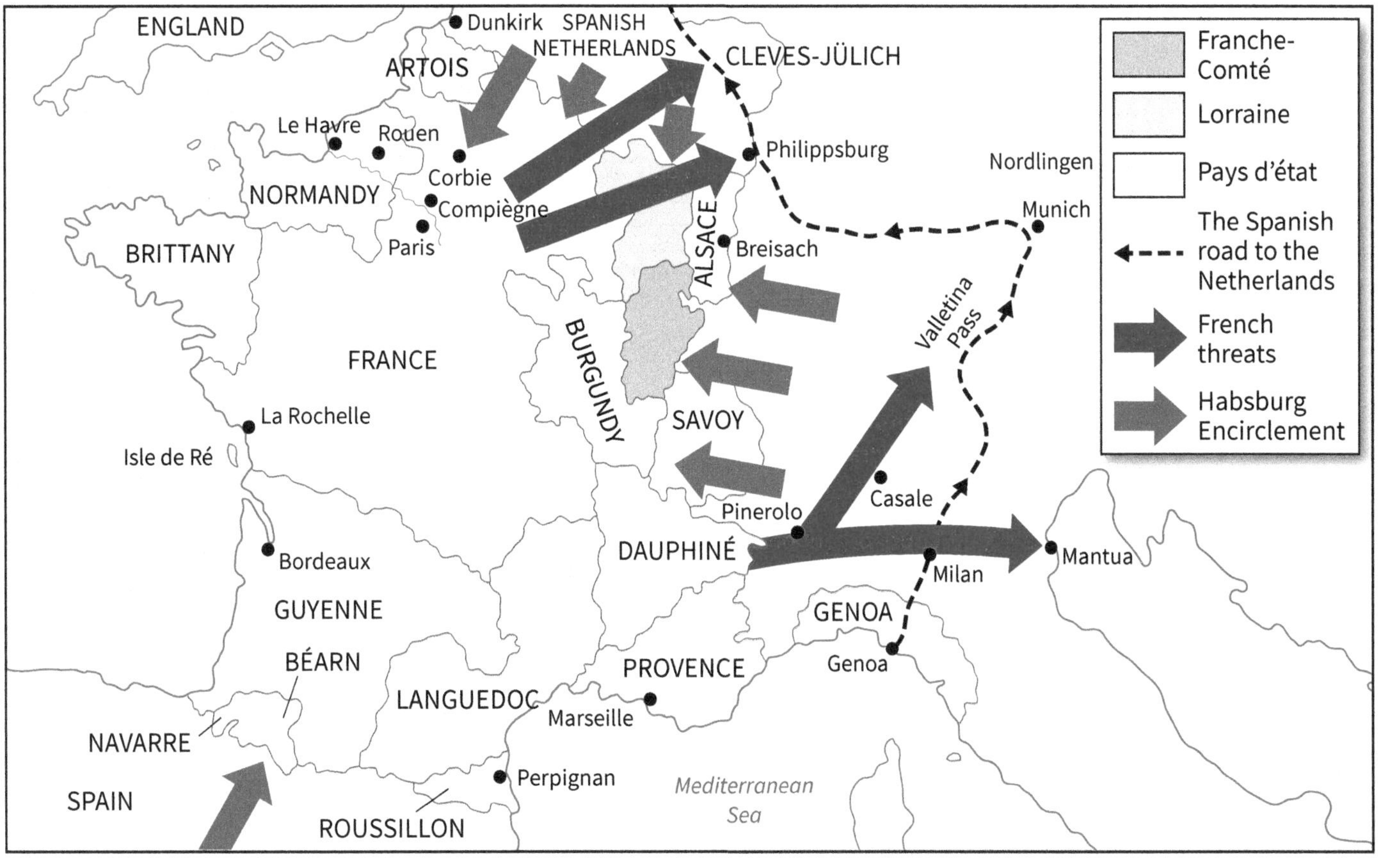

Figure 3.2: A map of France's borders in 1659

All of these were in evidence 1661–85.

Defensively, Louis had much to worry about in 1661. As Figure 3.3 shows, French borders were far from secure:

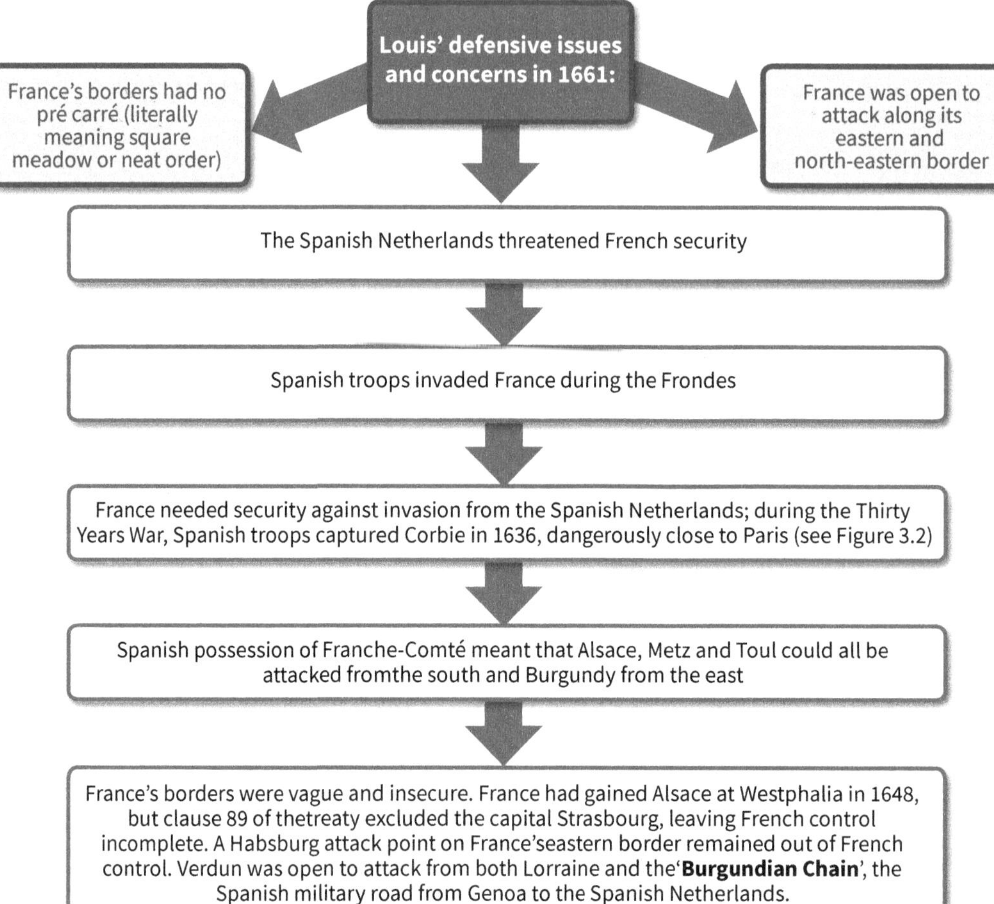

Figure 3.3: Reasons why Louis XIV had to consider defence of France as a key foreign policy aim after 1661

The confused state of French borders offended Louis' concern with order. Sébastien Le Prestre de Vauban was a military engineer and a marquis. He constantly emphasised the importance of maintaining defensible borders. This greatly appealed to Louis, as shown by Vauban's:

- promotions to Brigadier in 1674 and Commissioner General of Fortifications in 1678
- upgrades to the fortifications of over 300 cities 1667–1707
- construction of 37 new fortresses and military harbours.

Louis' dream of leading the Christian world and garnering German elector support to become Holy Roman Emperor also initially influenced his policy. This was encouraged by developments abroad, namely:

- Louis' allies in Bavaria (headed by Hermann Egon von Fürstenberg) secretly envisaged his election as Holy Roman Emperor in the case of the death of Leopold (Habsburg Emperor from 1658)
- Fürstenberg's brother's presence there meant pro-French support in Cologne
- The neutrality of Pfalz-Neuburg, Württemberg, Hanover and Osnabrück meant tacit support for the French.

- Some German electors (including Brandenburg, Saxony and Bavaria) no longer sought Habsburg protection of German Christian interests and were reluctant to join Leopold fighting the Ottoman Empire in 1663–4. Instead, they preferred to serve independently alongside French troops.
- Leopold's lack of a surviving male heir, until Charles' birth in 1678, signified that Louis could realistically imagine being backed as Holy Roman Emperor
- Louis' territorial gains following the War of Devolution (1667–68) and Dutch War (1672–9) and during Réunions 1681–84.

Louis' initial concern to enhance his kudos as Most Christian King was demonstrated in 1663–4 when he supplied 6,000 troops for Leopold against the Turks.

Louis also wished to enhance his dynastic honour; he envisaged the supremacy of Bourbon interests as a matter of personal principle and national interest. As highlighted in chapter 1, this involved pursuing his claim to the vast Spanish inheritance through his wife Maria Theresa. As we will see later in this chapter and in chapters 5 and 6, dynastic ambition was a smaller contributory factor in the king's policy until 1685 but it assumed much greater significance 1697–1702.

Gloire was important to Louis XIV. He wanted to project his (and therefore also France's) greatness with regards to frontier security, dynastic ambition and territorial control to buttress his propaganda. Louis' aggressive impulses came to the fore on numerous occasions, as explained in chapters 5 and 6. His motto was 'nec pluribus impar' – meaning 'not unequal to many'. This obscure boast has been taken by some historians to mean that the French king felt equal to taking on several enemies, so perhaps suggesting 'I can take on the whole world'. The extent of French military resources gave him good reason to believe this.

The extent of French military resources

Louis' quest for glory was fuelled by the fact that his army grew more quickly than that of any other state. His military resources included a hugely expanding and well-equipped army, an expanding navy and brilliant generals. The Sun King's huge army allowed him to dream big regarding his foreign policy ambitions. Warfare consumed 20% of total expenditure 1650–6, but considerably more from 1661:

Date:	Size of French army:	% increase over early 1630s levels:
1661	72,000 (approximate)	72%
1672	120,000	83%

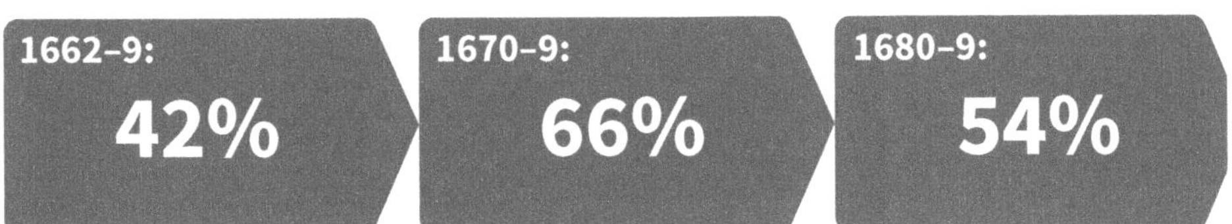

Figure 3.4: The French army in size and state expenditure

During the Dutch War (1672–9), the French army's average size was 40% more than it had been from 1635–59. Recruitment was incentivised by:

- regular pay
- tax exemption for good conduct.

Key terms

Magazine: magazines were stockpiles of food and weapons accessible by French border garrisons or France's armies when fighting outside or inside of France's borders.

At the height of the Dutch War, France's army had 66% more men than in 1667. Foreigners were attracted to enlist, including:

- 20,000 Swiss
- Piedmontese, Genoese, Germans, Irish and Hungarians.

Louis' army was made more prepared for anticipated wars. In 1661, Louis assumed the post of Colonel-general of Infantry. He then created a regular reserve of officers. This enabled prompt military mobilisation in 1667, when Louis attacked the Spanish Netherlands. Louis further increased the army's battle-readiness in 1668 by covertly absorbing officers who had allegedly been demobilised, into permanent formations.

Louis' increasing capacity for war was also reflected by Michel Le Tellier de Louvois' **magazine** system for feeding the army when it invaded. It also encompassed increasing the size of the infantry and artillery, new tactics (see the sections in this chapter on 'the role of Louvois' and 'the Military Academy' for further details) and army medical service improvements.

These included each regiment having its own field surgeon and hospital. In addition, permanent hospitals for troops were established in the rear and the Invalides was opened to give maimed and infirm soldiers security and honour.

As explained later in this chapter, Louis also had some outstandingly talented generals, especially:

Key terms

Glacis: artifical slopes to help deter and resist attack.

Chemin couvert: covered walkways allowed musketeers to shoot attacking enemies.

Bastions: projecting parts of a fortification built at an angle to the line of a wall, so as to allow defensive fire in several directions.

- Louis de Bourbon Condé – invaded Franche-Comté in 1668 and 1674
- Marshal Turenne – helped Louis overrun the Spanish Netherlands in 1667
- Sébastien Vauban – successfully directed 48 sieges, created a rationally designed barrier of fortresses to protect France's borders and perfected new ways of besieging and fortifying towns.

Vauban's fortification design included pointed bastions and detached outworks at the corners of star-shaped main fortresses. These:

- denied attackers any shelter (unlike older square and round towers)
- created angles for French soldiers defending fortresses to sweep the ditches in front of any wall with musket and canon fire
- enabled France to delay and repel allied invasion during the Spanish Succession War 1701–13 (see chapter 6).

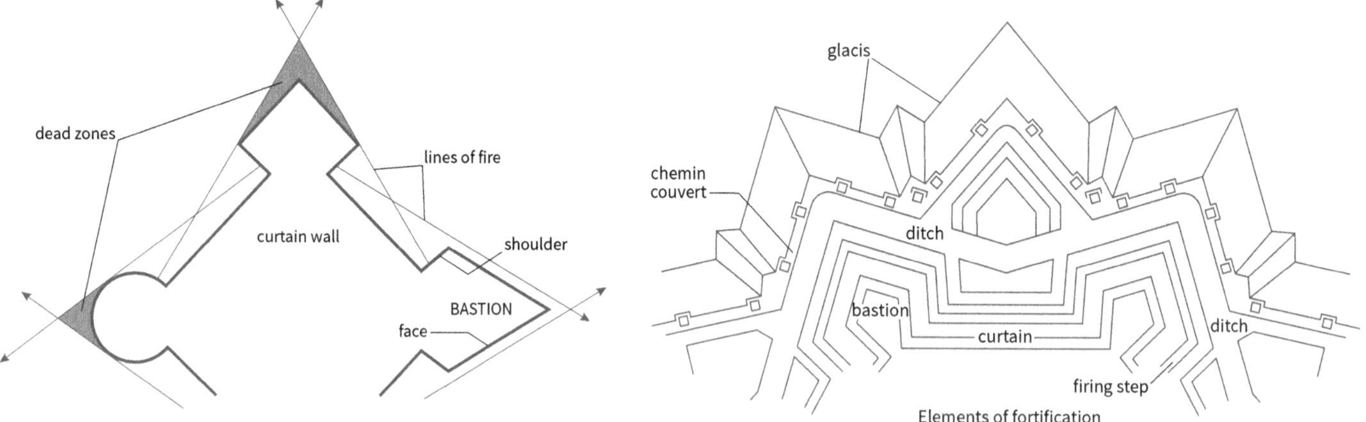

Figure 3.5: A typical Vauban's artillery fortress designed for defence

In 1661, Louis' navy consisted of rotting hulks and just 18 serviceable ships of the line. Colbert transformed this, building:

- 111 ships by 1671
- dockyards and arsenals at Rochefort, Dunkirk, Brest and Toulon
- a battle fleet with 31% more ships than the Dutch in 1680
- 117 ships and 30 galleys by 1683.

However, the extent of Louis' resources had serious limitations in reality.

As Turenne noted, an army over 50,000 men was awkward to supply and command. Feeding a large army became difficult as the Dutch War became prolonged. This led to the devastation of the Palatinate in 1674. Ill-discipline remained a serious issue. Desertion rates were high:

- 43% of Marshal Louis Vivonne's men ran away in 1677
- in 1678, the crack regiment of Champagne lost 68 men in just 10 days.

Exaggerated muster calls remained a serious problem. Captains borrowed **faggots** (men from other companies) for inspections so frequently that in 1667, Louvois introduced hanging in place of flogging and branding for detected 'faggots'. The fact remained that the strength of Louis' army was always greater on paper than in reality. Quality of recruitment was another issue. During the Dutch War, General Luxembourg (François-Henri de Montmorency) complained that his troops were 'deplorable… half of them children whom I shall have to send back to France'.[1]

Size, therefore, did not mean everything regarding Louis' military resources. These would enable him to succeed, but only up to a point and when his enemies were weak and isolated before 1685.

The Military Academy

Louis XIV inherited an irregular and ill-disciplined army. Obedience was instilled through hanging soldiers and nobles became officers more for personal gain than serving the state.

To counter this and to gratify his love of regimented order, Louis XIV started a basic military training system. This aimed to:

- bring on the next generation of officers
- formalise drill and training
- engender a battle culture of complete forbearance and unswerving obedience and discipline
- develop technical and engineering knowledge.

Louis created an elite military training school called the 'Musketeers of the King' in 1664. This was to recruit and train:

- nobles aged 16–25
- the most promising and best connected royal stable pages
- sons of leading court families
- Louis' son, the Grand Dauphin.

It offered the prestige of royal association. Both musketeer regiments that Louis created directly served him as their captain. It also aimed to create an elite modern professional officer corps. This was not without successes. The King's Musketeers developed a formidable reputation for reckless bravery and battlefield performance. They also provided leadership elsewhere in the French army. Guy Rowlands states that in the years 1674–89, 238 left to serve in other companies, often in a leadership capacity.

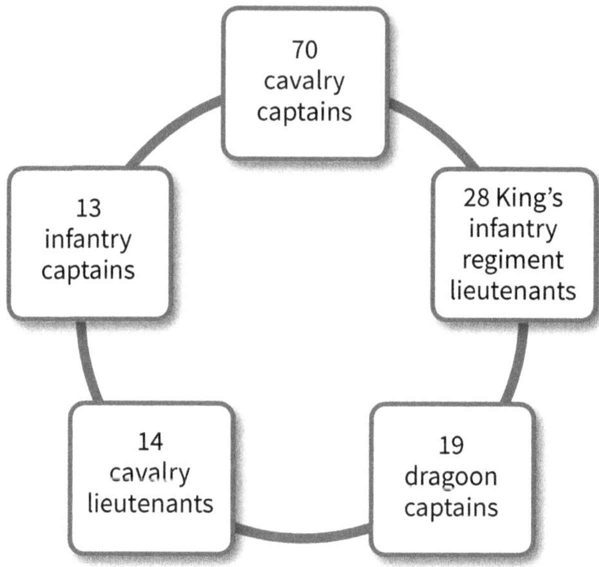

Figure 3.6: French army leadership positions filled by the King's Musketeers

Musketeer regiment success lasted beyond 1685. Between 1688 and 1715, the two musketeer regiments numbered 250 men each.

Military academy training became increasingly important during Louis' reign. It targeted young noblemen who were not wealthy or powerful enough to gain a place at court and was thriving by the early 1680s. This was down to two men who served Louis as Grand Écuyer (Grand Squire responsible for the royal stables and France's national military academy network):

- Louis de Lorraine, the Comte d'Armagnac (1666–1677)
- Henri de Lorraine, Comte de Brionne (1677–1718).

In 1668, a military academy was created at Metz. By the early 1680s, there were:

- 6 military academies in Paris
- 20 in the provinces.

However, academy training could be prohibitively expensive:

- despite subsidies from Louis, the musketeer regiments cost nobles 500 livres a year
- at least two-thirds of nobles avoided this form of military education.

Musketeer regiments also provided limited opportunities. Cavalry and infantry regiment colonels usually recruited their own illiterate and untrained recruits. Guy Rowlands notes that in 1688, there were only 4,000 nobles alive that had passed through a military academy. These numbers declined thereafter. Many academies closed in the 1690s, as nobles preferred serving in the royal stables.

Military training was extended in 1682 when Louvois established nine colleges, each with approximately 500 cadets. These offered:

- mathematics and arms manual training
- practical battlefield experience each summer
- a means of separating nobles from the perceived bad influence of less noble families
- a gratifying display of power for Louis, his family and attendant courtiers.

Louis enjoyed attending military parades and manoeuvres and he revolutionised new drills. These took place even in peacetime and taught soldiers to:

- stand their ground in the face of enemy fire
- rehearse practical mechanical movements (including musket loading and pike handling) so that they would become automatic whatever the enemy danger level
- march together in large troop bodies.

Infantry units drilled within their companies 5 a.m.–10 a.m., manoeuvred by brigade or battalion 4 p.m.–7p.m. and manoeuvred as a whole 24 company unit once a week. They were also taught to advance in linear formation at precisely 80 paces per minute while firing and reloading upon command by Jean Martinet (Louvois army inspector general 1667–72).

This perfectly suited Louis' love of regimented order, although there remained limits. John Lynn reports 'near mutiny' among cadets in Charlemont and Besançon in 1685, with two having to be executed.[2]

The role of Louvois

Louvois was the son of Michel le Tellier (war minister 1643–77). He started learning the ropes and sharing his father's responsibility as secretary of state for war in 1662. He frequently accompanied Louis' armies and often 'went alone to inspect, organise and make his presence felt and feared'.[3] Louvois was essentially in charge from 1670 (although his father did not resign until 1677). He joined the Conseil d'en haut in 1672 and became war minister in 1677.

Louvois did much to improve France's fighting capacity after 1661 by:

- improving royal army supply and control
- introducing a new promotion system
- taking strict disciplinary measures
- introducing new weapons.

French invasions of enemy territory would not be sustainable unless they were supported by an improved supply system. Unfed soldiers were more prone to ill-discipline, marauding and looting from local populations, including French. Louvois therefore established an extensive and permanent system of magazines alongside France's north-eastern border. These were centres for supplying:

- army food
- cavalry horse fodder
- cannon, cannonballs, grenades and gunpowder.

The magazine system extended the French army's operational range and eliminated the need to wait for spring herbage prior to invasion. Subsequently, French forces could amass along the Dutch border prior to invasion in 1672, with enough grain for 200,000 rations a day for 6 months.

Louvois also extended the crown's nominal control of the army at private contractors' expense. Previously, army units were named by and primarily loyal to their noble colonel, rather serving as regular units of the crown. Louvois tackled this through:

- 5 new royal administrative bureaux
- more rigidly worded contracts
- his overbearing personality.

Upon his death in 1691, 92% of infantry regiments bore permanent titles as regular royal army units.

Louvois provided a small but important step towards creating a military career ladder based upon ability rather than nobility (i.e. buying or inheriting a post). He did this by:

- introducing two unpurchaseable ranks – lieutenant colonel and major
- subjecting officers to promotion examinations and constant intendant monitoring
- requiring senior post applicants to amass more previous practical battlefield experience.

The impact of this was evident in 1684. When Louis created 27 new infantry regiments, all colonels appointed had previously served as either major or lieutenant colonel. Almost 56% had been captains in the King's regiments. However, birth and status still dominated the army's upper echelons; almost two-thirds of lieutenants-general were titled nobles. Only about 7% were non-nobles. Louvois' impact was therefore more evolutionary than revolutionary, as it was with his discipline improvement measures. Brutal punishments for delinquents included Jean Martinet's 12-thonged whip. Naarden governor Dupas was sentenced to execution for surrendering too easily in 1673. Others were rebuked for neglecting their regiments, regardless of reputation, including:

- Nogaret, a high-born captain and court reveller
- Lord Hamilton, who was threatened with being sent to the Bastille in 1685.

But ill-discipline still remained. In 1673, magazine supply looting was widespread. Between 1686 and 1695, 448 officers had to be stripped of their commands.

Louvois had more impact as a propagandist. In the 1680s, he commissioned almost 20 statues across France depicting Louis gloriously on horseback. He also overcame resistance to new weapons and tactics, including:

Innovation:	Details:
Bayonet charges	First used during the Dutch War.
Flintlocks	Guns that ignited gunpowder by a flint striking steel rather than a lit match; these loaded more quickly, misfired less and replaced muskets by 1679.
Increased use of artillery	Louvois increased the number of bombardier companies by 83%. These had an estimated maximum range of 2,500 yards, relative accuracy up to 500 yards and were brought under strict royal control.
Increased cavalry charges	New breeds of lighter horses allowed cavalrymen to gallop at the enemy with heavy sabre thrusts.
Mortar bombardment	Used during the 1680s, these were intended to bully, punish and terrorise enemies without risking French troops.
Socket bayonets	Developed by Vauban in the late 1680s, these allowed loading and firing without having to be removed.

Table 3.1: Summary of new weapons and tactics introduced by Louvois

Louvois therefore did much to feed Louis' appetite for war and use of brute force, as we will see in this next section and chapter 5.

France and Spain

The decline of Spanish military power

In the 17th century, a nation's military power was affected by many factors including its:

- population size
- extent of economic and financial resources
- army's numerical and defensive strength
- strength of military and political leadership
- level of internal stability and external allies.

In all of these aspects, Spain was increasingly weak relative to France, both before and after 1661. Although this was not obvious at the time, Spain represented a soft target against whom Louis could easily enhance his military prestige and territorial control.

Numerous factors underpinned Spanish military decline in the 17th century:

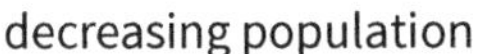

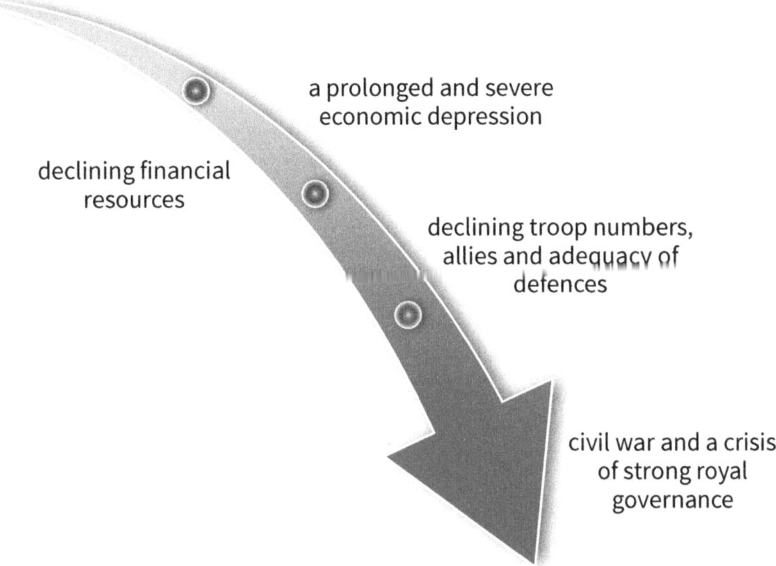

Figure 3.7: Reasons for Spanish military decline (1661)

France's population grew during the 17th century. Spain's declined (largely through plagues, civil wars and emigration):

Year:	Spain's population as a % of France's:
1600	40%
1650	34%
1700	23%

Table 3.2: The population of Spain compared to France

Spain's population decline undermined its military strength. Shrinking taxation yields meant less money available to fight war. So too did the disastrous loss of American bullion wealth from the 16th century. In the period 1631–60, there was a 75% drop in kilos of Spanish bullion relative to the period 1581–1630. During 1660–69, Spanish imports in pesos of South American bullion were 53% lower they had been in the period 1650–59.

Spain's economy suffered prolonged depression. This saw:

- declining industrial output from the 1620s
- the almost total collapse of Castilian manufacturing and banking
- four years of bad harvests from 1665–68.

Spain could not cope with a renewed war against France after 1661. In 1667, its debts were 221 million ducats – some 2.6 times higher than in 1598. This was partly caused by Spain's civil wars against Catalan separatists in the 1640s and 1650s and its prolonged, costly and humiliatingly unsuccessful campaign against Portuguese independence (1640–1668). This exposed the ramshackle state of Spain's army:

- 1665: A Spanish army was annihilated at Villaviciosa; Spain's undivided resources could only muster 20,000 troops.
- 1666: Spain still lacked the forces to go on the offensive, despite spending 4 million ducats on combatting Portuguese troops.
- 1667: Commander Don Juan José (Philip IV's illegitimate son) refused an order to lead the defence of the Spanish Low Countries.

Increasingly, the Spanish Netherlands were open to attack. Spanish troop numbers here fell by:

- 1640–1661: 73%
- 1661–1667: 39%.

Added to this was a crisis of effective political leadership. This was partly caused by Philip IV's declining health and years of Habsburg in-breeding. Philip IV died in 1665. He left his entire empire to his son, the syphilitic, paralytic three-year-old son Carlos. He was not expected to live until his fourth birthday and was challenged by his half-brother Don Juan.

Opportunity therefore knocked for Louis to attack Spain. The Spanish Netherlands were there for the taking, and so too seemingly was the rest of Spain's empire.

The War of Devolution

In 1667, Louis invaded the Spanish Netherlands. This started the War of Devolution (1667–8).

This overtly emotive propaganda claimed that invasion was necessary to put right a dynastic wrongdoing. Louis' stated intentions were purely to defend his family's succession rights which had been 'usurped' following Philip IV of Spain's death in 1665. The 'violation' Louis claimed related to his wife, Maria Theresa, who was the eldest daughter of Philip IV's first marriage. She was ignored entirely by Philip IV's will. Instead, the entire Spanish Empire was appallingly left to his three-year-old Carlos son.

Louis' lawyers thus used ancient Flemish '**Devolution law**' to justify his claiming and **partitioning** (dividing into separate parts) land in the Spanish Netherlands.

Key terms

Ancient Flemish **Devolution law** gave preference to daughters of a first marriage over the son of a second one. On this basis, Louis XIV pressed his wife's right to inherit territories in the Spanish Netherlands.

Voices from the past

Louis claimed dynastic concerns as his primary goal in the War of Devolution in a manifesto addressed to the Spanish court:

'It is not the ambition of possessing new states or the desire of winning glory by arms which inspires the Most Christian King with the desire of maintaining the rights of the queen his wife; but would it not be a shame for a king to allow all the privileges of blood and of law to be violated in the persons of himself, his wife and his son? As king, he feels obliged to prevent this injustice; as master, to oppose this usurpation; and, as father, to preserve the patrimony of his son. He has no desire to employ force to open the gates, but he wishes to be seen as a beneficent sun by the rays of his love'[4]

Comment upon the usefulness of Louis' manifesto for explaining his motives for attacking the Spanish Netherlands in 1667.

They argued that when a man had married for a second time, his property should go to the children of his first marriage. Unsurprisingly, the Spanish dismissed this outright. Louis' claims have been seen as fairly specious because:

- Devolution law only applied to property, not territory.
- Sick or not, Carlos was Philip's rightful heir.
- Philip had only consented to Maria Theresa's marriage to Louis on the grounds that she renounced her claim to the throne of Spain and its territories.

Louis' rhetoric for his invasion also largely differed from reality. Defensive concerns were clearly an issue preceding invasion, as was the opportunity to get some quick runs on the board in terms of *gloire*. Spain was in no position to cope with a French attack. Foreign affairs minister Hugues de Lionne skilfully ensured that Spain was left isolated with no allies, through diplomatic negotiation and bribery. Brandenburg, England, Sweden, Denmark and the League of German Princes had all promised to remain neutral in the event of a French attack. An annual subsidy of 2 million livres to Portugal also kept Spanish troops bogged down fighting the Portuguese.

With the Spanish Netherlands so lightly defended, the opportunity for lightning military victories was too hard to resist for Louis. The size of his 1667 invasion force was 50,000. By contrast, Castel Rodrigo, commander of the army defending the Spanish Netherlands, had only 20,000 troops at his disposal.

Aggressive opportunism, fuelled by a desire for *gloire*, therefore combined with defensive motives as the chief causes for the war. Attack would be the best form of defence.

If success is measured in battles won and how quickly an enemy could be humiliated, then the War of Devolution was arguably a clear triumph for Louis XIV.

Lightning victories were achieved as French troops easily outnumbered and outfought the Spanish. This was exemplified when the Prince de Condé overran Franche-Comté in just a fortnight. Turenne and Vauban were no less successful, capturing numerous significant towns such as Charleroi, Lille, Douai and Oudenarde.

In terms of land gained, the Devolution War also seemed successful. The 1668 Treaty of Aix-la-Chapelle allowed Louis to keep the towns he had gained in the Spanish Netherlands, in return for restoring France Comté to Spain. The towns gained afforded some level of security against Spanish attacks on France's north-eastern frontier. To the extent that Louis' war aims had been defensive, the outcome of the war and the negotiations that followed could be judged a success. Vauban had been recommending the construction of a **pré carré**. The gains of Saint Omer, Veurne and Cambrai respectively acted as just such buffer zones for Calais, Dunkirk (purchased back from the English in 1662) and Saint Quentin. This gave Louis the beginnings of what Vauban had recommended as essential to national security, as did Vauban's fortification of towns such as Lille and Ath. This shows that French security against

Key terms

Pré carré: a French term meaning 'back yard'. Vauban's intention was to create a defensive buffer zone at the French border as a protection against any hostile neighbours.

attack from the Spanish Netherlands was, at least to a point, a priority in the Devolution War and Peace of Aix-la-Chappelle in 1668, as illustrated by Figure 3.8:

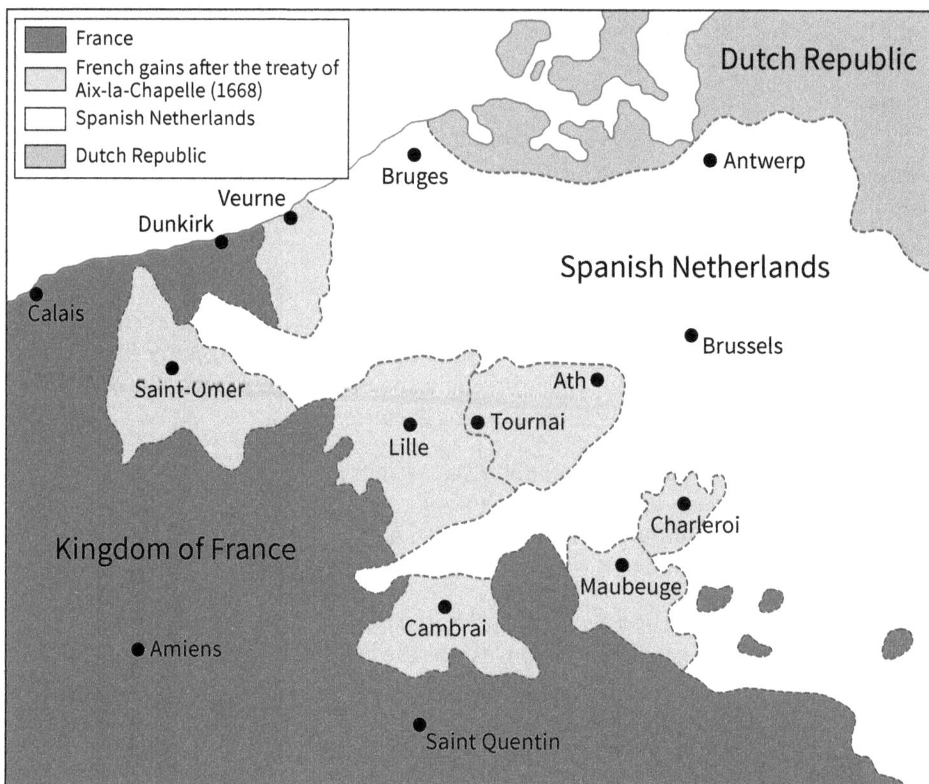

Figure 3.8: French gains in the Spanish Netherlands at the Treaty of Aix-la-Chapelle, 1668

French military dominance also led to a dynastic success and turning point in 1668. At the secret Treaty of Grémonville, Holy Roman Emperor Leopold I agreed to partition the Spanish Empire if Carlos died without heirs. This seemed only a matter of time. Moreover, it meant that Louis could return Franche-Comté, expecting that he would soon inherit it.

If dynastic factors were more of a **pretext** than an underlying priority going into the war, they assumed a greater significance as the war concluded, leaving Louis more open to the idea of compromise at the peace. However, the fact that all French land gained at Aix-la-Chappelle was in Walloon Flanders – where devolution law did not apply – suggests that he was not primarily motivated by dynastic factors.

The idea that Louis prioritised and succeeded in achieving a defensive pré carré can also be questioned. The territory gained from Lille to Ath and Charleroi seemed to negate the notion. Instead, it created **salients** (small territorial bulges) which could be easily attacked on three sides (see Figure 3.8). This seemed no more orderly, secure or even a border than in 1648. Louis' return of Franche-Comté to Spain in 1668 arguably further negated French security. Without Franche-Comté, French-held Alsace was vulnerable to attack from the south as shown in Figure 1.8. The fact that Louis later abandoned towns like Charleroi and Ath and kept Franche-Comté at the 1679 Treaty of Nijmegen shows that he later realised his mistakes and the need for a more defendable frontier.

Moreover, Louis' pre-war propaganda about fighting for blood – his wife's inheritance rights under devolution law – had not succeeded. His attack on the Spanish Netherlands was neither seen as dynastic nor defensive by countries he assumed would remain his natural supporters. Instead, it was clearly perceived as excessive, naked aggression and grounds for forming the Triple Alliance. This was an unexpected diplomatic setback for Louis. Sweden, England and the Dutch Republic – all previous allies of France – were prepared to fight to limit France to its 1659 borders. A Dutch propaganda medal showed van Beuningen – the Dutch instigator of the **Triple Alliance** – as Joshua holding back the sun in heavens, a clear celebration of the fact that the Dutch-inspired Triple Alliance had frustrated the Sun King's influence over Europe and more specifically, the Spanish lands. This showed that the Sun King's ambitions to be regarded as the leading European ruler, and make his 'most Christian' title really mean something, were already being challenged and would need some element of compromise, such as the return of France Comté. If Louis thought he could take on the whole world without taking account of international opinion and the European balance of power, then he was wrong.

Key terms

Triple Alliance: formed in 1668 when England and Scotland, Sweden, and the Dutch Republic came together to oppose French expansion in the War of Devolution.

Overall, Louis' successes in the Devolution War outweighed any setbacks. No alliance or foreign country actually fought against Louis and the scale of French lightning victories and *gloire* remained unparalleled. France Comté had been given up to curry international favour, but seemed likely to soon return in future due to Carlos' apparently impending death and the partition treaty with Leopold.

Although a minor irritant to Louis, the Triple Alliance was easily broken up, especially as England became a French ally again in the 1670 Treaty of Dover.

ACTIVITY 3.1

1 Prepare a mind map that shows Louis' main motives for fighting the Devolution War.

2 Copy and complete the following table for the War of Devolution:

War and dates:	Key battle victories/ details of successes:	Key defeat/ setback details, including diplomatic:	Peace Treaty gains:	Peace Treaty setbacks:	Overall how successful and why?:

Defensive and expansionist aims dominated the cause and conclusion of the war, although dynastic factors arguably assumed greater significance after the partition treaty with Leopold. In the case of the Dutch War, this was to be very different.

France and the Dutch Republic

Relations between Louis XIV and Charles II of England

Louis' initial foreign policy successes were partly aided and abetted by King Charles II of England and Scotland.

Charles was the son of Charles I, the Stuart king beheaded in England in 1649. After Oliver Cromwell's period as Lord Protector of England (1653–58), the monarchy's restoration seemed both popular and the best guarantee against social fragmentation. Charles II was family: the son of Louis' aunt Henrietta Maria and brother of Henrietta, who married Louis' brother Phillippe I, Duke of Orléans.

Charles was essentially bought off by Lionne to support French interests, as summarised in Figure 3.8. This was made possible by Mazarin's brief alliance with Cromwell after the Treaty of Westminster in 1655 (see chapter 1). This proved that collaboration was possible between England and France. In addition, Charles II was in financial difficulties: French subsidies paid for Charles II's army arrears, court, government and naval loans.

Between 1662 and 1685, Louis' relationship with Charles was generally beneficial to French foreign policy interests, although this was temporarily disrupted by England joining the Triple Alliance in 1668. It became harder to maintain from 1674.

Relations between Louis and Charles involved:

Mutually beneficial collaboration between 1662–5
A temporary and minor blip in this between 1665–8
Covert alliance from 1670 and joint fighting against the Dutch 1672–4
An increasing struggle to keep England neutral from 1674 until 1678
Renewed French subsidies in 1680
Charles' deathbed conversion to Catholicism in 1685.

Charles' openness to French subsidies 1662–5 undoubtedly served Louis' preparations for attacking Spain in 1667 and Holland in 1672 really well:

Date:	What Charles did:	How this benefited Louis:
1662	• Sold Dunkirk to Louis for 5 million livres • Helped support Portuguese troops against Spain in return for 2 million livres	• Gave him an excellent base for operations against the Spanish Netherlands • Diverted Spanish troops away from the Spanish Netherlands
1670	• Was persuaded by an annual subsidy of 3 million livres and the attractive Louis de Querouelle to leave the Triple Alliance and secretly sign the Treaty of Dover • Accepted 2 million livres in return for promising to declare himself a Catholic	• The Triple Alliance quickly disintegrated, leaving no one to counter French expansionism • Charles covertly committed England to assisting in attacking the Dutch • The Dutch would be politically isolated as Charles II seemed happy to nail his colours to the French Catholic mast.

Table 3.3: How Charles II benefited Louis' foreign policy

In 1665–7, Charles was at war with the Dutch, who Louis allied with from 1666. But this did little apparent damage to the mutual Anglo-French collaboration fostered in the years beforehand. Clyde Grose aptly states that 'the war between England and France, when finally declared in 1666, was scarcely more than a farce'.[5] Louis engaged very little time or money in this war. When Louis gathered an army to prevent Dutch humiliation, Charles blamed the war on Earl Clarendon (who he exiled in disgrace) and sent his sister Henrietta to start negotiating a peace.

The Triple Alliance in 1668 also did no major damage to Anglo-French relations. In 1668, Louis sent diplomat Charles Colbert (Marquis de Croissy and Jean-Baptiste Colbert's younger brother) with funds and gifts to placate anti-French English politicians, including Lord Arlington and the Duke of Buckingham. He also sent Charles II's sister, Henrietta Maria.

The ensuing Treaty of Dover reassured Louis that his next victim, the Dutch, would be outnumbered when attacked, and unaware of Charles' defection. This was because it was agreed covertly. The two kings promised to declare war against the United Provinces. Charles pledged 6,000 men to help the French attack by land and 50 men-of-war at sea.

However, an anti-Dutch alliance with Charles II was not sustainable. Anti-French factions became more dominant within his government after Thomas Osborne, Earl of Danby, took over the Treasury in 1673. He was:

- an avowed enemy of France and Catholicism
- dismayed at the secret Treaty of Dover and English naval losses
- opposed to any more money being spent on the war
- active in leading parliament to oppose spending any more money on the war.

French subsidies now failed to maintain English support against the Dutch. In 1674, England concluded a peace with the Dutch. French diplomacy now focused upon keeping England neutral. Charles and other leading political figures were secretly bribed behind Danby's back to continuingly not call parliament, thereby denying any opportunity for debate about whether England should join other countries, like Spain, which were now supporting the Dutch. Charles drove a harder bargain. In 1678, he declared his price was 6 million livres annually for three years (three times the amount offered by the French).

Louis refused Charles' subsidy requests once he had concluded his peace with the Dutch in 1678. Paul Barillon d'Amoncourt (French ambassador from 1677) ensured that French influence won the day by:

- successfully bribing many Lords – including Sir John Baber and Algernon Sidney – to help overthrow Danby in 1679
- bribing Charles to dissolve parliament again in 16[illegible], this was to counter parliament's plans for a Protestant regency government for Charles' brother James.
- Charles' deathbed conversion to Catholicism in 1685.

This apparently showed the supremacy of Catholicism, which was one of Louis' reasons for attacking the Dutch in 1672.

The Franco-Dutch War

Summary of key reasons for the war with the Dutch:

- Louis wanted to humiliate the Dutch and teach them a lesson for joining the Triple Alliance to limit French territorial gains.
- Louis had a natural underlying hatred of the Dutch.
- Lionne successfully isolated the Dutch.
- France had increased the size and strength of its army.
- There was no ministerial opposition to the war, but unequivocal support.

Anger, not strategy, prompted France's invasion of Holland in 1672. Louis sensed easy opportunities for enhancing his domestic and international reputation through lightning victories against a weak enemy. He acted impetuously – losing sight of his priority to be universally regarded as the 'Most Christian King'. Dynastic motives also seemed irrelevant. Aggressive opportunism, tinged with ideological hatred and the unchallenged belief that nothing could get in his way, was Louis' main driving force for attacking Holland in 1672.

Key terms

Hawk: Policy-makers who pursue an aggressive, warlike or inflexible policy.

Dove: Policy-makers who are willing to negotiate, compromise and find common ground.

ACTIVITY 3.2

1 Take detailed notes on:
- Louis' relations with Charles
- why Louis invaded Holland in 1672.

2 How important were the following factors for the French attack on the Dutch in 1672 and why?
- defence
- dynastic ambition
- *gloire*
- revenge.

3 Discussion activity: Based on what you have read in this chapter so far, to what extent were Louis' foreign-policy motives consistent?

Louis' view of the Dutch

Louis had never seen the Dutch as worthy allies, but rather as deserving victims. France had supported Dutch independence in 1648 and financed the Dutch in the Anglo-Dutch War from 1665, yet they had:

- joined the Triple Alliance which sought to bind France by its 1659 borders
- offended Louis' honour with their propaganda
- banned all French imports in 1672.

Ideologically, the Dutch Republic opposed everything that the France of Louis XIV stood for. As a republic, the Dutch had rejected the concept of divinely appointed monarchy. They found Louis' practice of strong, personal rule to be offensive to God, who was the only true king in their Calvinist view of the world. Dutch **Calvinism** was incompatible with Louis' orthodox Catholicism and was the very kind of 'heresy' he had vowed to extinguish in his coronation oath.

Louis also saw the Dutch as an isolated soft target. Lionne had easily dismantled the Triple Alliance. By 1672:

- Sweden had been bought off and promised to support a French attack.
- Brandenburg was Holland's ally.

The French domestic situation

France's expanding and increasingly well-equipped army augured well for a lightning humiliation of the Dutch. Louis' desire to teach what he called the Dutch 'maggots' a lesson was fully supported by:

- Colbert, as Dutch trade dominated in the Baltic, Atlantic and Levant
- **hawks** Condé and Turenne – they dominated after **dove** Lionne's retirement in 1671.

Against this backdrop and in keeping with many past and present invasions, the French aggressor portrayed itself as victim and vice versa. Dutch attempts to offer concessions to avoid war proved futile.

Voices from the past

Madame de Sévigné

Madame Françoise-Marguerite de Sévigné was a French aristocrat at Louis' court. She commented on the relations between France and the Dutch Republic:

'Yesterday, the Dutch ambassador presented his letter to the King who did not look at it although the Dutchman offered to read it. He pointed out that the States General had never acted other than in a polite way, yet this great army was prepared for attacking them. The King then spoke in a wonderfully majestic and gracious manner, said that he was aware that they were stirring up his enemies against him and that he considered it wise not to allow himself to be taken by surprise. He was powerful on land and sea in order to defend himself. He would do whatever he considered was necessary for his *gloire* and for the good of the state'.[6]

How successful was the Dutch War?

In terms of his objective of humiliating the Dutch, Louis experienced initial overall success in 1672, but ultimate failure.

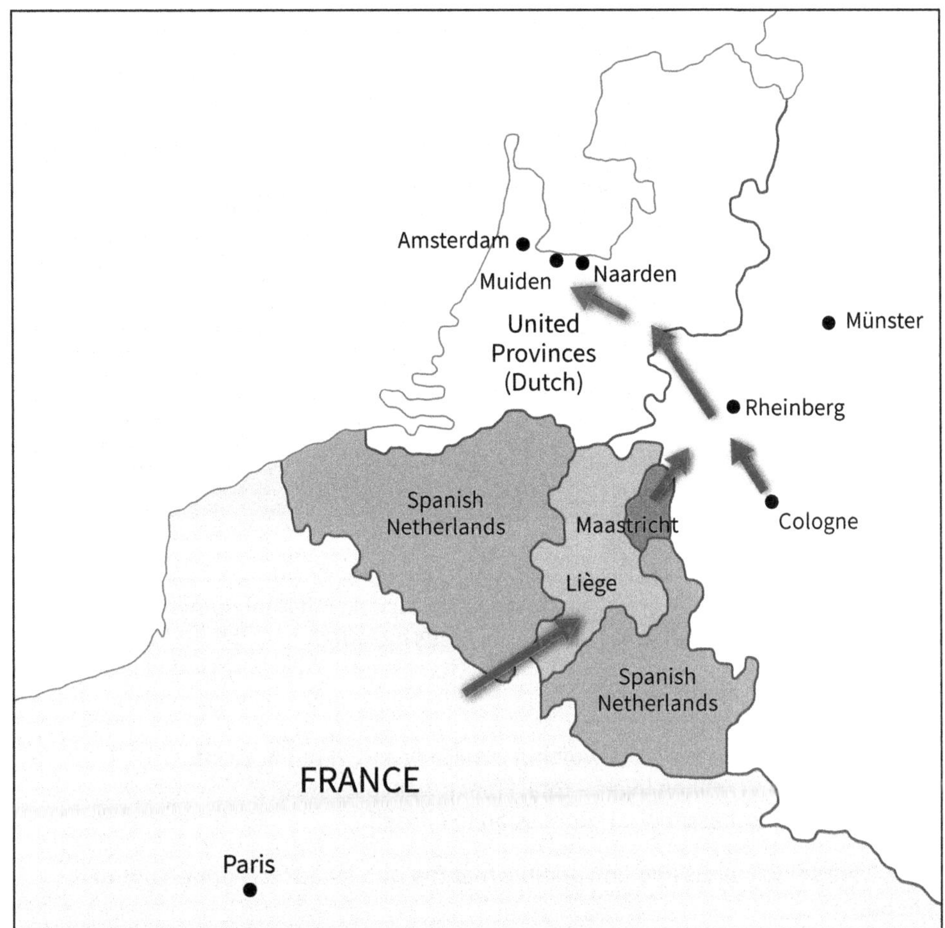

Figure 3.9: The route taken by French forces attacking Holland in 1672

Louis knew he had the Dutch where he wanted them, at least temporarily during June 1672:

'It is a good thing that I have prepared for so long for nothing has been lacking… I am in a position to instil fear into my enemies, astonishment to my neighbours and fear to the envious.'

By June 1672, the river Rhine had been crossed. Bossuet called this 'the wonder of the century' and Louis' heroism was immortalised in Le Brun's painting *The Crossing of The Rhine*.

The French captured over 40 Dutch towns in 1672. Dutch barrier forts were abandoned and *gloire* was enhanced by seizing Rheinberg and other Rhine strongholds. Yet tactical and diplomatic overconfidence and naivety cost Louis the lightning end to the war that he had envisaged in 1672.

Louis squandered chances for even greater success against the Dutch in June 1672. Firstly, he rejected Condé's offer to capture Amsterdam and slowed down the advance by insisting on being there in person to receive the surrender of each Dutch town. Secondly, he rejected generous peace terms offered by De Witt's government in June 1672, which included huge reparations and surrendering all territory south of the River Maas. This was far more than was actually gained in the Treaty of Nijmegen in 1679 in which France surrendered all Dutch territory captured.

Figure 3.10: Le Brun's *The Crossing of The Rhine*, 1672

Moreover, Louis' excessive greed and myopic obsession with total humiliation in negotiating peace in 1672 backfired. His demands included:

- the loss of all captured territory
- the end of anti-French tariffs
- the admission of Catholics to worship publically and to public posts
- reparations of 27 million livres – total French war costs in 1672
- annual Dutch ambassadorial submission to himself.

These were so ridiculous and unworkable that the Dutch had little option but to fight on.

The ensuing Dutch resistance took Louis by surprise. The opening of **dykes** at Muiden allowed seawater to flood land between Amsterdam and French forces, thereby ending all hopes of capturing it.

The Dutch government also would not surrender. William of Orange overthrew Jan De Witt's government and dedicated himself to spearheading Dutch defence and frustrating Louis XIV.

William of Orange was a member of a Dutch family which had been prominent in establishing Holland's independence. De Witt dominated Dutch politics while William was young. French aggression played into William's hands and he was appointed to head the country's defence.

William was fairly successful. Despite an invading force of 280,000, Louis could not defeat the Dutch decisively. What had started as an attempt at total humiliation became a prolonged stalemate that drained French finances, as explained in Chapter 2.

Certainly, French *gloire* was fuelled by victories in 1673, especially Louis' invasion of Franche-Comté and leading of the siege of its capital, Besançon. Vauban's capture of the powerful fortress of Maastricht in just 25 days was enshrined in positive representational culture by Le Brun (see Figure 3.10).

However, setbacks included:

- William's capture of Naarden
- the withdrawal of Munster and Cologne in 1673, followed by England in 1674, left France bereft of allies.

The Franco-Dutch War damaged Louis' reputation and sparked growing anti-French resentment across the continent. The violent destruction of crops, livestock, buildings, villages and towns led to civilian refugees fleeing from French troops and above all, a tarnishing of Louis' international image. Louis was now perceived as the main threat to stability in Western Europe. This enabled the Dutch to gain allies, including Leopold, Lorraine and Spain. In 1673, Leopold's general Montecucculi helped William to capture Bonn, an unexpected move which threatened French lines of communication and forced French withdrawal from Dutch provinces.

The war's character had changed from 1674. Turenne heightened international concern at French aggression by devastating the Palatinate and Turckheim. Leopold formed the Grand Alliance of The Hague in 1674 with the rulers of Mainz, Trier, Brandenburg and Palatinate. This threatened north east of Alsace. Dutch degradation would not happen, as highlighted by the following French setbacks from 1675–77:

- France's only ally, Sweden, was defeated by Brandenburg at the Battle of Fehrbellin. This left France to bear the brunt of fighting against the pro-Dutch alliance.
- The legendary general Condé retired, due to gout.
- The equally experienced and talismanic general Turenne was killed by a stray cannonball at the Battle of Salzbach in July 1675.
- Leopold's ally the Duke of Lorraine captured the strategically vital Philippsburg in 1676, exposing France's eastern border near Alsace to attack.
- No breakthrough happened on the Dutch frontier by 1677.

Figure 3.11: Death of Turenne, 1675

The Peace of Nijmegen

The peace at Nijmegen 1678–9 confirmed Louis' failure to achieve his early objectives. The French returned Maastricht – their sole Dutch conquest – to Holland and hugely reduced the tariffs imposed before the war – a setback to Colbert's mercantilist economic policy.

Another problem was Charles V of Lorraine's emergence as a devout anti-French ally of Leopold. Charles refused to accept any of Louis' terms. Louis now had a Habsburg puppet and potential future security risk on his north-western border of Alsace. In 1679, Louis was disappointed with Nijmegen, sacked foreign minister Simon Arnauld de Pomponne and wanted a new, tougher foreign policy (as shown in Extract A in the Practice Essay Questions section).

At the same time, Pomponne's sacking did not mean that Nijmegen had been a disaster. He was a member of the Arnaud family and had been offering protection to Jansenists. He also returned to serve Louis' Conseil d'en haut in 1671.

Sturdy goes too far in arguing that the Franco-Dutch War was the 'greatest mistake Louis had ever made'.[7] The Franco-Dutch war was hardly short of French success after 1673:

- Turenne won the Battle of Sinsheim in 1674, allowing control of the Palatinate; this denied the allies the opportunity to use the area as a base from which to attack France
- Vauban's daylight capture of Cambrai in 1677
- General Luxembourg's defeat of William of Orange at Cassel, 1677, with heavy Dutch and light French casualties
- the capture of Ghent and Ypres after sieges in 1678
- the Dutch economy was ruined by the war.

Louis ended the war with considerable tactical success at Nijmegen. Defensive motivations had superseded dynastic ones. Carlos had survived and Leopold emerged as a determined and well-supported ally of William of Orange. A certain realism was now apparent in Louis' foreign policy, at least for a while. He certainly succeeded in greatly enhancing French security and pré carré on his north eastern border, far more than he had in 1668.

Louis' decision to surrender forward bases in the Spanish Netherlands made good strategic defensive sense. He now had:

- fewer salient territories like Ath which could be attacked from three sides
- order on France's north-eastern border with the gains of towns in Flanders, including Aire, Ypres, Saint Omer, Cambrai and Bouchain
- a 160 kilometre strip of territory from the river Meuse; this provided a huge buffer zone for Calais, Dunkirk and Paris from Spanish attack, as Figure 3.12 shows:

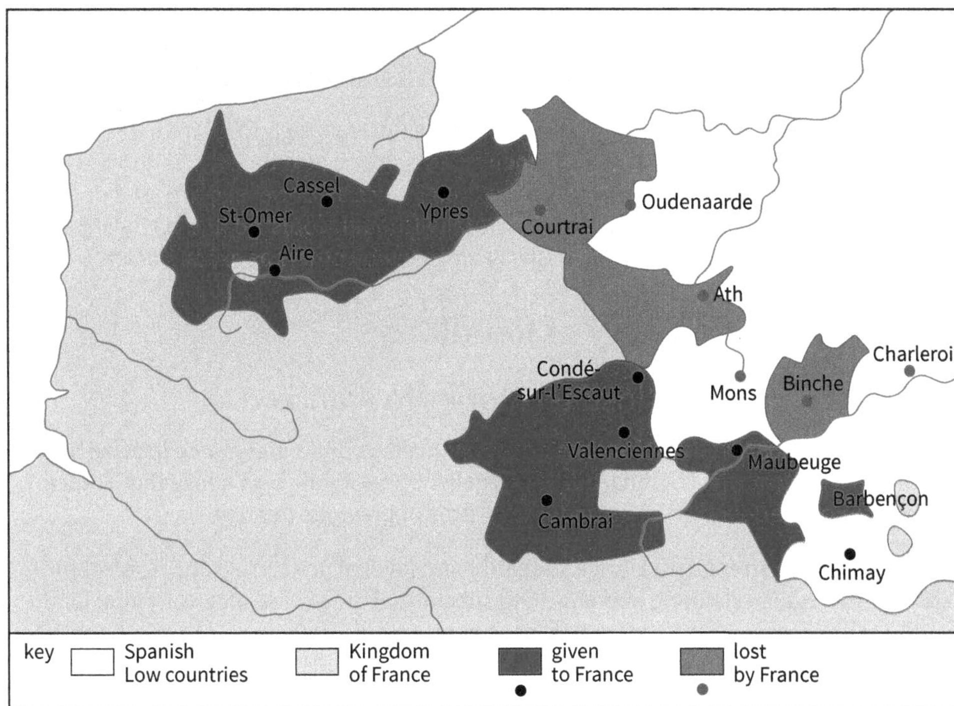

Figure 3.12: French territorial gains and losses at the Treaty of Nijmegen, 1678

France's eastern border security was further strengthened with by gaining Freiburg and above all, Franche-Comté; this prevented any attack on Alsace from the south.

Crucially, France was allowed to keep control of Lorraine after occupying it during 1678. This was vital for French security. The '**Spanish Road**', the route Spanish troops took to the Spanish Netherlands, ran through Lorraine. Charles V, Duke of Lorraine, had proved a loyal Habsburg servant and consistent enemy of Louis. This undoubtedly related to Louis having prevented him from taking up his dukedom in moves related to the Thirty Years War. Charles V had led the 1676 siege of Philippsburg and married Emperor Leopold's sister Eleanor of Austria in 1678. By controlling Lorraine, France could defend the north-western border of Alsace from Habsburg attack.

The glass of success therefore, was half full, not half empty. Certainly, Louis' arrogance and unswerving belief in the legitimacy and worth of his actions was undented, as shown by this note on the Dutch War from his *Mémoires*:

'Ambition and glory are always pardonable in a prince so young and blessed by fortune as I was... I fully rejoice in my clever conduct whereby I was able to extend the boundaries of my kingdom at the expense of my enemies'.[8]

Beneath this self-congratulatory interpretation of events lay a certain logic. The Sun King had:

- strengthened France's borders
- achieved battlefield successes and positive representational culture
- enhanced French supremacy over Spain
- seriously damaged the Dutch economy.

If French continental dominance was not a reality, it was certainly a widespread perception. As the Elector of Brandenburg noted:

'In the present state of affairs, no prince will find security and advantage unless in the friendship and alliance of the king of France.'[9]

ACTIVITY 3.3

1 Class discussions or homework tasks:
   - 'The Dutch War was a failure for Louis XIV'. How far do you agree?
   - 'The Dutch War was not defensive in any respect'. Present a case for and against this.

2 Make a living graph timeline of the Dutch War and its causes that plots:
   - successes
   - failures
   - turning points
   - Louis' original objective
   - French glory on the battlefield
   - Louis' international reputation
   - French security and the pré carré.

3 Reread the sources on the Dutch War throughout this chapter.
   - How useful are these for explaining how successful the Dutch War was for France 1672–9?
   - Which of these is the most and least convincing source and why?

Herein, however, lay a new problem; France was increasingly seen as a threat to peace and stability. The war damaged Louis' reputation and his ambitions to be seen as the leading Christian monarch of Europe, along with France's economy and finances.

Louis ignored all advice and continued to believe unswervingly in his own destiny and brilliance. This set the tone for French foreign policy next decade. So too did his continuing determination to further strengthen France's frontier security and order. Louvois' increasing dominance proved pivotal. Although Louis' goals may have been defensive, they were pursued aggressively and seen by others as expansionist.

France and the policy of Réunions

The drive to annex 'lost' territories to France

From 1680 to 1684, Louis' **Réunions** policy involved using military force to seize border territories for strategic reasons, but also legalistic investigation to allege that France had acquired certain territories under the terms of previous treaties.

Louis sought to strengthen France's security and level of pré carré along its eastern border by 'legally' claiming and annexing substantial areas of strategically vital land. Although defensively motivated, this was aggressively pursued and provoked the War of Reunions with Spain and widespread condemnation.

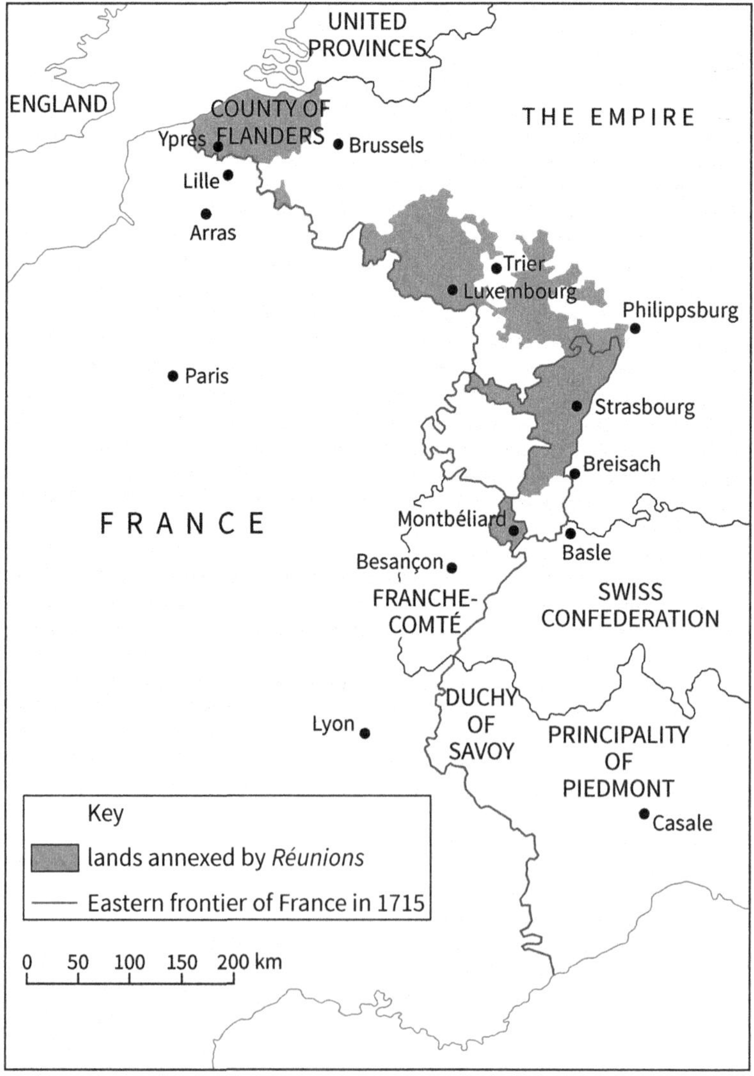

Figure 3.13: France's eastern border and the territories seized by different means, 1680–84

Voices from the past

Honoré Courtin

Honoré Courtin, French ambassador to Sweden, could see as early as 1673 that France was seen as a threat and the king's reputation had been damaged, as he wrote to Louvois in September:

> The king is doubtless the world's greatest prince. He can remain so with a peace settlement that all of Europe would consider very honourable for him and very advantageous for his state. Thus I have trouble understanding why His Majesty wants to jeopardise this happiness and risk exposing himself to future troubles, which might indeed serve to show off his courage and valour but will doubtless serve to be the ruin of his subjects... If one wishes to reflect in all seriousness and good faith on the internal affairs of the state, is it not recognised that funds are depleted, that most of the money has left the kingdom and will not return while war continues to ruin commerce? [10]

Louis set his legal advisers to exploit any vagueness they could find in the Treaties of Münster (1648) and Nijmegen (1679). His intention was to find legal justifications for extending his authority over disputed border areas in order to further enhance French security.

Special law courts called '**Chambres de Réunions**' were established to investigate French claims to different territories. This included researching their status as dependencies under different rulers and powers, sometimes over periods extending back into the Middle Ages. The intention was to prove that they had either originally been French, and so should be French again, or had become French as a result of one or another treaty. Unsurprisingly, the accusation was that where a French claim could not be found, one was manufactured.

Louis calculated that French seizures of territory by these means would be unopposed because his rivals were not at that point in a position to stand up to him. Leopold I, for example, was now fighting the Turks who had reached the gates of his capital city, Vienna, in July 1683. Spain simply lacked allies.

In short, Louis' foreign policy 1680–4 was characterised by unbridled opportunism, constant plunder and intermittent aggression, justified on the grounds of securing France from perpetual threats to its security.

Luxembourg, Casale and Strasbourg

Luxembourg

Luxembourg was a Spanish territory. In 1681, Louis used a 'Chambre de Réunion' in Metz to decree that the county of Chiny in Luxembourg had once belonged to Metz, to send French troops to seize Chiny and then other parts of Luxembourg (claimed to be dependent upon Chiny), and to blockade and starve the Spanish fortress city of Luxembourg.

When starving Spanish troops attacked the French blockade in the winter of 1681–2, Louis retaliated by:

- invading the Spanish Netherlands
- devastating the lands around Courtrai
- approving mortar shell bombardment of the city.

Spain responded by declaring war on France in October 1683, but received no help from Emperor Leopold, who was bogged down repelling Turkish invaders from his lands. Louis exploited this and used Vauban to bombard, besiege and capture the city of Luxembourg in 1684.

Casale

What Louis could not claim through Réunions, he bought and invaded. Casale was a Spanish fortress city in northern Italy, which provided a bridgehead across the Alps for Habsburg troops. Louis wished to protect France's south-eastern border from attack and bribed Casale's self-indulgent and penniless leader, the duke of Mantua, to surrender to French forces on 30 September 1681.

Strasbourg

On the same day, Louis stunned the rest of Europe by capturing Strasbourg, the capital of Alsace. No claim could be found affecting Strasbourg. However, according to Louvois, Leopold I was rumoured to be planning to send troops there. Accordingly, it was simply seized anyway by 30,000 French troops.

Key terms

Free Imperial City: a self-governing city within the territories of the Holy Roman Empire. It was run by the city council under the Emperor, and was not answerable to a prince or bishop.

Strasbourg was a **Free Imperial City**. Outside French control, Strasbourg left French possession of Alsace incomplete. Holding a bridge that was a vital crossing point over the Rhine, it seemed a logical extension of the concept of 'pré carré' to take control of it, especially since that bridge had been used by Imperial troops to invade France during the 30 Years War. The city had allowed Leopold I's troops to invade Alsace on no fewer than three occasions during the Dutch War. It had entered into alliance with Lorraine – a Habsburg collaborator and ally – during the Franco-Dutch Wars. Unsurprisingly, Louis wanted it in French hands to increase his eastern border security.

Was Louis XIV's policy defensive?

Historians have rightly emphasised the defensive rationale and benefits of Louis' actions. Vauban's fortifications of Casale, Strasbourg and all other gained land points to a defensive strategy. So too does the seizure of Montbéliard. This county linked Alsace with Franche-Comté and once in enemy hands would, as historian John Lynn has pointed out, have allowed the invasion of both. By claiming Montbéliard, Louis was securing both Franche-Comté and Alsace from potential Habsburg invasion, and adding to his pré carré, as it linked both regions together.

Security and defensive concerns were certainly utmost in Louis' mind when he captured Strasbourg in 1681. Without Strasbourg, French control of Alsace, border security and pré carré was seriously incomplete. Louis was able to force the different towns of Alsace, but not the capital Strasbourg, to swear oaths of allegiance to the French crown. Louis targeted taking control of various gateways through which France could still be attacked after 1679. One of these was Zweibrücken. Although supposedly under Swedish control, this position had allowed Habsburg troops to cross the Rhine and attack France during the Dutch war.

Louis' expansion of his borders after 1680, therefore, was to a large extent driven by a defensive impulse.

Was Louis' policy offensive?

However, it would be wrong to pigeonhole Louis' actions 1680–4 as being purely defensive. His motivations were more complex, opportunist and pragmatic than first appears. His desire to dominate was at least as strong as his desire to defend. This was apparent in:

- Louis' private comment that 'Alsace was a passage for our troops into Germany'[11]
- His lack of any legal claim whatsoever to Strasbourg and insistence that the city should cease all Protestant worship (despite Protestantism in Alsace having been protected under the terms of the 1648 Peace of Westphalia).
- His lack of restraint with Réunions; when offered the choice of Dinant or Charlemont, he took both.

Louis' actions became increasingly aggressive after 1683, so much so that many have actually questioned whether he had any kind of coherent and consistent policy. A big reason for this is likely to have been the growing influence over Louis of Louvois, the belligerent Secretary of State for War, especially after Colbert's death in 1683. This left Louvois the dominant force within the Conseil d'en haut (or ministerial council of state), as did the appointment of Louvois' ally Le Pelletier as Controlleur-Général and the removal of Colbert's son Seignelay as Secretary for Navy.

Bereft of any moderating influence among his advisers, therefore, Louis became increasingly prone to more aggressive actions, especially during 1684. That year, the French navy bombarded Genoa, burning it to the ground.

What had started as a defensive expansion to enhance French security now gave way to naked aggression and outright terror. This was exemplified by Louvois' ravaging of the Spanish Low Countries in 1684. His instructions for 20 villages around Charleroi to be burned to the ground – leaving innocent helpless people homeless during the winter – make particularly grim reading:

'The king, having been informed that the Spaniards put to the torch barns full of fodder and grain situated at the extremities of the villages of Avenelle and Sepmenier.... commanded me to inform you that he wishes you to burn twenty villages as close as possible to Charleroi, and that you distribute handbills saying that it is in retaliation for the burning of these two barns; the king's will is that you take the necessary steps so that not a single house in these villages remains standing; that in the future you receive word of a similar thing, you will act in like manner without awaiting further orders from His Majesty...'[12]

Louis' reputation

Small wonder therefore, that Louis XIV's actions outraged European opinion at the time. If Reunions had initially been intended as defensive, they were perceived as anything but. Charles XI, King of Sweden, broke off diplomatic relations. No less disgusted were the Duke of Württemberg and Elector of Trier, who appealed to the **imperial diet** (assembly) against Louis' Reunions. Moreover, the writings of the German philosopher Gottfried Leibniz indicated that Louis had lost both all sense of legitimacy, and the backing of his traditional supporters; he was seen as devoted to his own aggrandisement with no sense of principle or restraint. As historian David Maland says, 'After 1672, the French decided that the King no longer needed to justify his enterprises to the world.'[13]

Louis' reputation for naked self-interest has been questioned. Maland states that Leopold refused Louis' help fighting the Turks. But this neglects the facts that Louis was widely denigrated for ignoring Innocent XI's request in 1683 to help defend Vienna from attack from the Turks. Louis had also told the Turkish Sultan that he would not oppose him attacking Leopold. As a result, Louis was now widely perceived as a rogue who needed to be cut down to size.

One parody of Louis' title was when critics dubbed him the '**Most Christian Turk**'. This subversive critique was specifically to do with his attacking the Habsburgs just when they were under pressure from the Ottoman Mehmet IV in 1684, and then again in 1688. These attacks were then popularised by pamphleteers.

The true scale of German anti-Louis outrage and damage to Louis' international standing is revealed in Leibniz's bitter satire of Louis' foreign policy called 'Mars Christianissimus'. Meaning 'Most Christian God of War', this was a bitter parody of Louis' official title as French king, 'Rex Christianissimus' (most Christian king, a title awarded to his ancestors by the pope). Here was anti-French propaganda at its most impassioned with the overt aim of stirring up anti-Louis feeling across Europe.

Francophobic feeling seriously tarnished Louis XIV's international reputation. The Rhine princes, who had traditionally looked to France for protection against Habsburg incursion and threats to their independence, were no longer French allies. Neither was Sweden, from whom Louis had seized the duchy of Zweibrücken. Whatever claim Louis might put forward to be the defender of Christendom, all Europe could see that it was Leopold who was leading the fight against the advancing armies of the Islamic Ottoman Empire. Louis was now widely accused of shameless self-interest and exploiting Leopold's engagement with the Turks to plunder from the emperor's allies and pursue an increasingly aggressive foreign policy. By contrast, Leopold was seen as nobly defending Christendom after winning the battles of Vienna and Kahlenberg in 1683. In his insatiable pursuit of defensive pré carré and dominance, Louis had also scored a spectacular reputational own goal.

However, it would be wrong to exaggerate the setbacks and neglect the successes of Louis' actions up to 1685. What Louis had lost in terms of his international reputation, he also certainly gained at a domestic level. Réunions massively increased Louis' reputational *gloire* within France. Huge amounts of land had been taken and nobody had dared or succeeded in challenging France. Louis basked in an unprecedented outpouring of praise and positive representational culture within France. Catholics delighted by his order that Strasbourg should cease being Protestant. Commemorative medals and paintings enshrined the glory of the capture of Strasbourg and Casale, while the Paris city gates now depicted Louis as the triumphant God Hercules conquering his enemies – legendary and positive representational cultural status confirmed in one.

None of Louis' victims could stop him in his tracks. His gamble that nobody would or could stop him basically worked. The Dutch Republic, Sweden, Austria and Spain had talked the talk of uniting to defend the peace treaty borders of 1648 and 1678–9 by signing the Treaty of Hague in 1681. But none of these countries, aside from Spain briefly in 1683, was prepared actually to fight France. Turkish incursions to the gates of Vienna in 1683 left Leopold unable to commit any troops to war. When Spain attempted to oust French forces from Luxembourg in 1683, it had no allies whatsoever and was easily defeated.

Arguably, Sweden's alienation and loss as a French ally was insignificant. Sweden's declining population and defeat at Fehrbellin made its support of dubious ongoing value to France, especially after French subsidies (financial support) returned Brandenburg as an ally in its place.

If Louis' motto of 'not unequal to many' had been challenged during the Dutch War, by 1685 it was enhanced, and significantly so.

The Truce of Ratisbon

Louis had succeeded in greatly enhancing his domestic standing, even if his international and moral reputation had been harmed. He also largely strengthened French security, while the whole notion of pré carré and French dominance over Europe seemed more complete than at any other time. This was confirmed at the Truce of Ratisbon, in August 1684. This was a truce, not a permanent settlement. It thus accepted France could retain the territories gained through its policy of Réunions, and that it could keep Strasbourg and Luxembourg – for the next 20 years. Louis' actions had a high degree of success in terms of territory, defence and his reputation within France.

Internationally he had engendered widespread resentment and discontent, and this laid the foundations of the **League of Augsburg** (a topic to which we return in Chapter 5); once the state of Europe changed and became less favourable to Louis in the years ahead, he would reap what he had sown. For this reason, success was not complete in 1685.

ACTIVITY 3.4

Write full definitions of the following terms:

- Réunions
- Pré carré
- Montbeliard
- Louvois
- Charleroi
- Most Christian King
- Most Christian Turk
- Most Christian Mars.

ACTIVITY 3.5

1 Take detailed notes on what French foreign policy 1680–84, including Réunions, was intended to achieve.

2 Copy and complete this table, giving an overview of Louis' foreign policy:

War:	Dates:	Treaty names and dates:

3 Make a living graph of French foreign policy 1661–85 that shows the relative importance of defensive, aggressive and reputational (domestic and international *gloire*) factors.

4 Make a living graph titled 'How successful was French foreign policy 1661–85' that shows the big picture of successes and failures for each of the Devolution, Dutch and Reunions wars.

Timeline

1648	Peace of Westphalia
1648	Treaties of Münster
1662	Dunkirk purchased back from the English
1665	Philip IV of Spain died
1667	Louis invaded the Spanish Netherlands
1667	Louis started the War of Devolution
1668	Treaty of Aix-la-Chapelle
1668	Secret Treaty of Grémonville
1668	Return of Franche-Comté to Spain
1670	Treaty of Dover
1671	Lionne's retirement
1672	Dutch ban on all French imports
1672	Louis' attack on the Dutch
1674	Leopold formed the Grand Alliance of The Hague
1679	Treaty of Nijmegen
1675	General Turenne killed at Salzbach and Brandenburg defeated Sweden at Fehrbellin
1679	Louis sacked foreign minister Simon Arnauld de Pomponne
1674	Turenne won the Battle of Sinsheim
1677	Vauban captured Cambrai
1677	General Luxembourg's defeat of William of Orange at Cassel
1678	Capture of Ghent and Ypres
1681	French troops occupied Strasbourg and Casale
1681	Treaty of The Hague

Figure 3.14: Commemorative coin celebrating Strasbourg's surrender in 1681

1683	Turkish army reached the outskirts of Vienna
1684	Louvois' ravaging of the Spanish Low Countries
1684	Truce of Ratisbon

Practice essay questions

1 'Defensively intended, aggressively pursued.' Explain why you agree or disagree with this view of French foreign policy 1680–84?

2 To what extent did Louis achieve his aims through his Réunions policy of 1680–84?

3 'Aggressive intent by Louis XIV and ultimate French failure.' Explain why you agree or disagree with this view of the Dutch War.

4 'French security was a highly significant factor far Louis XIV's foreign policy in the War of Devolution.' Explain why you agree or disagree with this view.

5 'The War of Devolution was more successful than the Dutch War for France.' Explain why you agree or disagree with this view.

6 With reference to these sources and your understanding of the historical context, which of these two sources is more valuable in explaining French foreign policy between 1681–84?

Extract A

Extract of the registers of the French Royal Chamber of Reunions established at Metz on 21 April 1681:

'Louis, by the grace of God King of France and Navarre, to the chief officer chamber which we have established in our town of Metz,...our Attorney General has uncovered that it appears from several titles and documents that the County of Chiny, with its dependencies, is a territory which has always been under our protection and still is today, according to the custom of Beaumont-en-Argone of which we are sovereign. And that the said County of Chiny with its dependencies is a fief of the Duchy of Bar, of which we are sovereign, and that the people of Chiny have for a long time taken their lawsuits to Montmédy, a town which...was ceded to us by the Treaty of Pyrenees in 1659, and confirmed by the Treaties of Nijmegen in 1679.'

David Smith, *Louis XIV*, Cambridge: Cambridge University Press; 1992, p. 84

Extract B

From the German philosopher Gottfried Wilhelm Leibniz's anti-French pamphlet, '**Mars Christianissimus**' (meaning Most Christian War God), published in 1684):

'As early as the year 1672, it was resolved in France that the King would, in the future, no longer to give reasons to the world for his enterprises...Since the Peace of Pyrenees has been broken and trampled underfoot at the first opportunity, it must be recognised that whoever henceforth trusts the word of France is very stupid and deserves to be deceived. That is why the Dutch, the Spanish, the Emperor and other allies who negotiated at [Nijmegen] will sooner or later be punished for their credulity... We have seen that Louis' aims went further than mere bravado... and that the ambition of the Most Christian King was quite egocentric and looked as much to profit as to glory'.

Gottfried Wilhelm Leibniz, *Political Writings*, ed. P. Riley,Cambridge, 1988, pp. 121–45.

Chapter summary

You should now have a good understanding of Louis XIV's foreign policy in the period 1661–1685, and why he fought a series of wars. You will also have learnt about what different historians have written about the extent to which his foreign policy in this period can be considered a success, and to have formed your own views. From reading this chapter, you will also have grasped:

- how important different French foreign-policy motives were in this period
- Louis' main foreign policy aims and priorities, but also how these changed
- the relative importance of different factors in the formulation and execution of policy, including defence, dynasticism, *gloire* and expansion
- the role played by various ministers and military leaders.

End notes

1 Treasure G. *Louis XIV*. Harlow: Longman; 2001. p. 140.

2 Lynn J. *Giant of the Grand Siècle*. Cambridge: Cambridge University Press; 1997. p. 273.

3 Campbell P. *Louis XIV, 1661–1715*. London: Routledge; 1993. p. 55–6.

4 Louis' manifesto sent to the Spanish Court, 1667. Cited in Wilkinson R. *Louis XIV, France and Europe, 1661–1715*. London: Hodder & Stoughton; 1993. p. 102.

5 Grose C. Louis XIV's Financial Relations with Charles II and the English Parliament. *The Journal of Modern History*. 1929; 1(2): 177–204.

6 Wilkinson R. *Louis XIV*. London: Hodder & Stoughton Educational; 2003. p. 105.

7 Sturdy D. *Louis XIV*. London: Palgrave. Macmillan Press; 1998. p. 139.

8 Treasure G. *Louis XIV*. Harlow: Longman; 2001. p. 174.

9 Wilkinson R. *Louis XIV*. London: Hodder & Stoughton Educational; 2002. p. 107.

10 Campbell P. *Louis XIV, 1661-1715*. London: Routledge; 1993. p. 149.

11 Treasure G. *Louis XIV*. Harlow: Longman; 2001. p. 206.

12 Louvois (February, 1684). Cited by Wilkinson R. *Louis XIV*. London: Hodder & Stoughton Educational; 2002. p.113

13 Maland, D. *Europe in the Seventeenth Century*. London: Macmillan Education; 1986. p. 349–50.

PART 2: LOUIS XIV IN DECLINE, 1685–1715

4 Challenges at home, 1685–1715

We now turn to the situation in France itself during the final 30 years of Louis XIV's long reign, and the political, financial, economic, religious and social challenges he faced. Much of what you study will enable you to see the consequences of earlier decisions and policies. You will also observe the continuing attempts to turn around an increasingly desperate situation. You will need to take account of both the personalities involved and the underlying forces that drove the challenges Louis faced, and come to a judgment about how well he handled these. We will look into:

- the personal monarchy: the strengths and weaknesses of royal government; the influence of Madame de Maintenon
- finance and the economy: problems after Colbert; the costs of war
- Louis XIV and the Church: Gallicanism; relations with Huguenots; Jansenists and Quietists
- pressures from below: social divisions; problems with the regions; discontent and popular protests.

The personal monarchy

The strengths and weaknesses of royal government

Louis XIV's governmental strengths arguably outweighed his weaknesses, but only at the centre and start of his reign. His authority after 1685 was sometimes constrained and sometimes confident. Overall, Louis achieved an illusion of unrestricted political power which became much harder to sustain after 1685, especially in the provinces.

Louis had always prided himself on manipulating his conciliar government (employing just 16 ministers between 1661–1715) and the ministers serving him. Louvois did serve Louis, commissioning 20 public square statues to promote Louis' *gloire* in 1685–6. In the period 1685–91, however, Louis' continuing capacity to rule personally waned. Waylaid by an anal fistula in 1687, Louis was less capable of exerting personal authority and reining in Louvois, who apparently dominated royal decision-making. French foreign and anti-Huguenot policies certainly became increasingly aggressive, damaging Louis' Most Christian King international reputation and reflecting Louvois' growing influence over royal policy in relation to the following areas:

- continuing the dragonnade persecution and terrorising of Huguenots
- violently seizing Avignon in 1688, causing defeat in the Cologne election and an anti-French alliance to declare a war that France could ill afford in 1688–9 (see Chapter 5).
- authorising civilian atrocities in the Palatinate region along France's eastern border in 1688 and extending this as a routine matter of policy to other German towns during 1689–90 (see Chapter 5).

Louis' apparent lack of control of his war minister was demonstrated when Louvois disregarded Louis' refusal to approve the burning of the town of Treves in 1690 and issued the order himself. Louvois then reportedly informed Louis that he had done so to spare the Sun King's conscience the agony of issuing this order. He also defied one of Louis' orders in 1691 as French troops besieged Mons, with Louis in attendance. Arguably, this shows that in Louvois' eyes at least, that he was a law unto himself and that Louis could be defied.

However, Louis remained capable of asserting his authority over Louvois. Upon learning of Louvois' impertinence in 1689, he reportedly reacted furiously, grabbed the fireplace tongs and was only prevented from smashing Louvois' head in by Madame de Maintenon. Louis further indicated his ongoing capacity for personal rule by:

- overriding Louvois' order and saving Treves from being burned in 1690
- preparing a lettre de cachet to send Louvois to the Bastille and strongly rebuking him in his council chamber for defying him in 1691. Louvois left this in utter despair and died almost immediately afterwards, either through a shock induced heart-attack or stroke or swallowing poison
- suppressing all investigations into Louvois' death
- assuming total control of military strategy from 1691 and reducing Louvois' son, Barbezieux, to overseeing army supplies.

Louis also maintained a capacity for control and coercion in his relationships with the parlements, and in his manipulation of the paulette (an annual tax magistrates paid that allowed them to transfer their office, often to a son). In 1701, some 5.67 million livres came into the royal coffers through the paulette. In 1702, Louis' Controlleur-Général Michel Chamillart ignored protests by Paris Parlement **First President** Achille III de Harlay against paying a further 5.67 million livres in paulette, and obtained the full payment after threatening to create new offices to make up for any revenue shortfall. Structures of strong royal control existed alongside the virtual financial exploitation of the elites in Franche-Comté.

Key terms

Franche-Comté: a previously autonomous province which was given to France by the 1679 Treaty of Nymegen.

This was evident in the:

- abolition of its provincial estates
- royal control of a new parlement in **Franche-Comté's** largest city Besançon through Louis' ally (and attorney general) Gabriel Boisot and other compliant royal supporters
- close intendant control of taxation
- regular payment of a fixed subsidy from local nobles (often borrowed on their own personal credit) to deter the creation of new offices.

Intendants offered the strengths of receiving annual ministerial instructions and constant scrutiny, experience and acting in an investigatory, supervisory or disciplinary role on Louis' behalf.

They fulfilled multiple tasks, including:

- rooting out administrative and financial corruption
- ensuring good relations between civilians and military
- overseeing local justice and equitable tax distribution and collection
- zealously enforcing anti-Huguenot policies.

Louis arguably also exhibited strong government outside Paris by:

- extending indirect taxation to a range of consumer goods (see: Problems after Colbert)
- surviving and dealing with crises, including organising alms (hand-outs) for the poor during the 1694 famine and quashing of grain riots in Lyon in 1709.

However, the extent of royal authority hardly increased across all France's provinces. Outside Paris, Louis faced an increasing struggle for control.

Intendants provided huge information, but little infrastructural control. France remained insufficiently governed. Brittany had no intendant until 1689. Intendants were unpaid, overburdened and often easily corrupted. Some falsified reports, as in Aix and Provence, and others met wilful obstruction. Most intendants defied royal authority by:

- relying upon judicial and financial officier sub-delegates, despite their frequent inefficiency, dishonesty and non-compliance
- blocking royal attempts to squeeze more money from sub-delegate office prices.

Louis' government could not even enforce its own three-year intendant safeguard. Many intendents effectively monopolised their position, including Languedoc intendant Nicolas Lamoignon (1685–1719).

Nor could it sustain any crackdown on corruption. Tax farmers' accounts were not submitted to intendants. In 1692, municipal officiers could repurchase offices that they already held. This netted valuable finance for war, including 100,000 livres from Dijon's major, but allowed corrupt officials to continue embezzling public funds, as in Nérac and Condom.

Compromise with the local elites remained a key part of government in Franche-Comté, where loans to the crown were made conditional upon guarantees of magistrates' privileges and office property rights.

The crown's relationship *appeared* to change with the introduction of new taxes which challenged the principle of tax exemption, the **capitation** (1695) and **dixième** (1710).

Key terms

Capitation: a direct tax on all men, including the privileged, except the clergy, introduced in 1695, collected until 1699 and renewed in a very watered down version (with many privileged exemptions and regional variations) in 1701.

Dixième: a 10% (royal) tax upon wealth and private revenues, introduced in, and collected from, 1710. This taxed wealth from land, manufactures, paid work and offices and was based, at least in part, on self-assessment. It taxed both the privileged and non-privileged, but privileged classes – the clergy and nobility, continued to pay a significantly reduced amount.

In reality, however, continuity and compromise remained the order of the day; Louis had no interest in alienating his natural supporters and sources of financed loans. Thus:

- the capitation was only kept until 1699.
- Alsace, Flanders and Franche-Comté immediately purchased exemptions.
- So widespread was the scale of special deals and exemptions upon its reintroduction in 1701, that its yield was triflingly small.

The dixième netted 96 million livres in four years, but saw ongoing defiance of royal authority:

- 75% of Auvergne's nobility refused to declare
- Lyon's merchants also resisted registering and paying.

Provincial tax collection invited inefficiency, dishonesty and avoidance. Pays d'état taxes were only paid after deductions of collectors' fees and estate local charges (e.g. for road maintenance). Pays d'états and newly acquired territories (Flanders, Roussillon, Franche-Comté and Alsace) continually underpaid their taxes and flouted royal authority with breath-taking impertinence:

- They paid an indirect trade tax rather than taille. This was subject to suspension of investigations of unpaid noble taxes in Brittany and fluctuating trade.
- Their estates paid a negotiated cash gift, called the don gratuit, but yields from this declined in real terms between 1689–97 and 1702–13.
- Languedoc paid much less of a don gratuit from 1708.

Equitable taxation and submission of the provincial elites to royal authority largely remained a pipe dream. Pays d'états remained scandalously undertaxed, paying just 10% of the taille yielded from the pays d'élection in 1687. Overall, pays d'états paid 4.5 million livres. This was just 5% of total ordinary revenue charges. Some 22%–44% was deducted as local charges.

Institutional opposition was routine outside Paris. Pays d'état defiance of royal judicial edicts and nearly 400 differences in laws continued. Colbert's uncle Henri Pussort bemoaned France's reputation of enforcing ordinances 'more inefficiently than any other state'.[1]

Weaknesses in royal authority in the provinces were matched by flaws in the centre of Louis' regime after 1685. Tameness outweighed talent in his choice of post-Colbertian finance ministers, who increased offices, **rentes** and **tax farm** costs, thereby undermining royal financial control (see: Finance and the economy). Royal finances were increasingly ramshackle in the years between 1689 and 1713, with net revenue contributing just 25%–33% towards total expenditure.

Louis' control of government and appointments was dubious after 1685. Michel Chamillart was overburdened as finance and war minister. Recruitment of Jansenist sympathiser Antoine de Noailles as Archbishop of Paris in 1695 owed much to Madame de Maintenon and backfired (see: The influence of Madame de Maintenon).

Louis also lost the Paris Parlement's support by:

- jettisoning his Gallican religious policy in 1693
- inviting papal condemnation of Jansenism.

In 1713, the Paris Parlement remonstrated against the Bull Unigenitus, supported by Parisian Archbishop Noailles and many clergy.

Perception wise, Versailles created a magnificent and enviable illusion of Louis' authority. Strict courtier rules at Versailles suited Louis' love of regimentation and competition for royal favour. Offences included:

- turning a back on him
- emptying his chamber pot without first kneeling down.

In reality, however, Versailles only allowed very limited domination of the elites. As shown in Chapter 2: The role of Versailles, it housed only a few of the French nobility. Symbolically, it increasingly reflected the limits and decline of Louis' power which was so obvious in other areas. Malarial fever, overcrowding and a lack of toilets caused serious hygiene issues and weekly cleansing of faeces and dirt from hallways in 1715.

Neither Versailles nor Louis' machinery of spin could prevent an increasing torrent of criticism and negative representational culture, as explained later.

Thus, although Louis' government undoubtedly had many strengths, these were increasingly offset by weaknesses by 1715.

The influence of Madame de Maintenon

Madame de Maintenon was born Françoise d'Aubigné. The widow of a crippled burlesque comedy author 25 years her senior, she became the governess of Louis XIV and Madame de Montespan's illegitimate children from 1669 and was named the Marquise de Maintenon after her estate's name. She charmed Louis by speaking to him as an equal and by not immediately succumbing to his advances. She came to Versailles in 1680 and secretly became Louis' second wife after Maria Theresa's death in 1683.

Perception outweighed reality regarding Maintenon's influence. Powerful court opponents loathed her, accusing her of harmfully duping and manipulating Louis. Yet her actual influence was limited. She fulfilled a contributory role as Louis' confidant and spiritual mentor, not a primary political role affecting government policy. Louis' absolutism was increasingly challenged by the Paris Parlement and the French clergy by 1715 over his anti-Jansenist policies, but politically, he remained his own man.

Figure 4.1: Madame de Maintenon

The idea of Madame de Maintenon's excessive manipulation of Louis stems from two witnesses. The Duc de Saint-Simon portrayed her as a ruthless schemer who feigned religious devotion to exploit Louis' fear of sin. Liselotte, the Princess Palatine, Elizabeth Charlotte (wife of the Duc d'Orléans and Louis XIV's sister-in-law) blamed her for almost every royal blunder.

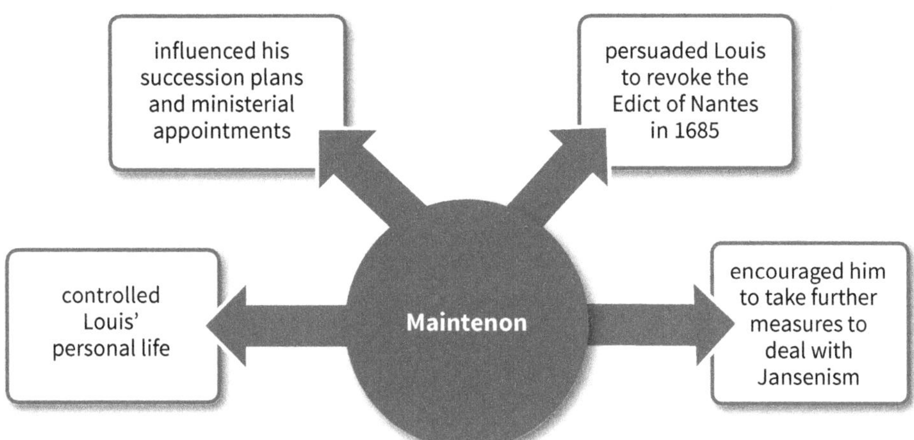

Figure 4.2: Maintenon as described by Saint-Simon and Louis' sister-in-law, Princess Palatine Elizabeth Charlotte

Maintenon apparently had some personal influence over Louis. As governess, she developed soft spots for the Ducs de Maine and Toulouse and encouraged Louis to make them princes of the blood in 1714 to secure his succession. She also effectively tamed her tiger, confining Louis to sexual intercourse within their marriage. Her confessor Paul Godet des Marais and Archbishop of Cambrai François Fénelon encouraged her to regard Louis' salvation as her central responsibility. This involved urging Louis to atone for his sexual promiscuity and create a more pious atmosphere at court. Italian diplomat Graf Girolamo Velo reported that under Maintenon's guidance, Louis frequently received the sacraments in 1692. Louis called Maintenon 'Your Firmness' and appreciated her spiritual mentoring, claiming 'She helped me in everything, especially in saving my soul'.[2]

Maintenon's simple existence as Louis XIV's secret second wife arguably damaged the king's reputation among influential contemporaries. After his defeat at the Battle of Oudenarde (1708) during the Spanish Succession War, the English propaganda piece '*The French King's Wedding*' (1708) mocked Louis for trying to keep his relationship with Maintenon secret and inferred that Louis was weak in relation to Maintenon, bordering on impotent:

> 'The Plagues of War and Wife Consent,
> To send the King a Packing,
> You cannot give your Spouse Content,
> For she'll always be lacking.'[3]

However, Maintenon's personal influence over Louis is exaggerated. Louis' Jesuit confessors had already instilled in him the need for sin atonement, especially Père La Chaise. Maintenon questioned her own impact too, stating that Louis thought 'too little about God'.[4] Desperation over a looming Bourbon dynastic emergency from 1711 outweighed Maintenon's role in Louis legitimising Maine and Toulouse.

By 1714, the Dauphin, two grandsons and a great grandson had died. Maintenon therefore encouraged personal choices that Louis had overwhelming reasons to have already made.

Education was a more tangible but still inflated area of influence. Maintenon secured 1.4 million livres and architect Mansart from Louis to design her boarding school at Saint Cyr. As school general director from 1686, she persuaded Louis to assign Jean Racine to write *Esther* in 1689 for Saint Cyr's schoolgirls, a spectacular production costing 14,000 livres.

The choice of play implicitly (and its prologue explicitly) flattered Maintenon's self-given status as Louis' chaste queen and saviour. Its performance was attended by ministers, the Dauphin, courtiers, Paris Parlement members and Louis' exiled cousin King James II/VII.

However, Maintenon neither controlled Louis over Saint Cyr nor fully controlled the school itself. By providing for daughters of nobles impoverished or killed serving the state, Saint Cyr matched Louis' obsession with regulated conformity. Crucially, Louis, not Maintenon, selected students and the building design. With Père La Chaise, he decided the uniform and rules. Maintenon's influence again had obvious limits.

Recruitment of friends is another area of perceived importance. Maintenon succeeded in recruiting many clients as ladies-in-waiting 1683–1715, including:

- Mademoiselles de Ventadour and Châtillon in Liselotte's household
- Madame de Dangeau to the Dauphine's and Duchesse de Bourgogne's household.

Maintenon also influenced:

- Michel Chamillart's appointment as Saint Cyr intendant and Controlleur-Général in 1699
- her friend Louis Antoine de Noailles appointment as Archbishop of Paris (1695), against the wishes of Louis' confessor, Père La Chaise
- Daniel-François Voysin's appointment as war minister (1709).

However, Louis had other good reasons, aside from Maintenon's encouragement, to make these appointments:

- As a former finance intendant for nine years, Chamillart offered experience and an amenable personality. He was well liked at court. This contrasted with predecessor Ponchartrain's willingness to clash with Louis. Declining tax farm profitability (with 50.6 million livres' debt by 1697) also explains Pontchartrain's fall from grace.
- Ex-Bishop of Châlons Noailles had been a model clergyman and offered a long family history serving Bourbon kings. He was also recommended by François Fénelon, the Dauphin's tutor 1689–97.
- Conscientious administrator Voysin was trusted by Louis and recommended by Chamillart.

Liselotte claimed in May 1701 that:

'Since the king was not very wise, the old woman and his confessor made him believe everything they wished. The ministers for the most part are only creatures of the old turd'.[5]

Such claims, however, seem questionable. Conseil d'état meetings and consultations sometimes occurred in Maintenon's apartments, where she met Louis each evening. She sometimes discussed statecraft and supported Louis' actions, such as accepting Carlos' will in 1700. Roman clergy and the Pope reportedly approached her as an 'informal diplomatic actor' when wanting something from Louis. But Maintenon's political influence is largely overstated. Her presence at Louis' council was occasional, not regular. She never spent any time preparing for council. She spent two of every three days at Saint Cyr from 6 a.m., suggesting a willingness to retreat away from Louis' government and court.

Louis never relaxed his control of government nor altered any major political decision due to disagreement with Maintenon.

By her own admission, she limited herself to Louis' salvation:

'The king will only allow his Ministers to talk to him about business. He was displeased because the Nuncio addressed himself to me… I can only groan over the turn that matters have taken.'[6]

Overall, Maintenon was a supporter of Louis' policies rather than primary instigator. Louis' sense of dynastic duty underpinned his acceptance of Carlos' will, as did Leopold's frosty response to the partition treaties before 1700. Liselotte blamed her for the Edict of Fontainebleau:

'The old whore and Père La Chaise convinced the King that all the sins he had committed with Madame de Montespan would be forgiven if he banished the Protestants, and therein lay the road to heaven. This the poor King believed and that is how the persecution of the Protestants began'[7]

Historical circumstances suggest that this was only partly true. As explained earlier, Louis had many reasons to believe that Protestantism was finished and to try and steal Leopold's thunder as defender of Christendom. Le Tellier and Louvois instigated the Edict of Fontainebleau, not Maintenon and she disapproved of the violent conversion methods after 1685.

Maintenon's influence with Jansenism has also been embellished. She encouraged Port-Royal's destruction and further anti-Jansenist action, but so too did:

- Pope Clement XI
- Louis' Jesuit advisers since childhood
- Pontchartrain
- Lieutenant General of Police d'Argenson
- France's Ambassador to Rome.

Louis had many other reasons independent of Maintenon's encouragement to renew his assault on Jansenism, as explained later. His new confessor Charles-Maurice Le Tellier advised crushing 'this nest of heresy'.[8]

Maintenon was inadvertently influential in initially encouraging **Quietism**, but so were Fénelon and Madame Guyon, as explained below. Her banishment to her room for a month over this issue showed an inability to manipulate Louis and she was only part of the team who backed Louis in condemning Quietism.

Influential though she appeared to some of her contemporaries, Madame de Maintenon was really quite limited in her influence over the Sun King after 1685.

Finance and the economy

Problems after Colbert

Colbert envisaged an abundance of money to buttress state power and grandeur, not the chronic absence of funds so apparent after his death. Between 1683 and 1715, France's finance and economy were overseen by:

- Claude Le Peletier, 1683–9
- Phélypeaux de Pontchartrain, 1689–99
- Michel Chamillart, 1699–1708
- Nicolas Desmaretz, 1708–15.

ACTIVITY 4.1

1. Prepare for a debate on the motion 'Madame de Maintenon had no influence on government policy'. Make notes on both sides before deciding which side you find more convincing. Take a vote before and after a class debate to see if people change their minds as a result of hearing the arguments, and analyse what things affected their (and your) views.
2. How valid is Liselotte's assessment of Louis' reasons for revoking the Edict of Nantes in 1685?

Under their tenures, traditional revenue sources (taxation and borrowing) became increasingly inadequate. Two decades of almost continuous war prompted new financial policies that were short term, counterproductive and downright naive. Economic growth stagnated. Against a backdrop of spiralling agricultural depression, depopulation and systemic manufacturing decline, France's economy was incapable of generating the wealth on the scale required by Louis' wars of increasing attrition. By 1715, France's finances and economy were exhausted to the point of almost collapse.

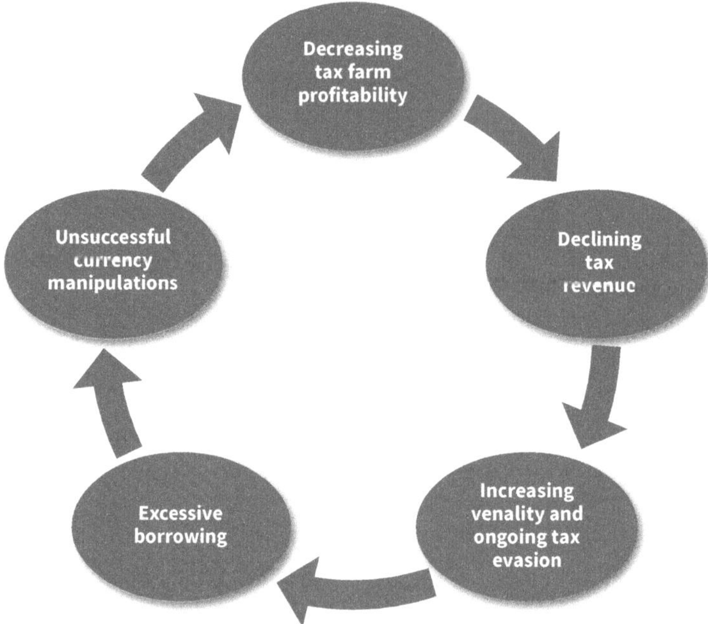

Figure 4.3: Reasons why French finances deteriorated so badly after Colbert

After 1687, taxation revenues were incapable of meeting Louis' growing expenses. This was partly caused by mismanagement of tax farms. In 1687, Le Peletier replaced Colbert's single tax-farm lease with two leases and inexplicably lowered the price below takings – a policy continued by Pontchartrain. This increased the charges, thus reducing the net income and so destroying tax-farm profitability:

Tax farm charges as a percentage comparison to the sum reaching the Treasury:	
1685	40.5
1689	48
1692	63
1693	93
1694	121
1695	147
1697	265
1703	320
1705	318
1707	345

Table 4.1: Tax farm charges as a percentage comparison to the sum reaching the Treasury 1685–1707

Embezzlement and tax evasion were increasingly rife. By 1708, tax farms brought in just over half the income of the late 1680s. Dwindling salt and wine consumption further depressed tax farm values. So too did an exponential rise in salt smuggling involving criminal gangs of several hundred royal troops.

In 1709, Desmaretz bemoaned that tax farms were under two-thirds their ordinary value. The paltry 18 million livres netted in 1712 could not even meet 10% of annual government expenses.

Declining tax-farm profitability had a serious debilitating effect upon royal finances. So too did the increasingly expensive and inefficient taille:

Date:	Charges as a % of taille owed:	% of taille reaching the Treasury:
1685	18%	64%
1697	31%	58%
1699	32%	39%
1706	32%	43%

Table 4.2: The increasing inefficiency of taille collection 1685–1706

Between 1683 and 1715, France's tax base was dwindling, overburdened and incapable of meeting rising state expenditure. Severe famine in 1692–4 and the winter of 1708–9 caused depopulation, as explained later. New taxes on the nobility and clergy – the 1695 capitation and 1710 dixième – made little headway due to entrenched opposition. Pontchartrain and Chamillart's increasing resort to office sales resulted in 70,000–80,000 officiers by 1709, all of whom were tax exempt.

With costs and debts soaring, taxation revenue was in catastrophic freefall:

Date:	Percentage of tax lost in charges:	Percentage reaching royal treasury:
1683	20	80
1715	72	28

Table 4.3: Inefficencies in tax collection, 1683–1715

Increasing venality was short-sighted. Office sales raised an estimated 900,000 livres 1690–1715, but this was offset by huge rises in officier salaries (**gages**). By 1699, these cost 51% more than in 1683. Allowing for currency depreciation, gages almost doubled 1683–1715.

Increasing use of cash investment interest offers to investors was also extremely counterproductive. The government paid 8.33% annually on rentes 1688–97 and 6%–7% 1702–13. **Tontines** offered unsustainable 12.5%–14% interest rates to investors in 1693. Rentes were a total asset liability; those launched since 1702 produced under one third of expected investment by 1713. By 1715, state liability of fixed rate interest rentes was nine times higher than in 1683.

Key terms

Gages: salaries of office holders (officiers).

Tontines: a form of government borrowing through compound interest *rentes* (loans and government bonds); they were extremely costly to the government.

Equally reckless was Chamillart's 8% and 10% cash investment interest offers to investors in 1702 and 1705. Borrowing against future tax revenue became established practice. By September 1707, 72% of 1708 revenue had been consumed in advance. By 1709, Desmaretz had assigned over 53 million livres from revenues dating as far ahead as 1717!

Over 40 currency manipulations 1686–1709 proved equally counterproductive. These attempted to:

- inflate money supply
- generate more disposable income
- revalue coins upwards against the livre
- devalue the livre against gold and silver.

This increased credit and the costs of transferring money abroad; it meant that royal funding of the army soon produced diminishing returns. In real terms, amounts raised through currency manipulations 1689–1709 fell by 40%. Chamillart's 1704 reminting was particularly disastrous, raising just 38% of the amount raised in 1689.

France's economy stagnated and declined badly and was unable to generate the wealth required for growing expenditure. Not every part of France's economy was depressed after 1685. Regional studies highlight continued vibrancy in some sectors and regions.

Provence appeared to revive from the 1680s, well before France as a whole. French trade with Spain, Antilles and Levant continued and even grew. Marseille revived from the 1690s and privateering netted 220 million livres in total prizes 1689–1713. Iron production remained strong, with 211 iron forges in 1693. Cloth manufacturing revived until 1708. Wool production rose 23% overall 1700–15 and threefold in Languedoc 1703–13, stimulated by growing wartime army demand.

Overall, however, economic recession was severe across much of France. Declining gabelle revenues indicated falling consumption and productivity. This was prompted by increasing indirect taxes from the 1690s. These affected:

1702	Playing cards
1704	Ice sales
1706	Wigs
1708	Oil
1709	Oysters

Government duties consumed as much as 50% of sale values. This increased prices and decreased demand and profit margins. So too did higher prices for raw wool. The period 1683–1715 was not prosperous for the woollen industry in many regions, especially from 1690:

- Alençon, Burgundy and Bourbonnais' intendants reported 'greatly diminished' serge production by 1698–99.
- Moncoutant in Lower Poitou saw a 63% decrease in master craftsmen by 1714 and a 40% fall in woollen piece production 1692–1704.

Wool production was depressed in Flanders, Champagne and Picardy:

Date:	Fact:
1697	66% and 80% drop in looms making a specific cloth in Lille and Valenciennes and its disappearance from Menin altogether
1699	• 93% drop in Tours' loom numbers and 75% fall in its woollen industry employment • Reims' 50% drop in looms from 1686 • Mézières had just 8% of looms left.

Table 4.4: Signs of economic depression within the French woollen industry 1697–99

Economic decline was also characterised by declining profits at Abbeville's Van Robais factory and the negative performance of Norman wool manufacture from 1709, after the removal of royal orders.

Linen and hemp production also stagnated. They were hit by high English and Dutch tariffs from the late 1680s and disruption from the Nine Years War to foreign trade routes. In 1699, Lyon's intendant reported that fustian output was just 10% of its former volume. By 1699 Alençon and Rouen's hemp production was 50% lower than they had been in 1683.

Manufacturing goods demand was further lowered by the twin effect of rising tax burdens and inflation, especially in wheat prices 1692–4, as explained later. Against this backdrop and starved of royal subsidies, luxury goods industries struggled. Colbert's showpiece Gobelins factory closed in 1694 until the Nine Years War ended, while lace manufacturing practically disappeared in Auvergne by 1700 and in Languedoc by 1708.

Emigration of skilled Huguenot labour after 1685 blighted French manufacturing production, at least to an extent. Rouen, Reims, Tours and Nîmes lost half of their workers. Lyon lost 75% of its silk workers by 1702. Even the loss of non-Huguenot skilled labour was a problem. 4,500 Catholics emigrated to England due to the depressed nature of weaving in Normandy. Excessive government regulation created deplorable conditions which drove many workers out of the country, such as from Bourbonnais' rug and furniture industry in 1699.

Agriculture continued to be neglected and remained depressed. Land values had fallen by 40% by 1686, while disposable money available for taxation and consumer spending was negated by:

- hyperinflationary bread prices in 1692–4 and 1709
- low wheat prices in Aix in 1688–9, which depressed peasant incomes.

Post Colbert, money was conspicuous by its absence. At the very time when almost constant war increased royal debts to dangerous new levels, financial revenue and economic productivity both declined severely.

The costs of war

Louis' wars made increasingly rapacious demands upon government expenditure, far more than before 1661 and after 1670. The Dutch War consumed 66% of revenue and further increased costs through the chain reaction shown in Figure 4.4.

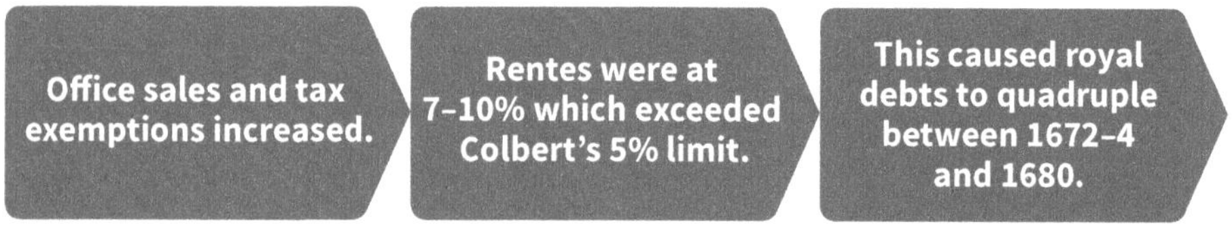

Office sales and tax exemptions increased. → **Rentes were at 7–10% which exceeded Colbert's 5% limit.** → **This caused royal debts to quadruple between 1672–4 and 1680.**

Figure 4.4: The damaging impact of the Dutch War upon royal finances

However, this was dwarfed by exponential rises in war expenditure after 1685. War dominated 22 of the last 30 years of Louis' reign and increasingly drained and exhausted royal finances, as shown in Table 4.5 and Table 4.6, detailing the date and % increase in government expenditure.

Date:	% of total expenditure devoted to warfare:
1630–49	35%
1650–6	20%
1662–9	42%
1670–9	66%
1680–9	54%

Table 4.5: France's expenditure on warfare as percentage of total royal expenditure 1630–95

Date:	% increase in government expenditure from 1670:
1680	20%
1685	61%
1690	47%
1700	42%
1711	71%
1714	61%

Table 4.6: Date and % increase in government expenditure 1670–1714

Louis' wars from 1688 placed intolerable burdens upon Colbert's financial system. No longer could ordinary revenues sustain Louis' growing revenue needs. Fighting a range of enemies caused:

- increasing demands for pay, food and equipment
- suspension of budgetary controls
- increasing venality
- open and hidden borrowing at hyperinflationary interest rates
- increasingly desperate subsidies to try and gain allies.

Louis' desperation for allies saw more than 1.85 million livres paid to Hanover and 2 million to Denmark and Münster in failed attempts to woo them into supporting French armies. Savoy also became a recipient of French aid after leaving the coalition in 1696.

Louis' occupations of Lorraine and Savoy brought heavy costs. He tried but failed completely to pass these onto the occupied local populations. In 1693–4, bad harvests in Lorraine weakened yields from gabelle and étapes (a military tax for passing troops). Louis' aim of taking maximum revenue from Savoy at minimal cost saw crippling billeting, fortification bills and tax demands. But these only partly succeeded. Subsistence problems left communities incapable of paying charges; after a good harvest in 1694 depressed Savoy wheat prices, most locals lacked money and could not pay the French capitation tax.

Unable to make war pay for itself, Pontchartrain resorted to increasingly desperate and counterproductive ways of trying to make ends meet. He failed. The Nine Years War was a tipping point in royal control over finance and debt. Between 1688 and 1697, royal debt increased fivefold. By 1695, the crown was unable to borrow more money, forcing a failed attempt to make all people pay capitation tax on their social or office-based status. This raised just 59 million livres before abolition in 1698 – less than 14% of cumulative state expenditure for 1697–8. Its failure is explained further in the social divisions section. Colbert had warned that France could only stand a 35 million livres annual deficit. By 1697, this limit had been exceeded by 68%.

Harmed by these costs and additional debts accrued from increasing rentes and office sales, France sorely needed peace. Instead, by 1702, it was again at war. Facing a huge enemy coalition in a war that demanded France send forces well beyond its frontiers, this stretched the country's military logistics and resource capacity. Louis' early ambition in the War of the Spanish Succession quickly outran available resources and achievements. The costs were driven up by a growing wealth transfer problem, and increasing burdens, first of occupation, and then of defeat. Let's examine those three in turn.

Growing wealth-transfer problem

Having assumed the lead for defending Spanish lands, France found itself committed on several locations in different directions. The Spanish Netherlands, Milan, Naples, Sicily and Spanish Iberian territories all required substantial French army egagement and vast financial expenditure.

France had to move money to armies and allies abroad on a far greater scale than 1688–97. This incurred heavy exchange costs. France's Italian campaign required expensive money and credit transfers through Lyon and Italian centres. Subsequently, this consumed a disproportionately high share of revenue, with costs almost doubling 1702–5. Louis' huge-scale Iberian campaign from Andalusia to Catalonia also greatly strained French resources. All this was made worse by underdeveloped local financial infrastructures and limited funding sources.

Increasing burdens of occupation

After 1700, France's occupations further burdened rather than boosted war revenue. From 1700, income from enemy territory provided just 10% of total military spending. This limited the army's potential to live off foreign lands. Louis preferred not fully occupying Lorraine and keeping the Duke friendly to dissuade him from aiding the allies. This meant that:

- Lorraine paid very little towards French occupation.
- Louis paid supply transportation costs and customs duties in full.
- Lorraine remained open to all foreign trade, allowing French coinage intended for troop pay to pass to the Dutch and Empire.

Proposed direct taxes for Savoy were 50% and 350% heavier than the burdens on pays d'élections and pays d'états, respectively. But Louis failed to make Savoy pay for various reasons:

- Pre-existing poverty and embezzlement negated taille returns; by 1705, the deficit between expenses and tax revenue was 58,000 livres.
- Heavy raiding from local bandits drained further capital, with 33,000 livres stolen in February 1705.
- Violent storms in 1706 meant the taille had to be lowered by 50,000 livres.

Louis would not make Lorraine pay and he could not make Savoy do so. By the summer of 1708, there was a catalogue of unpaid taxes stretching back to 1706. This further debilitated French finances.

Increasing burdens of defeat

In 1704, over 200,000 livres was lost after France's crushing defeat at Blenheim. In 1706, defeats at Ramilles and Turin wrecked Chamillart's ability to maintain confidence in Mint bills. In 1709, defeats at Malplaquet and the subsequent losses of Tournai and Mons made it harder to finance the war effort through taxation, as the Allies were now lodged in French northern provinces.

In short, rising war costs had multiple causes from 1702. As Guy Rowlands notes, the 'costs of strategic overextension was compounded by the costs of failure'.[9]

The Spanish Succession War was the straw that broke the camel's back of royal financial stability. Between 1702 and 1713, average royal debt was 118 million livres – 71% higher than Colbert's deficit limit warning. This became 78% higher 1705–7. Annual war costs from 1704 were over three times more than the total amount spent 1662–71. By 1715, total debt had reached an intoxicatingly high 1.8–2.3 billion livres – some 35 to 45 times higher than disposable income.

Louis' wars after 1685 brought other costs. Manufacturing demand was depressed, as shown earlier in this chapter. Economic stagnation was an undoubted price of almost endless conflict until 1713. During war years, Touraine saw 86% less involvement in tanning and leather-making. At the same time, 77% of Rouen's sugar refineries ceased operations by 1709 due to hostilities.

Politically, Louis also paid a price. The crown seemingly lost all control and discipline over revenue and expenditure, and the plot, over fiscal policy, turning a blind eye to financial irregularity. Colbert and Le Peletier's routine checks on royal money handlers' annual accounts stopped, thereby diverting attention from the state's ramshackle creditworthiness and that of its financiers. By 1714, accounts from 1700 onwards had still not been checked. By 1706, borrowing constituted 85% of annual royal finances. Such unsustainably high debt levels almost cost Louis huge territorial and dynastic losses in 1709 when he offered generous surrender terms. Only Allied greed prevented Louis paying a much higher price than at Utrecht in 1713.

ACTIVITY 4.2

Was war the greatest threat to the French economy and government solvency during the reign of Louis XIV?

Mounting war costs from 1710 highlighted continuing royal failure to make the elites contribute fairly in taxation. War cost over ten times more from 1710 than the paltry 22.5 million raised from Desmaretz's dixième.

Louis confessed to loving war 'too much'. Indeed, his final two wars had severely damaged French financial and economic stability and highlighted the increasing extent to which his royal control was no more than nominal.

Louis XIV and the Church

Gallicanism

Gallicanism demanded keeping the pope at arms' length and French ecclesiastical independence. Louis' relations with Rome were sometimes warmer, sometimes cooler; this variation weakened perceptions of his Gallicanism.

Louis initially maintained a skilful compromise, keeping Gallican supporters on board and avoiding complete schism with Rome. Louis was pragmatic and averted being totally manipulated by Gallicanism. However, his approach of embracing, then abandoning, Gallicanism badly backfired.

After 1685, Louis pleased both Parlement and Sorbonne by locking horns with Pope Innocent XI over French diplomatic asylum in Rome (January and November 1687) and the Cologne election (June–September 1688). These things led to a breakdown of relations with Innocent XI by 1689.

Louis' renewed Gallican zeal followed Pope Innocent's lukewarm reaction to the revocation of the Edict of Nantes. Innocent failed to approve (as Louis expected) as he:

- resented Louis' régale extension and Four Gallican Articles (see Chapter 2)
- preferred French help to fight the Turks and defend Christendom
- condemned anti-Protestant violence and forcible conversions.

Innocent provoked further Gallican confrontation in January 1687 when he removed French embassy immunity from inspection by Vatican officials pursuing criminals. Louis immediately took Gallican umbrage, rushed to victim-status and resorted to military might to assert diplomatic right. He did this by:

- dispatching the bullish Marquis de Lavardin and several hundred men to fortify France's embassy in Rome
- ordering Lavardin to obstruct Vatican officials from catching criminals exploiting diplomatic immunity.

However, Innocent was no pushover. He retaliated publicly by excommunicating Lavardin, and secretly by informing Louis that he and his ministers were also excommunicated. Louis responded by rewarding Lavardin with the Order of the Holy Ghost and unleashing anti-papal propaganda. This accused Innocent of:

- mad Francophobia
- persuading Leopold to attack France.

Louis' confrontational Gallican response proved self-defeating. When Cologne Archbishop Maximilian-Henry died in 1688, Louis needed papal endorsement of his election candidate von Fürstenberg, to maintain control of a strategically vital city. Louis tried appeasing, persuading and threatening Innocent by invading Italy. He failed. Innocent rebuffed all negotiation and intimidation attempts. After a disputed election, he was entitled to have the final say and chose Habsburg candidate, Bavarian Joseph-Clement as Archbishop.

Wounded Gallican pride saw Louis retaliate violently in the autumn of 1688. He seized papal state Avignon and imposed Fürstenburg by force. This horrified European opinion and hardened international resolve to check French aggression.

When Innocent died in 1689, Louis realised it was time to mend his fences with Rome by:

- restoring Avignon
- withdrawing the Gallican Articles and compromising over the régale; this entailed withdrawing his claim to extend this to all of France in 1693.

This was vital. Innocent had refused to consecrate newly appointed bishops, leaving a third of bishoprics without ecclesiastical direction. Louis averted total ultramontanist schism and kept Gallican supporters on side by:

- still allowing the Gallican Articles to be read and taught
- never sending bishops' apologies to the pope
- keeping disputed régale income.

Ultimately, however, Louis' Gallicanism waned and came back to bite him when he dashed his supporters' hopes. His struggle with Jansenism and Quietism (see: Louis XIV and the Church in this chapter) pushed him into ever closer collaboration with Rome. When 40 Sorbonne theologians justified Jansenist rights to respectful silence in the Case of Conscience, Louis accepted Pope Clement XI's condemnation in his 1703 **Cum nuper**. Although applauded by papal nuncio Gualterio, it appalled Parlement President de Harlay. Supported by Chancellor Pontchartrain, he resisted Louis' lettres de cachet ordering acceptance of papal condemnation of the theologians.

Further Gallican unease came in 1705 when Louis accepted Clement's Bull *Vineam Domini*. This required all bishops to condemn respectful silence, and affirmed papal infallibility over faith and doctrine. Gallican opposition saw three propositions which stated:

- bishops' rights over the pope for judging doctrinal issues
- papal rulings over the church were only binding after ecclesiastical discussion
- acceptance required the collective judgment of the General Assembly of Clergy.

In 1713, Louis ignited Gallican furies by attempting to forcibly register the Bull Unigenitus. This condemned 101 Jansenist propositions and applauded 'the zeal of our most dear son in Jesus Christ, Louis the Most Christian King of France'[10]

Unigenitus horrified Gallicans by inviting concessions to papal infallibility. In February 1714, Paris Parlement **Advocate General** Joly de Fleury described articles 90, 91 and 92 as: 'dangerous to the liberties of the Gallican Church, the maxims of the Realm, the authority of kings, the independence of the Crown and the loyalty due him by his subjects'[11]

Louis' attempt to force through the bull's registration was opposed by:

- 15 bishops
- Paris Archbishop Noailles
- Paris Parlement remonstrance
- Nearly half the Sorbonne's theologians; by refusing to register the bull 'purely and simply'[12]
- Chancellor Pontchartrain, who resigned when asked to discipline the bishop of Metz.

Louis' U-turn on anti-papal policies ultimately backfired. He had failed to manage Gallican expectations and had lost the support of his once most natural supporters.

Relations with Huguenots

In 1685 Louis issued the Edict of Fontainebleau in which he revoked the 1585 Edict of Nantes. The latter had granted the Huguenots limited freedom of religion (see Louis XIV and the Church in Chapter 2). Although many French Catholics approved of the Edict of Nantes Revocation, some did not. Louis basked in much domestic propaganda after Fontainebleau, but failed to stamp out Huguenot Protestantism. Increasing persecution from 1685 did some harm both to Louis' reputation and to France's economy. His relations with the Huguenots largely disappointed success wise, but not totally.

The Edict of Fontainebleau delighted most Catholics. In October 1685, Madame de Sévigné stated that 'nothing is as beautiful as what it holds and never did a king do, or will a king ever do, such a memorable deed'.[13] Public enthusiasm and gratitude was expressed by the clergy. In Le Tellier's funeral oration in January 1686, Bossuet, Bishop of Meaux, exclaimed:

'Let us not fail to proclaim this miracle of our age... Let us raise our acclamations even to the skies.... this new Theodosius, this new Marcion, this new Charlemagne... You have confirmed the faith; you have exterminated heretics. This is the crowning achievement of your reign which thereby gains a character of its own. Because of you heresy is no more'.[14]

Jesuit court preacher Louis Bourdaloue agreed. In November 1686, he preached at Versailles that:

'I address these words to a king who, in order to triumph over the enemies of his state, has accomplished miracles of such renown that posterity will not credit it... and who, in order to triumph over the enemies of the Church, is today performing such miracles of zeal that we who witness them can scarcely believe our eyes.'[15]

The support of men so possessed by Louis' efforts to extinguish Huguenotism greatly assisted the royal missionary effort. Bourdaloue was dispatched to Languedoc and Fénelon to Saintonge, where he converted a third of all priests. Missionary squads distributed 500,000 volumes of instructions reinforcing revocation rhetoric.

However, enforcement soon descended into deplorable violence, seemingly encouraged by Louvois. This included:

- public executions
- dragging relapsed heretics' naked corpses through the streets
- leaving them on rubbish tips to be eaten by rats
- arranging them in obscene positions.

Many were naturally shocked and offended. Matignon, Bishop of Condom, protected local Huguenots from royal troops. Montgaillard, Bishop of Saint-Pons, condemned dragonnades forces 'who spit and trample on the Eucharist' in two letters published in February 1686 by Pierre Jurieu.[16] Such fluent and emotive anti-revocation propaganda could not be offset by royal propaganda. Exiled philosopher Pierre Bayle wrote: 'The Roman Catholic Church is nothing but a fury and a whore'.[17]

Protestant preachers Jurieu, Bayle and Jacques Basnage encouraged active opposition in the name of liberty of the conscience. Externally, Louis' reputation was undoubtedly damaged. Huguenot exiles provided the perfect propaganda gift to William of Orange. This assisted his overthrow of James II/VII and development of the League of Augsburg. German protestant princes were appalled by anti-Huguenot violence. Brandenburg severed all relations with Louis.

Some 200,000 Huguenots – 27% – fled France. Sébastien Le Prestre de Vauban, the military engineer and marshal who had recommended the policy of a pré carré, deplored this as utterly counterproductive, claiming that it:

- brought about the ruin of trade and loss of specie
- provided William of Orange with 10,000–12,000 soldiers, Marshal Schomberg, 600 officers and 8,000–9,000 sailors.

The Huguenot **diaspora** certainly deprived France some of its most industrious, skilled, wealthiest and loyal subjects. This contributed to economic stagnation after 1685:

- 50% of all workers left Reims, Tours, Rouen and Nimes.
- Huguenot depopulation blighted Sedan wool manufacturing and apparently caused drastic decline in Alençon, Saint Quentin, Rennes, Nantes, and Vitré's linen production.

Hatters, clothworkers, clockmakers, shipwrights and papermakers were lost, along with 75% of Lyon's silk workers. France's loss was very much its enemies' gain:

Country:	Number of Huguenots immigrants:
Holland	65,000 (mostly clothworkers)
England	40,000
Brandenburg	20,000

Table 4.7: Huguenot emigration from France after 1685

Huguenot emigration to Holland apparently caused specie drainage. Between 1696 and 1700, Bank of Amsterdam deposits were 45% higher than 1681–85.

The revocation's reputational and economic damage have been exaggerated. As explained in Chapters 3 and 5, Louis and Louvois had already shocked and offended international opinion, thereby facilitating William's rise to power and anti-French alliance.

War did more economic damage than the Revocation. Not all emigrants after 1685 were Protestant:

- Most immigrants arriving in England were Catholic.
- 4,500 Catholic weavers fled Normandy for better pay and employment opportunities in England.

Dauphiné, Picardy and Normandy were harder hit economically after 1685 than Languedoc, Poitou, Angoumois, Touraine, Maine and Lyonnais. Tours' and Lyon's silk-making was already declining before the Revocation.

No large-scale wool manufactory folded due to the Revocation. Protestant entrepreneurship was not always indispensable:

- Languedoc and Normandy cloth production did not seriously decline. Elbeuf fine cloth production flourished when taken over by Catholic merchants; from 1690, they employed 8,000 workers and annually produced 9,000–10,000 drapery pieces valued at 2 million livres.
- Protestant drapery production enjoyed royal protection and thrived at Abbeville and Caen; here Protestant Massieu employed a 99% Catholic workforce.
- Catholic Gilbert Paignon took over and maintained Brie wool production from 1686.
- Catholics sustained France's sugar refineries from 1685.
- Knit stocking production and metallurgy actually improved from 1685.

Above all, most Protestants – about 75% – stayed in France. Revocation contributed to, but did not cause French economic decline from 1685.

Louis failed to extinguish Huguenotism. Children were to be removed if new converts did not perform their Catholic duties. Involvement in secret meetings was punishable by death, prison or the galleys from 1686. However, Huguenot defiance was strong:

- 200,000 fled France rather than convert. 1,450 were sent to the galleys.
- 1,000 Huguenots were deported from Cévennes for attending secret meetings 1686–9.
- About 60 meetings occurred in Cévennes and lower Languedoc 1685–1700.
- Mass was commonly avoided in regions where Protestants were numerous after dragonnades left.

Huguenot resistance proved a thorn in Louis' side. The 1702 Cévennes revolt was a major Huguenot revolt using guerrilla warfare tactics in a mountainous region of Languedoc. It took three years to suppress, tying down some 20,000 men and Louis' best general, Villars, during 1704 (the year of Blenheim). Louis could ill afford this when outnumbered and outfought on the Spanish Succession battlefields. Sporadic fighting continued in the Cévennes until 1710. Huguenotism was energetically resisting royal authority, not extinguished.

Figure 4.5: *The Cévennes Revolt*, 1703, painting by Samuel Bastide

Jansenists and Quietists

Jansenists

Louis' desperation to destroy Jansenism before 1715 saw him increasingly collaborate with the pope, bringing pressure to bear on Port-Royal's tiny isolated convent of aging nuns. Ultimately, Louis won some battles but lost his war against Jansenism. By 1715, this was rekindled rather than repressed.

Papal denunciation of Jansenism renewed in 1690 when Alexander VIII condemned 31 Jansenist propositions. In 1694, Innocent XII condemned the five propositions outright, thereby invalidating the Peace of the Church.

Opportunity to strike at Port-Royal arose with the deaths of several of its long-time friends and defenders, including Bishop of Angers Henri Arnauld 1692, Pierre Nicole and Claude Lancelot 1695 and Madame de Sévigné 1696.

Port-Royal offered an increasingly soft target. 75% of its original nuns had died by 1710; more than half of those remaining were in their fifties.

Jansenism's unrelentingly and increasingly outspoken nature also invited retaliation. Arnauld's 20-chapter *Phantom of Jansenism* (1686) accused Louis of:

- abusing lettres de cachet
- despotism
- peddling falsehoods about Jansenism, which was neither heretical nor rebellious.

In 1694, Arnauld warned of continual war against the Jesuits' anti-Jansenist formulary. Pasquier Quesnel's inflammatory *Moral Reflections on the New Testament* (1678) infuriated Louis. It was enlarged and reprinted in 1692 and recommended from 1695 by Noailles. Quesnel offended Louis by emphasising the human spirit's futility and implicitly anti-authoritarianism: 'An unjust excommunication ought not to prevent us from doing our duty'[18]

Jansenist provocation gave Louis three final straws from 1703:

Jansenist submission of the 'Case of Conscience' raised the question of absolution for a cleric who condemned the five propositions but refused 'with respect and silence' to attribute them to Jansen. This reignited royal interest in enforcing the anti-Jansenist Formulary. Pope Clement XI thus ruled against Jansenists and ordered Quesnel's arrest.

This provided further grounds to destroy Jansenism in 1703. Quesnel's confiscated papers emphasised Jansenism was not bound to obey any pope, bishop or king and had a widespread network of committed sympathisers. This indicated that Jansenists remained enemies of the state and a dissident Republican threat.

Louis subsequently invited papal condemnation of Jansenism to destroy it. He was encouraged by his Jesuit advisers who were exasperated at incessant complaints, petitions and ongoing recalcitrance from Port-Royal, as shown in Figure 4.6:

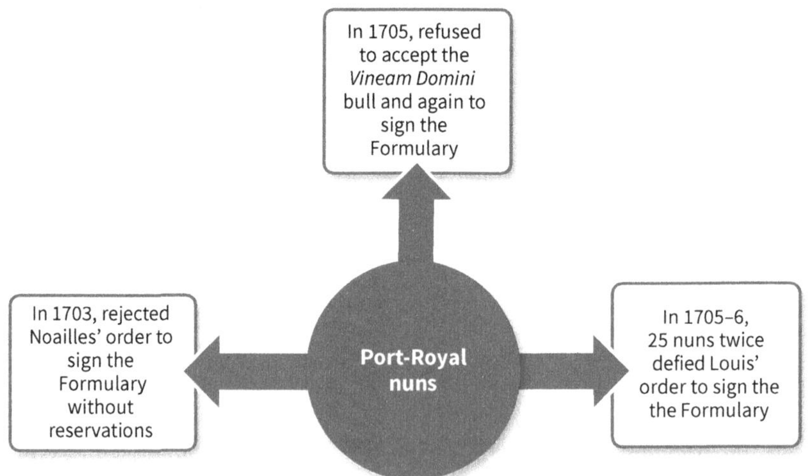

Figure 4.6: Why Louis saw Port-Royal as a challenge to his authority by 1710

This hardened Louis' resolve to extinguish Port-Royal. When the nuns refused to let the new abbess chosen by Louis enter in 1709, 300 archers and three police officers were dispatched to arrest and disperse the nuns, destroy the Port-Royal buildings, and exhume around 3,000 corpses including leading Jansenists.

Louis had seemingly won his anti-Jansenist campaign. But his actions were seen as immoral. Endless emotive writings defended Port-Royal's memory and its sisters' Christian heroism. They also highlighted Jesuit immorality including looting and chopping corpses' heads and limbs off to fit into small transportation boxes.

In his management of Jansenism, Louis ultimately lost the backing of his natural Gallican supporters. Louis' ambition of quickly seeing off Jansenism certainly outran his achievement. In 1708, the Paris Parlement took eight months to register Clement XI's bull supporting Louis. It also rejected the 1713 Bull Unigenitus (condemning 101 propositions from Quesnel's book), horrified at the scope of papal interference.

Unigenitus provoked a rejection of royal and papal 'despotism' and declarations of open Jansenist allegiance:

- An estimated 86% Parisian bishops opposed Unigenitus.
- 87% of Sorbonne theologians, 17 bishops and 3,000 parish priests also opposed it nationally.
- By 1715, 12% of clerics opposed Louis' order to publish the bull, which was revoked after 1715.

Louis failed to contain Jansenism. He left a deeply divided Church and kingdom, a clear Gallican schism and a reinvigorated Jansenist movement, with widespread support.

Quietists

Quietism was a religious sect that emphasised:

- an individual's ability to communicate with God
- total surrender to the will of God
- rejection of the self and all worldly impulses.

This undermined many prerequisites of Catholic worship, including sermons, sacraments, ceremony and atonement for sin.

Quietism became an issue from 1687 when prolific author Madame Guyon wrote a *Short and Very Easy Way of Praying*:

'Our surrender ought to be an entire leaving of ourselves in the hands of God, forgetting ourselves in a great measure and thinking only of God... As to the practice of this virtue, it consists in a continued forsaking and losing of self-will in the will of God; in renouncing all particular self-inclinations as soon as we feel them arise in us...'[19]

Guyon's influence grew when she was tasked by Madame de Maintenon with developing a more spiritual focus at Saint Cyr. The girls were overly excitable after performing Racine's play *Esther* (specially written around a biblical subject), but Guyon soon made her Quietist mark. Contemplation superseded study; teachers and students spent less time studying than lying meditating on the chapel floor.

Quietism's suppression was initiated by Maintenon's concerned confessor, the Bishop of Chartres. He persuaded Maintenon to condemn and not condone Guyon. Maintenon duly obliged. Guyon was dismissed and confined to a convent, then imprisoned, then exiled; her books were burned.

Suppressing Quietism was not straightforward, but was ultimately successful. Guyon won over the Dauphin's tutor and Cambrai Archbishop, François Fénelon. He defended Guyon's books. However, Louis, Maintenon and Bossuet combined against Fénelon.

ACTIVITY 4.3

1. Why and how did Louis:
   - persecute the Huguenots?
   - renew his persecution of the Jansenists?
   - take measures to silence Quietism?
2. How successful was Louis in each of these actions and why?
3. How significant was Gallicanism as a factor in Louis' religious policies?
4. 'Jansenism was the greatest threat to Louis XIV's authority.' How far do you agree?
5. 'Louis' religious policies were largely a failure.' How far do you agree and why?

- He was isolated, banished to Cambrai and forced to condemn his own books.
- Guyon's works were censured.

Louis silenced Quietism but not Fénelon. He became a stern critic of Louis (see Pressures from below in this chapter).

Pressures from below

Social divisions

France remained deeply divided socially, as well as religiously, after 1685. Huge gaps existed between the haves and have-nots of its Estate system.

As we saw in Chapter 1, French analysis of society conventionally assumed the existence of three social groups called 'estates'. The first was the clergy. The second was the nobility, comprising the 'robe' and 'sword' nobility. The third was the remainder, including the bourgeoisie and peasantry (see Chapter 1)

Opportunities for self-enrichment abounded for bankers who funded Louis' armies in the field, *traitants* financiers and wealthy bourgeois office holders. Opportunities also occurred for the elites to evade and exploit taxation. Both the clergy and nobility managed to sidestep half-hearted royal attempts at challenging their most coveted symbol of privilege – immunity from taxation. This left an increasingly disproportionate burden on the lower orders, as did appalling levels of socio-economic poverty across many urban centres and regions of France.

Nothing enshrined social division more in Louis XIV's France than the Church. Its leadership became increasingly aristocratic. Between 1661 and 1715, the number of self-made careerist bishops fell 22%. In selecting Archbishops, Louis preferred nobility to ability. Aristocrats like Noailles were chosen for their perceived lameness and silence on social problems.

Figure 4.7: A later image showing 'The Three Estates' and increasing burdens upon the Third Estate

Between 1688 and 1697, the Church paid increasing annual dons gratuits, averaging over 6.5 million livres. But it remained incredibly wealthy and grossly undertaxed, wriggling out of paying the 1695 capitation and 1710 dixième:

- Royal financial desperation allowed the Church and nobility to retain tax exemption.
- Maintaining this status symbol cost the Church six times the amount that they owed in taxation.
- At best, the Church contributed just 5% of royal income and borrowing.

The First Estate could pay tax, but did not. In 1710, it paid 24 million livres from loans and clerical funds to remove itself altogether from the dixième.

This added to the ordinary tax and tithe burdens of the lower orders. It also showed the ubiquitous wealth of the elites and their determination to use it to maintain existing privileges.

The Spanish Succession War increased social division, allowing rich bankers to profiteer through hyperinflationary money transfer charges:

- In 1703, the cost of sending money to Milan was 8.5%, and a further 14.5%.
- Merchant bankers Antoine and Daniel Hogguer charged 34.48 million livres for remitting money to Italy in 1706; this represented an extortionate 101% handling charge.
- Financier Samuel Bernard lent Louis' army in Flanders a million livres a month at 16% interest.

The scale of private financier profiteering after 1702 is highlighted by Desmaretz's assessment of debts owed in 1708:[20]

Debt owed to Bernard for loans made to maintain the army	11,000,000 livres
Debt owed to the Hogguer brothers for loans made in 1706 to maintain the army in Italy	5,000,000 livres
Bills of the subfarmers of the aides	7,200,000 livres
Interest owed (on debts and charges)	27,991,665 livres

Table 4.8: Nicolas Desmaretz's assessment of royal debts owed in 1708

Equally lucrative were traitant commissions. Contracted by the royal council to manage ad-hoc taxes, venal office sales and forced loans, traitants frequently:

- delayed handing money over
- used funds to make profitable loans accruing 20%–32% investment returns
- added their own charges; these averaged a 23% cut of revenues collected 1689–1715 and a notional 36% rake-off from **affaires extraordinaires** 1700–7. Royal tax demands subsequently increased upon the overtaxed lower orders.

The Duc de Saint-Simon misleadingly portrayed sword nobles' **usurpation** by robe nobles. Outside the royal bureaucracy, the sword nobility dominated the best jobs in the church, army and navy. They also monopolised provincial governorships and major ambassadorial positions of Louis' fellow monarchs in London, Madrid and Vienna. The nobility embodied privilege and social division on a huge scale. In around 66% of France, nobles were completely or generally exempted from direct taxation. They also profited from it and doggedly obstructed royal attacks on their vested social interests.

In 1695, Pontchartrain proposed his capitation tax based on social or office status. The nobility resisted paying, buying exemptions on such a scale that it was abandoned in 1698. This exacerbated both the royal debt and the Third Estate's tax burden. After the capitation was reinstated in 1701, its burden was increased by one third over that of 1695–8. In 1705, Chamillart further impoverished commoners by increasing capitation by 10% hike in capitation; this disproportionately hit those who could not buy tax exemption.

Desmaretz's 1710 dixième placed a 10% tax on all private revenues from land, property, investments and venal office, but was resisted by the elites who bought exemption. It also invited avoidance by being based on self-assessment. A recent estimate is of 70% underassessment.

Social divisions were also apparent within the royal administration. Sword nobles were excluded from ministerial government. Wealthy bourgeois social climbers increasingly bought venal office positions (including Controllers of Perruques in 1706!). This gave them pensions, tax exemption and increasing wages:

Year:	Officier salaries (in millions of livres):
1683	23
1699	47
1715	84

Table 4.9: The growing expense of officier salaries 1683–1715

Officier wages escalated to such a point (Table 4.9) that they typically absorbed all cash received for office sales and extensions within 12 years.

All of this stood in stark contrast to the widespread poverty in many peasant and worker communities across France as explained below.

Problems in the regions

Not all regions suffered the same type and extent of problems after 1685. Some thrived while others saw three main forms of rampant poverty:

- deteriorating living conditions
- economic stagnation
- agricultural distress.

Overall living standards fell from 1685, especially for the 80% of people who depended upon agriculture. Good harvests in 1686–7 depressed prices as supply exceeded demand causing regional poverty. Widespread bread shortages and incidences of peasants eating nothing but acorns and boiled grass were reported in Cévennes, Poitou and Saintonge. Widespread rural poverty was also uncovered in:

- Maine and Orléannais in 1687; peasants reportedly relied upon alms and black bread. This bread cost a large proportion of a peasant's derisory budget and was barely fit for consumption, comprising stalks, scaly chaff seed casings, tree bark, grass and sawdust.
- Auvergne in 1689: 75% of people ate roots and grasses for 3–4 months a year.

Worse still were general crop failures and famine 1692–4. This particularly hit northern, eastern, and central regions by 1693:[21]

Region:	Average % price change of wheat from 1670–90:
North	185
Seine-Loire	221
East	155
Central	133
Southeast	68

Table 4.10: Impact of crop failures and famine across different regions of France by 1693

By 1694, wheat prices were over four times their 1686–90 average. Intendants in Burgundy, Provence and Languedoc obstructed grain sales to big cities and seized boats in several main river ports. Regions with more plentiful supplies – such as the west – falsified stock reports to prevent grain losses. Wheat prices therefore rocketed in cities – by almost 80% in Paris and Toulouse.

This negated taxation yields, economic demand and Third Estate living standards, as shown below in Table 4.11:

Place:	Problem by 1692–94:
Reims	Almost 50% of people were reduced to beggary Trade totally stopped.
Béarn	15,000 people had no resources whatever
Lyon	Grain shortages provoked worker violence
Limoges	70,000 people were reduced to beggary
Moulins	There were 26,000 beggars and 5,000 wretchedly poor.

Table 4.11: The fall in Third Estate living standards

By 1698–1700, economic stagnation also depressed living standards in many areas. Unemployment, vagrancy and beggary increased in Tours, Laval, Orléans, Alençon and Bourbonnais. Vitry-le-François saw a 90% decline in wool manufacturing employment. Auvergne had 95% fewer paid lace-makers than under Colbert.

Additional suffering was caused by agrarian depression and conscription of 200,000 peasants by 1715. These exacerbated growing agricultural labour shortages and increased labour wages which hurt farm owners' profits. Fields were left untended – 28% less land was being tilled in Albi (Languedoc) by 1699. Contemporary estimates were dire. Net farm yields were 50% lower than 1661 and rural property income a third lower than the 1660–70s.

Members of the Third Estate suffered different problems at different times. War, tariffs and unemployment meant prices and therefore peasant farmer incomes remained depressed from 1701–7. Harvest failure and an ensuing widespread famine from 1708 meant that bread became unaffordable to the masses. Prices rocketed (by 400% in Picardy, 112% in Paris and Toulouse and 189% in Pontoise) and bakeries were pillaged.

Extremely harsh minus-forty-degree winter temperatures in 1709 also devastated many regions, destroying crops and livestock and leaving vineyards barren for five years. It also caused a crisis mentality and wheat-hoarding in Champagne, Franche-Comté and Burgundy. Burgundy competed with Lyon for wheat. 300 soldiers had to be detached to prevent grain hoarding in Auxonne. With supplies rationed, Lyon bread prices rocketed, consuming 85% of a skilled artisan's wages with a family of four. Lyon hoarded bread it bought up, thereby causing 50% bread price increases in the surrounding region.

Additional problems lay in depopulation. An estimated 6% of the population died in 1693–4 – proportionately more than during the First World War. Although the south-east suffered relatively less, deaths in the south-west increased by 345% and by over 200% in Seine-Loire and central France. In 1709–10, deaths increased 140% in the east and 116% in the southeast. This exacerbated declining economic demand, labour supplies, numbers of marriages and taxation yields. Less people alive meant less people to buy goods, supply labour, marry and pay tax.

Regional poverty massively hindered taxation collection and returns. By 1703, popular resistance against tax receivers was common. Some **Généralités** saw considerable arrears by 1707. By 1709, economic failure in northern France meant months of unpaid tax revenues. Troops had to be sent to Bourges in 1710 to collect the **ustencile** – a tax to pay for army living expenses.

Many regions actively avoided paying taxes. Alsace, Franche-Comté and Flanders immediately purchased capitation exemption. Alsace did similarly from the dixième in 1711. Violent local anti-dixième protests erupted in Béarn, Périgord, La Rochelle, Picardy, Limousin, Normandy, Touraine and Montauban.

Additional problems occurred in 1715 when widespread plague devastated many provinces and their livestock as shown in Table 4.12:

Region:	**Losses:**
Burgundy	72,000 cattle
Metz	32,000 cattle 24,000 sheep 18,000 horses

Table 4.12: Livestock losses resulting from the 1711 plague

This plethora of regional problems provided fertile grounds for social discontent and popular protest.

Discontent and popular protests

A nation's health can be gauged by the levels of popular discontent and protest, and by the state's response to such things. On all counts, France was increasingly – if not totally – unhealthy 1685–1715. Various outspoken intellectuals criticised royal policies and demanded various alternatives, to little avail. Resistance, riot and revolt ignited across different regions, cities and social strata. The royal response was more high-handed than helpful.

Mounting criticism of royal policies came from the 'Burgundy circle' – intellectuals trying to influence the Duke of Burgundy, 'le petit Dauphin', seen as a future king. These included:

- Cambrai Archbishop Fénelon
- Rouen government official Pierre le Pesant Boisguilbert
- Marshal and military engineer Sébastien Vauban.

Fénelon lamented Louis' wars and public suffering in an unflinching letter sent to (but probably unread by) Louis:

'Your people, whom you should love as your own children, and who have hitherto loved you so passionately, are now dying of hunger. Cultivation of the land is almost abandoned; the towns and the countryside are becoming depopulated; all trades are languishing and no longer produce workmen. All commerce is destroyed. Thus you have drained away half the inner strength of your state in order to make and defend useless conquests outside it. Instead of drawing money from this poor people, you should give them alms and feed them. The whole of France is no longer anything more than a great, devastated hospital, with no provisions.'[22]

Fénelon also criticised sovereign power's faults in his audacious fantasy *Les aventures de Télémaque* (1699). This portrayed the king as failing to listen and neglecting peace, recommended free trade, and stressed the horrors of war and arbitrary power. By 1711, Fénelon was advising Burgundy to reduce:

- royal expenses and court
- numbers of officials
- taxation, so agriculture and industry would flourish.

Increasing poverty in Rouen made Boisguilbert, a radical anti-Colbertiste and Jansenist, predisposed to criticising Louis for mismanaging France. So too did his investigations into social problems in 1696 and 1707. Boisguilbert corresponded with government ministers over two decades, proposing **laissez-faire** alternatives to mercantilist obsession over money as the source of wealth. Instead, he urged a focus upon farm production and raising all subjects' well-being.

Speak like a historian

Laissez-faire is a French term meaning 'leave it to happen'. The expression (which Boisguilbert may well have coined, though others later adopted it) emphasises a policy of minimising state or government interference in the economy, allowing producers and customers to negotiate the quantity, quality and prices of products and services.

Discussion point

Contrast this with the mercantilism of Colbert which we discussed in Chapter 2. Do some further research into the two approaches: what do you think are their attractions and disadvantages? Was either the answer to France's economic problems under Louis XIV?

Boisguilbert's 1695 *Le Détail de la France, sous le règne présent* (Description of France under the Current Reign) depicted all classes' ruin, openly criticised royal policy and demanded:

- taille abolition
- removal of 'criminal' taxes on farm products and damaging indirect taxes.

Vauban also criticised royal policy, lobbying for reform from 1689. His research blamed depopulation upon harsh taxation and criticised its increasing inefficiency and inequality. Vauban wanted taxation to be made proportionate to wealth, and peasant labour as the primary focus of French wealth generation.

ACTIVITY 4.4

Was taxation the greatest destabilising force in French society under Louis XIV?

Popular protest took many different forms. In 1702, Huguenot **Camisard** guerrillas in the Cévennes mountains revolted against extreme conversion methods. The house of Chief inquisitor Abbot Chayla was torched and he was stabbed 52 times after jumping out! Ambush tactics, local support and terrain knowledge made the Camisards difficult to defeat. Civil war bogged down substantial royal forces and Villars continued until 1710. Languedoc also saw sustained non-payment of the taille. Table 4.13 shows how urban riots affected France.

Date:	Location:
1692	Lyon, Marseille and Arles
1693	Rouen
1696 and 1709	Marseille, Arles and Dijon
1685, 1695, 1704 & 1711	Amiens (labour insurgency)

Table 4.13: Urban riots in France's regions

Social participation in revolt varied. Nobles sometimes led collective crowd actions. Women seized grain in La Ferté-Imbault in central France in 1692 and stopped grain traders in Rogin in eastern France, 1693. In 1709 alone:

- Dieppe's bourgeoisie and commoners alike stole grain.
- bourgeois and soldiers stole grain in Valenciennes.
- Anjou, Paris and Rouen women spinners rioted alongside the bourgeoisie.
- Rouen bourgeoisie and textile workers rioted.

The government addressed the symptoms of these problems, but not the causes. In 1693–4 and 1709, alms and spending on housing for the homeless was increased, but **reaction** was preferred over **reform**:

- 1701–1708, troops were used to enforce taxation in Languedoc.
- In 1709, troops dispelled a crowd blocking wheat shipments along the Marne.
- In 1710, troops were sent to keep order in Paris and many provinces.

Ultimately, the Burgundy circle lacked a cutting edge; its increasing criticisms prompted no major reform. Power outweighed persuasion in deciding the argument. Neither the capitation nor dixième succeeded in making the elites pay their fair share of taxation. Vauban's 1707 book ***Projet d'une Dîme royale*** was condemned and his arrest ordered before he died. Boisguilbert was snubbed by Pontchartrain and Chamillart. He was exiled for three months in 1707 and largely ignored thereafter. Burgundy's death in 1712 sealed matters once and for all – removing a future potential figurehead for reform.

By suppressing revolts and failing to implement social, economic and fiscal reforms, therefore, Louis left behind a society that was deeply divided and prone to unrest. A cocktail of unresolved problems stored up the future for further conflicts that ultimately came to the fore at the end of the 18th century in the French Revolution.

Timeline

1669	Françoise d'Aubigné (later Madame de Maintenon) became governess to Louis XIV and Madame de Montespan's illegitimate children
1673	Parlement's remonstrance revoked
1675	Turenne killed
1680	Madame de Maintenon came to Versailles
1683	Madame de Maintenon secretly became Louis' second wife after Maria Theresa's death
1683–9	Claude Le Peletier finance minister
1685	Large-scale Huguenot emigration begins
1685	Edict of Fontainebleau Revocation of the 1598 Edict of Nantes
1686	Condé retired
1686	Madame De Maintenon general director boarding school at Saint Cyr
1687	Avignon seized causing defeat in the Cologne election
1687	Le Peletier replaced Colbert's single tax-farm lease with two leases and lowered the price below takings
1687	Louis in conflict with Pope Innocent XI over French diplomatic asylum in Rome (January and November)
1687	Louis XIV affected by anal fistula
1688	Cologne Archbishop Maximilian-Henry died
1688	Louis in conflict with Pope Innocent XI over the Cologne election (June – September)
1688	Louis seized papal state Avignon and imposed Fürstenburg as Cologne archbishop
1688	Nine Years War broke out
1689	Jean Racine writes *Esther* for Saint Cyr's schoolgirls
1689	Pope Innocent XI died
1689	Vauban became critic of royal policy
1689–1699	Phélypeaux de Pontchartrain finance minister
1692–4	Hyperinflationary bread prices
1693	Louis lost Paris Parlement's support by ending Gallican policy and inviting papal condemnation of Jansenism
1694	Officer-training schools abandoned due to riotous and disorderly behaviour
1695	Failed attempt began to make all people pay capitation tax on their social or office-based status
1695	Jansenist sympathiser Antoine Noailles became Archbishop of Paris

1695	Luxembourg died
1695	Pontchartrain's capitation tax based on social or office status
1699–1708	Michel Chamillart finance minister
1701	War of the Spanish Succession broke out
1702	Cévennes revolt
1703	Pope Clement XI's *Cum nuper* condemned Jansenist claim to right to respectful silence in the Case of Conscience
1704	France defeated at Blenheim
1705	Louis accepted Clement's *Bull Vineam Domini* requiring all bishops to condemn respectful silence, and affirmed papal infallibility over faith and doctrine
1705	Chamillart increased capitation by 10%
1706	France defeated at Ramilles and Turin
1707	Vauban's published a *Projet d'une Dîme royale*
1708–1715	Nicolas Desmaretz finance minister
1709	Daniel-François Voysin appointed war minster
1709	Hyperinflationary bread prices
1710	Desmaretz's dixième placed a 10% tax on all private revenues from land, property, investments and venal office
1713	Louis attempted forcibly to register the Bull Unigenitus; Paris Parlement remonstrated
1713	Treaty of Utrecht
1714	Ducs de Maine and Toulouse made princes of the blood to secure the royal succession
1714	The Dauphin, two grandsons and a great grandson had died

Practice essay questions

1. 'Louis lost control of his government in the years 1685–1699.' Assess the validity of this view.
2. 'Madame de Mainteron exerted a dominant influence over Louis XIV.' Assess the validity of this view.
3. 'The Spanish Succession War was the biggest problem facing French finances after 1702.' Assess the validity of this view.
4. 'Social disorder in 1709 was the most serious threat Louis XIV faced at the end of his reign.' Assess the validity of this view.
5. 'The loss of Huguenots after the Devocation of the Edict of Nantes did no damage to France.' Assess the validity of this view.
6. With reference to these sources and your understanding of the historical context, assess the value of these three sources to an historian studying the problems facing Louis XIV at the end of his reign.

Extract A

Jean-Baptiste Antoine Colbert, Marquis de Seignelay (1651–90), was Colbert's son and Louis XIV's Secretary of Navy from 1683. In 1687, he wrote this letter to Pierre Arnoul, Intendant of La Rochelle:

'I am very comfortable telling you that you are mistaken on the subject of the persons who leave the kingdom, when you say that the damage is not great and that that does not diminish commerce. And you should be persuaded that the greatest ill that can happen to a state is the loss of a large number of subjects who leave, who take their industry to foreign lands and enrich them at the cost of the kingdom, and that is what you must prevent with all your might in the full extent of your department.'

Seignelay to Pierre Arnoul, Intendant of La Rochelle, 6 June 1687, cited by David Smith, *Louis XIV*. Cambridge: Cambridge University Press; 1992. p. 40

Extract B

Part of a letter sent by Archbishop of Cambrai Francois de Salignac de la Mothe-Fénelon, addressed to Louis XIV, although probably never read by him (historians believe this was in Madame de Maintenon's possession in 1695).

'Your people, whom you should love as your own children, and who have hitherto loved you so passionately, are now dying of hunger. Cultivation of the land is almost completely abandoned; the towns and the countryside are becoming depopulated; all the trades are languishing and no longer produce workmen... All commerce is destroyed. Thus you have drained away the inner half of you state in order to make empty conquests outside it. Instead of drawing money from this poor people, you should give them alms and feed them. The whole of France is no longer anything more than a great, devastated hospital, with no provisions.'

Peter Campbell, *Louis XIV: 1661–1715*. London: Routledge; 1993, p. 129

Extract C

A letter from Controller General Nicolas Desmaretz to Madame de Maintenon, 26 July 1709, asking for continued backing in his post:

'Allow me to remind you that you that having been entrusted with the control of finances in the month of February last year, at a time when everything seemed hopeless, I arranged for more than 288,000,000 livres of expenditure, which have provided the means to re-establish and twice dispatch on campaign the most beautiful armies to be seen.

In the eighteenth months since I was honoured with the place of Controller-General, the King has reduced the taille by 4,200,000 livres. The revenues from Flanders have gone down by nearly 3,000,000 livres because of the fall of Menin and of Lille. The King has ordered the supply of grain to Paris, and has provided funds for bringing it from abroad for Guyenne.'

Peter Campbell, *Louis XIV: 1661–1715*. London: Routledge; 1993, p. 129

Chapter summary

You should now have a good understanding of Louis XIV's domestic problems and policies in the period 1685–1715, including how they related to his foreign-policy decisions. You will also have learned about what different people said about the situation at the time as well as what historians have written about it more recently and you will have begun to form your own views. From reading this chapter, you will be able to:

- assess the strengths and weaknesses of royal government
- understand and evaluate Madame de Maintenon's influence
- understand the financial and economic problems after Colbert including the costs of war
- know and assess Louis' policies towards Gallicanism, the Huguenots, Jansenists and Quietists
- understand the social situation, including social divisions, problems in the regions, discontent and popular protests.

End notes

[1] Maland D. *Europe in the Seventeenth Century*. London: Macmillan Education; 1966. p. 299.

[2] Catholic Encyclopedia: Marquise de Maintenon. Newadvent.org. 2016. Available from: http://www.newadvent.org/cathen/09548b.htm

[3] Burke P. *The Fabrication of Louis XIV*. New Haven: Yale University Press; 1992. p. 142.

[4] Treasure G. *Louis XIV*. England: Longman; 2001. p. 222.

[5] Liselotte to the Electress of Hanover. Cited by Boislisle A. Le Secret de la Poste sous le règne de Louis XIV. *Annuaire Bulletin de la société de l'histoire de France*. 1890. p. 231.

[6] Williams H. N. *Madame de Montespan and Louis XIV*. Rockville, Marylands Wildside Press; 2009. p. 310.

[7] Cited by Elisabeth C, Kroll M. *Letters from Liselotte 1652-1722*. London: Gollancz; 1970. p. 52.

[8] Strayer B. *Suffering Saints: Jansenists and Convulsionnaires in Paris 1640–1799*. Brighton: Sussex Academic Press; 2012. p. 148–9.

[9] Adapted from Sturdy D. *Louis XIV*. Houndmills, Basingstoke, Hampshire: Macmillan Press; 1998. p. 52.

[10] Rowlands G. Louis XIV, Vittorio Amedeo II and French military failure in Italy, 1689-96. T*he English Historical Review*. 2000; 115(462): 534–569.

[11] Pope Clement XI (September 1713). Cited by Smith D. *Louis XIV*. Cambridge: Cambridge University Press; 1992. p. 70.

[12] Strayer B. *Suffering Saints 11*. Brighton: Sussex Academic Press; 2012. p. 161.

[13] Ibid. p. 161.

[14] The reactions in France and abroad. Musée virtuel du Protestantisme. Museeprotestant.org. 2016. Available from: http://www.museeprotestant.org/en/notice/the-reactions-in-france-and-abroad/

[15] Bossuet funeral oration (January 1686). Cited by Wilkinson R. *Louis XIV, France and Europe, 1661–1715*. London: Hodder & Stoughton; 1993. p. 43.

[16] Sermon by Louis Bourdaloue (1 November 1686). Cited by Smith D. *Louis XIV*. Cambridge: Cambridge University Press; 1992. p. 75–6.

[17] Treasure G. *Louis XIV*. Harlow: Longman; 2001. p. 227.

[18] Ibid. p. 227 & 232; Wilkinson R. *Louis XIV, France and Europe, 1661–1715*. London: Hodder & Stoughton; 1993. p. 41.

[19] Cited by Treasure G. *Louis XIV*. Harlow, England: Longman; 2001. p.321.

[20] Wilkinson R. *Louis XIV, France and Europe, 1661–1715*. London: Hodder & Stoughton; 1993. p. 48.

[21] Cited by McCollim G. *Louis XIV's Assault on Privilege*. Rochester, NY: University of Rochester Press; 2012. p. 43.

[22] O Gráda C. Chevet J. Famine and Market in Ancient Regime France. *The Journal of Economic History*. 2002; Vol. 62, No.3, p. 718–9 & 730.

5 Challenges in Europe, 1685–1697

We will look into:

- the challenge of William of Orange: the Dutch-English alliance after the Glorious Revolution of 1688
- the Grand Alliance: the League of Augsburg and the anti-French alliance between Protestant states; the Empire and Spain
- the Nine Years War: outbreak, course and outcome; the war in Europe; the war in North America, the Caribbean and Asia; the Peace of Ryswick 1697
- the new balance of power: the position of France in relation to the European powers by 1697; the impact of years of war on France's economic and military resources; the prospects of future wars.

The challenge of William of Orange

The Dutch-English alliance after the Glorious Revolution of 1688

In 1685, there seemed little prospect of a challenge to Louis XIV, especially from England. Charles II's proclivity to accept French subsidies and his deathbed conversion to Catholicism left Louis confident that England would remain compliant with, if not also a complicit supporter of, his foreign policy. When the Roman Catholic James II/VII became king of England and Scotland in February of that year, his authority appeared secure: a king's son, a king's brother, the undoubted heir to the throne would now receive the crown with the full backing of Parliament. Louis saw the prospect of further collaboration with England.

Instead, he found himself facing confrontation from 1688. English Parliamentarians, afraid of their Catholic king and his policies, invited James' son-in-law William of Orange to overthrow King James. Almost overnight, England changed from a French ally to a Dutch one. A king friendly to Louis was replaced by Louis' arch-nemesis.

Key terms

In the **Glorious Revolution** a Roman Catholic king was overthrown by the governing elite of a Protestant state. The following year James' daughter Mary and her husband William were proclaimed joint rulers and a Bill of Rights was passed that limited royal powers and strengthened Parliament's rights. This was a major change (so a revolution) which established certain freedoms with minimal loss of life (so glorious). Although Mary had the more direct claim to the throne, William insisted on this joint arrangement, and as a result he remained king by himself after Mary's death in 1694.

The Glorious Revolution of 1688

The **Glorious Revolution** was a coup undertaken with the support of a foreign army. It saw King James II overthrown by English parliamentarians, supported by Louis' protestant enemy William of Orange. William invaded with a Dutch army, but in response to an invitation from the members of the establishment who had finally decided that they didn't trust James. Up to this point, Louis might have regarded the French relationship with England as well established:

- Charles II's mother was Louis' aunt.
- Charles II and James II had spent part of their years of exile in France, dependent on Louis XIV's financial support.
- James II had looked set to maintain the alliance.

Now England was no longer a French ally. Worse, it was now bound to support William in his campaign against France, for the Dutch leader was keen to employ England's abundant financial, naval and military resources, and, to wage war against Louis with a large international coalition called the Grand Alliance. William's path to power in England had been supported by three main factors:

- *James II's alienation of the elites*: Louis' ally James II was himself a significant reason why the French King's Dutch adversary was able to assume control of England in 1688. A Catholic, James seemed to pose a worrying threat to the Church of England and the Anglican status quo. The English tended to assume that Catholicism meant extremism. The executions of Protestants by the 16th century Roman Catholic Queen Mary I and the Catholic attempt to assassinate James I in the Gunpowder Plot of 1605 were still common knowledge. Gripped by the fear that another such Popish conspiracy was in the making, the English Earls of Danby and Halifax, together with Bishop of London Henry Compton, wrote to William of Orange in June 1688, pledging their support and calling upon him to invade with an army. Table 5.1 sums up some of the reasons why:

Date:	What James did to lose support:
1687	Took measures to secure freedom of worship for Catholics, suspend penal laws against them and allow them to serve in public office.
1673	Allowed his conversion to Roman Catholicism to become public knowledge.
June 1688	Had a son James Edward Stuart. This presented the prospect of a Catholic dynasty. This terrified the Anglican Tory elites and made William seem an attractive puppet Protestant alternative.

Table 5.1: Reasons why James II lost support

- *William's plans to invade England and harness its resources against Louis*: William had been planning to take over England and been assembling an invasion force of 21,000 men, before he was given the green light by the English elites. His main reason was quite simple – to bring the English into war against France and to prevent (or disrupt) any Anglo-French alliance; with additional resources at his disposal, he hoped to defeat Louis and restrict him to his 1659 borders.

Voices from the past

Claude Louis Hector de Villars

Claude Louis Hector de Villars came from an impoverished noble family. One of Louis XIV's most successful soldiers, he was made Prince de Martigues, and Marquis (then Duc) de Villars, Vicomte de Melun and a Marshal General. In the following extract, he comments on the French court's attitude to the deposed English king.

'The court hesitated to its policy, whether it should be to aid King James, about to be attacked, or should prevent peace with the Turks which was being made and which would bring down upon us the whole forces of the Emperor and the Empire. M. de Louvois ... decided upon the second course. In effect nothing was more important to us than to secure so powerful a diversion in our favour as that of the Turks. Besides, what prospect was there that so great a revolution could take place in England without great trouble and discord? This suited us better than settled government under King James.'[1]

1 What would you say was the gist of this passage? Paraphrase it in plain, modern English.
2 Why do you think Louvois favoured preventing peace with the Turks to defending James II? What were the results of this decision?

- *James II's inaction when William landed*: Louis had seen in James II a potentially useful military ally. In reality, James II was anything but. He put up no fight against William when faced by invasion, even though he had assembled a 25,000 strong army to defend England from the summer of 1688. Anti-Catholic riots and the desertions of his own daughter Anne, his nephew Lord Cornbury, his son-in-law William of Orange, and long-standing supporter the Duke of Marlborough prompted James to run away to London. So too did his declining health. Within four days, James had retreated from Salisbury – where he intended to intercept William. He was then permitted to flee to France which allowed parliament to claim he had abdicated. James' invasion of Ireland in March 1689 with 6,000 French troops ultimately failed; he was defeated by William in the 1690 Battle of the Boyne.

By 1689, William was England's king. Louis' role in this abrupt change has often been neglected. Basic tactical mistakes allowed William to invade and achieve his goal of including England in a powerful anti-French coalition. Louvois had been acutely aware of the need to help defend James II in 1688, but instead had opted for an altogether different policy option and practically welcomed an invasion as an opportunity for profiting from a weakened and divided England facing another civil war.

Instead of intervening directly in England, French soldiers were sent to capture Philippsburg and devastate the Palatinate from September 1688 until 1689. This policy of **scorched earth** was intended to deprive the enemy of resources for attacking France. It also greatly benefited William of Orange and indirectly facilitated his invasion as:

- it meant that there were no French troops on the Dutch border; as a result, William of Orange knew that the Dutch Republic would not be attacked while he was distracted in England
- it was the ultimate propaganda gift for William to harness anti-French opinion to support a coalition for war; the razing of Heidelberg and Mannheim (March 1689) confirmed Louis' image as a rogue who needed cutting down to size.

Timeline: How William overthrew James II in 1688 and built the Grand Alliance

By November 1688	Louis' archenemy William of Orange had landed unopposed at Torbay in England	Louis' ally James II put up no fight and fled to London
By January 1689	William was crowned English King	England's large powerful navy, substantial financial resources and potentially effective army were now placed under the control of the man whose life ambition it was to frustrate and defeat Louis XIV
By May 1689	William had formed a powerful anti-Louis coalition called the Grand Alliance	It included England, the United Provinces, Lorraine and the Habsburg Empire. By 1690, Savoy and Spain had also joined

Louis had miscalculated to a large extent. He overestimated James' capabilities as an ally and underestimated William. In 1688–9, events moved quickly – and not in Louis' favour.

Key terms

Attila: comparing King Louis with Attila intentionally suggested that he was a barbaric threat to civilisation, like the fifth-century king of the Huns who had once threatened to overwhelm the Roman Empire.

ACTIVITY 5.1

1. Write brief notes summing up the key challenges Louis faced after 1685. Which do you think were the most significant and why?
2. Present a summary of how each of the following allowed William to take over England in 1688:
   - James II's mistakes
   - Louvois' mistakes.
3. How useful is the source of Duras addressing Louvois and the source from Louvois himself for telling us why Louis faced war with the Grand Alliance in 1689–90?

The Grand Alliance

By 1689, William had assembled the Grand Alliance – a huge anti-French international coalition including Emperor Leopold I, the Dutch, Lorraine, Spain, Savoy and German Protestant princes. They aimed to make Louis surrender all his territorial gains since 1661 and formally declared war on France in May 1689.

Louis did much to provoke this. In March 1689, he supplied 6,000 troops to help James try and provoke an armed Irish rebellion against William. This failed and garnered English opinion against Louis and James. Equally repugnant was premeditated French aggression during 1688–90, including:

- Mannheim's destruction in March 1689
- Louvois' troops razing to the ground 20 major German towns by 1690, including Worms and Speyer (May 1689).

Louis therefore achieved what no Habsburg emperor had been able to: he united European opinion against France. He was dubbed a monster and a French **Attila**, a scenario that experienced French Marshal Duras warned about in May 1689:

'The pain of having to destroy cities as considerable as Worms and Speyer leads me to put before his Majesty the bad effect that such desolation would have on his reputation and *gloire* in the world'.[2]

Louvois also bullied the neighbouring Duchy of Savoy in 1690. He demanded that, unless Duke Vittorio Amedeo immediately send 2,000 infantrymen – half of Savoy's army – to fight alongside French forces or help attack Spanish held Milan, he 'be punished in a manner that he remembers for the rest of his life'.[3]

Small wonder therefore that Savoy and Spain both joined the Grand Alliance against Louis by 1690.

Louvois' confrontation therefore legitimised William's coalition. Historians have dated Louis' failure to rein in Louvois back to 1685, when the Sun King was debilitated from long surgical operations on an anal fistula. But William's Grand Alliance now became Louis' major source of discomfort from 1689, harnessing England's resources and against France as head of a huge anti-French war alliance.

ACTIVITY 5.2

Write a few sentences of definition or brief comments on:

- the Glorious Revolution
- Louvois
- Devastation of the Palatinate
- Vittorio Amedeo.

The League of Augsburg and the anti-French alliance between Protestant states, the Empire and Spain

The League of Augsburg was a defensive alliance formed by the princes of Franconia and the Rhineland in 1686. By 1688, it included Brandenburg, Bavaria, The Elector of the Palatinate, Saxony, Spain, Sweden, the United Provinces and the Emperor. The league's existence arose from:

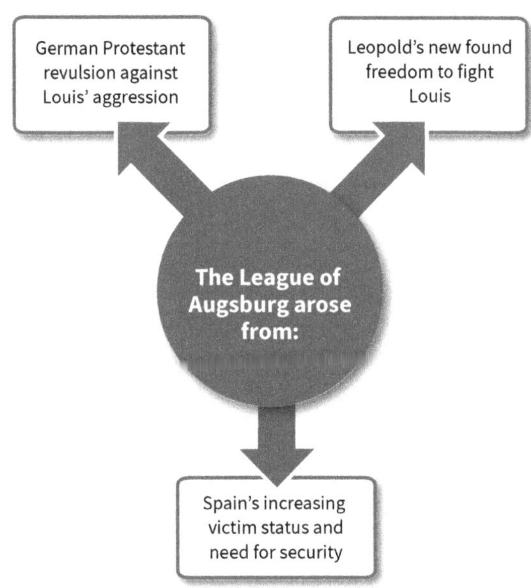

Figure 5.1: Motives for the creation of the League of Augsburg

As highlighted in chapters 2 and 3, the violent aspects of Louis' anti-Huguenot and Réunion policies provided the ultimate propaganda gift to his enemies. Some 200,000 Huguenots fled France. Many had horror stories of French 'terror'. This deeply shocked Protestants abroad, especially in the Dutch Republic, England, Scotland and the German states. Now they were united in defending Protestantism against French aggression. To this end, German Protestant states were inspired by:

- German philosopher Leibniz's call for an alliance of smaller German states and the Dutch Republic
- the Elector of Brandenburg's Minister President Paul von Fuchs declaration that only understanding between Brandenburg, the United Provinces and England would deliver Europe 'from the universal yoke of France'.[4]
- Brandenburg's 'defensive alliance' with Emperor Leopold from March 1686.

The League of Augsburg also arose from a changing state of Europe. From 1686–7, Leopold had relative freedom from the Ottoman threat and an improved opportunity to attack France. Habsburg victories over the Turks along the Danube at Buda in 1686 and Mohács in 1687, gave the Emperor the very kind of opportunities he had dreamed of:

- to lead a large and expanding alliance with Spain to wage war on Louis XIV
- to regain those territories France had acquired during previous conflicts and the period of Réunions
- to undermine France's ability to wage aggressive campaigns against its neighbours
- to legitimise this by presenting himself as the defender of sovereign German Protestant states' liberty and independence.

Leopold had been given moral consent to attack France after Pope Innocent XI declared: 'War with France is the only prompt and effective means of bringing her to compensate all of Europe for a part of all the wrongs and injustices that she has committed.'[5]

Taking it further

How useful is Innocent XI's advice to Leopold and the League of Augsburg to our understanding of his reasons for going to war in 1688?

Spain's desperate need for security and willingness to unite with German Protestant states and Leopold were accentuated by French aggression during and after the War of Réunions (1683–4). The Emperor's increasing success against the Turks made him appeal increasingly to Spain as a safe bet as an ally in protecting it from French expansionism. The violent nature of French actions against Spain at Charleroi and Luxembourg (explained in chapter 3) gave Spain renewed need for protection and victim status, which aided its task in finding allies with a common anti-French cause. So too did:

- Louvois' bombardment of Genoa in 1684; this used 13,300 bombs and destroyed two thirds of the city after the Genoese refused to hand over galleys built for the Spanish
- French invasion of the small Protestant territory of the Vaudois valley during 1685–6. This was a punishment for harbouring Huguenots emigrants and involved 7,000–8,000 men. This alarmed Spain, as Vaudois was to the south west of Turin and was therefore dangerously close to Milan and other Spanish territories in northern Italy.

The League of Augsburg's rapid development and heightened willingness for an offensive action against France undoubtedly had much to do with the increasingly threatening and aggressive nature of Louis' foreign policy from 1687–8:

Timeline

1687	Louis demanded that Leopold recognise Réunions as permanant and increased French military presence in Rome.
Nov 1687	Louis quarrelled with the pope and violently seized the papel of Avignon.
Sept 1688	Louis threatened the pope for choosing Joseph Clement as Archbishop of Cologne above the French candidate Fürstenberg.
Sept 1688	Louis issued an ultimatum and gave the German Protestant princes and Leopold just 3 months to agree to the following demands: • that all his gains from Réunions and 1684 Truce of Ratisbon must be made permanent • that his sister-in-law Elizabeth Charlotte, should be paid an indemnity for renouncing her claim to the Palatinate • that Fürstenberg be appointed Archbishop of Cologne.
Sept 1688	France's invasion of Cologne, Baden and the Palatinate (and devastations of the latter two regions) confirmed Leibnitz's image of Louis as the 'most Christian Mars and Turk'.
1688	Louis installed Fürstenberg as Archbishop of Cologne by force and captured Philippsburg.
1688	Louis had violently seized the papel state of Avignon.

Such intimidating, hostile and antagonistic actions caused extreme resentment and fear of French expansion, not just among German lands, but across Europe. Louis was not just a threat to Protestantism itself, but to the independence of German states that had once looked to France for protection against Habsburg imperialism. Louis' actions hardened opinion against him and united his opponents. He seemed more and more the extremist barbaric threat that Leibnitz had portrayed him as in 1685.

Jules-Louis Bolé de Chamlay was a diplomat and one of Louvois' generals. When Louis decided to threaten the pope with war, he sent Chamlay to insist Innocent XI back the French candidate Fürstenburg as Archbishop of Cologne after the death of Maximilian Henry in June 1688.

'Any refusal by His Holiness to grant the necessary bulls would only serve to set off a war in the Empire which it would be hard to end, and which would cause Christendom to lose all those advantages which have been secured because I have not wished to profit from favourable circumstances to press the claims of my Crown against neighbouring states ... while the Emperor's forces were occupied in Hungary.'[6]

Louis was talking up his own decision not to take advantage of Habsburg weakness during 1686–7, when the Emperor had been engaged in pushing the Ottoman Turks out of Hungary.

The League of Augsburg sensed an attempt at French intimidation. The major beneficiaries of this were Louis' enemies William of Orange and Leopold. Unintentionally, Louis' actions had contributed significantly to the growth of the anti-French alliance, the start of conflict in 1688, and its proliferation during 1689–90. Louis' invasions of the Palatinate, Cologne and Philippsburg were the sparks that lit the fire of conflict.

With remarkable speed, several countries sprang to arms against Louis. Leopold prepared to march on the Upper Rhine (the upstream, southern part of the strategically important north-flowing river), while troops from Brandenburg and

ACTIVITY 5.3

What does Chamlay's diplomatic note to the pope tell us about the increasing challenges Louis faced within Europe by 1688? Write a paragraph putting the source into context and explaining what it contributes to our understanding of the French diplomatic position.

ACTIVITY 5.4

Research the following and write a few sentences about each of them, noting both what happened and what significance it had:

- League of Augsburg
- Seizure of Avignon
- Cologne election
- Louis' ultimatum September 1688.

Saxony proceeded to the Rhine's lower reaches. The Nine Years War had begun, with William about to soon take over in England and do all he could to support Leopold. The Sun King's foreign policy success was now in serious danger of being eclipsed.

Louis' intentions

Although it is easy to blame the anti-French alliance upon Louis and caricature French foreign policy from 1685 as purely hostile, this obscures the full context affecting Louis' actions and the rise of the anti-French coalition from 1686. Louis claimed **dynastic** motives for invading the Palatinate and had a growing conviction that:

- such action was essential for defending France (and especially Alsace)
- conflict was inevitable in 1688.

Louis' foreign policy should not therefore, just be pigeonholed as expansionist or aggressive, at least not in terms of its underlying intentions.

The Sun King knew Leopold and the Elector of the Palatinate were threats to French security. In his later *Mémoire des raisons*, Louis argued:

'By which the King is obliged to resume his Arms, and which ought to persuade all Christendom of the Sincere Intentions of his Majesty for the Establishment of the Public Tranquillity. His majesty ... had always been advertised of the design that the Emperor had formed for a long time to attack France, as soon as he shall have made peace with the Turks.'[7]

In addition to laying all blame for conflict at Leopold's door, Louis also cited dynastic and defensive reasons for his invasion of the Palatinate, claiming that his aims were to:

'putting a stop to the unjust courses and violent usurpations of the Elector Palatine; and to cause a restitution to **Madame**, the Sister in Law to his Majesty, of what in right belongs to her by Succession from her Father and Brother, and timely to prevent all the Leagues, and preparations of War that have at length forced him to bring his Arms to the Banks of the *Rhine*, and to attack those places by which the Emperor might with most ease and renew and maintain a War against France.'[8]

Such emotive propaganda usefully shows:

- Louis' attempt to absolve himself of all responsibility and blame for war in 1688
- his perception in September 1688 that conflict was inevitable, which provided his rationale for crossing the Rhine and invading the Palatinate and Philippsburg
- his view that he was defending both family and strategic interests; France had been provoked into conflict by the Emperor and his willing collaborator, the new Elector of the Palatinate from 1685.

By sending troops to the Palatinate in 1688, Louis was asserting the rights of his sister-in-law Elizabeth Charlotte. She was the sister of the Elector Palatine Charles II, a Protestant ally of the French king. When he died childless in 1685, the Palatine passed to his Catholic cousin (also Leopold's godfather) Philip William, the Count of Neuburg. Louis decided Elizabeth Charlotte had a valid counter claim.

Louis' appeals for arbitration by the pope or at least some form of compensation was ignored. Leopold and the German Princes rejected all of Louis' appeals and denied his sister-in-law's claims.

This offended Louis' sense of dynastic honour and created a new issue of national security. Lying north of Alsace, and alarmingly close to it, the Palatinate region was strategically vital to France. With Leopold's godfather in place as Elector, Habsburg troops could now be stationed there, as well as Philippsburg, Cologne and in the Duchy of Lorraine.

Here was the very kind of nightmare scenario that Louis most feared:

- a growing threat from the Emperor and his allies to the security of Alsace and Strasbourg
- the distinct possibility of Habsburg encirclement through territories all along France's eastern border.

The Archbishop of Cologne and Elector of the Palatinate were now allied with the Emperor. Another Leopold ally, the Elector of Bavaria, was now eyeing up the Spanish Netherlands, with Leopold's full support, thereby reviving the threat of invasion from the north east. For the security conscious Louis, pre-emptive attack was the only form of defence. This is highlighted by the map in Figure 5.2:

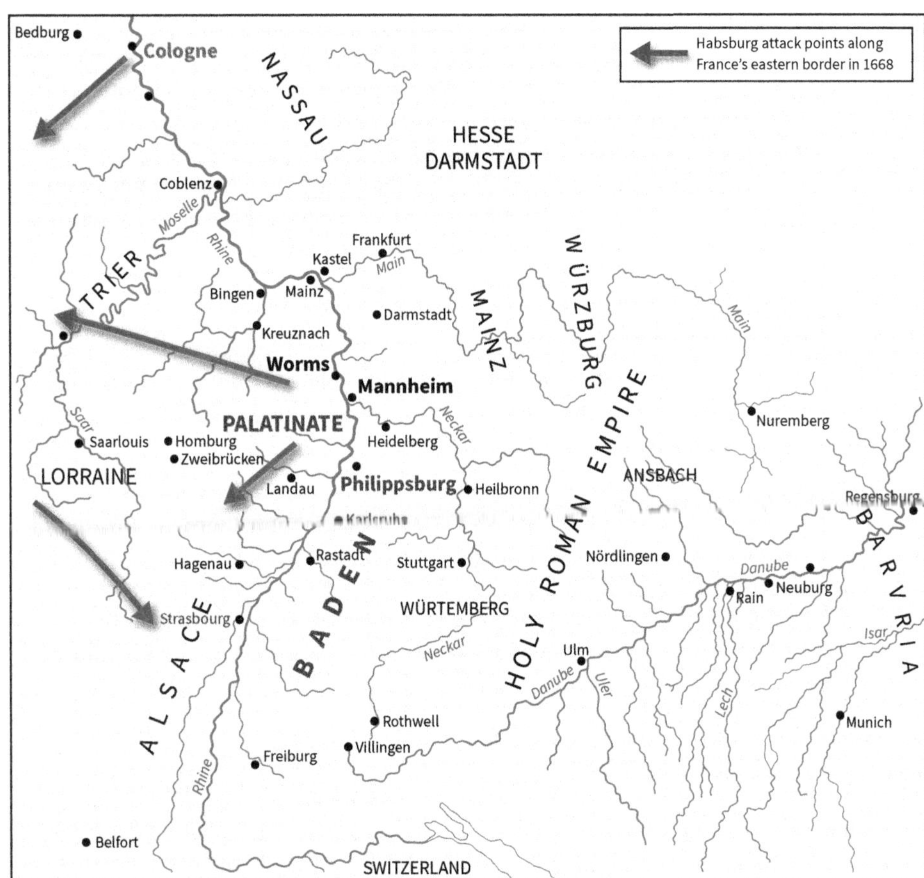

Figure 5.2: Potential threats to French security in 1688, as perceived by Louis XIV

Louis' aggression in 1688–9 was therefore motivated by his defensive desire to head off new threats to France's national security. By attacking the Palatinate, Baden and Philippsburg, and imposing his ally Fürstenberg as Archbishop in Cologne, Louis was pre-emptively defending France from what he saw as an inevitable attack from Leopold and his supporters, in the Palatinate and the expanding coalition of German allies. Devastation of the Palatinate and Baden in 1688 offered security by a tried and tested policy of scorched earth, preventing enemy troops from establishing themselves so precariously close to Alsace and Strasbourg, building up supplies and bases and linking up with the Duke of Lorraine, who still opposed French gains from Nijmegen (1679).

Louis rightly sensed that it was only a matter of time before Leopold would attack France, although he vigorously went about trying to prevent this. Leopold had vowed to retake Alsace and had the full partisan support of Pope Innocent XI, with whom he appeared in a new threatening league.

Figure 5.3: Leopold I

With his improving national security, new-found support from the pope and confirmed hero status as the defender of Christendom, Leopold wasted no time, from 1685 onwards, in negating and sabotaging French diplomatic interests, as the summary in Table 5.2 shows:

Date:	What Leopold did:
1685	Refused all offers to convert the Truce of Ratisbon into a permanent peace. Denied Louis' sister-in-law's inheritance rights in the Palatinate and with the support of German princes, refused Louis' offer of arbitration by the pope, leaving his godfather Phillip William, the Count of Neuburg, the Elector of the Palatinate.
1686	Openly rejected all lands gained by Réunions (including Strasbourg) by forming the League of Augsburg. This guaranteed Leopold's rights in the Palatinate and vowed to restrict France to the lands gained by the 1648 Westphalia. It also offered the Elector of Bavaria, land in the Spanish Netherlands – which would place a willing Leopold ally on France's north eastern border. As the diarist Dagneau recorded, the League of Augsburg seemed to be 'directed uniquely against France'.[9]
1687	Refused repeated offers to convert the Truce of Ratisbon into a permanent peace.
June 1688	Colluded with the pope to deny 'an elected bishop's rights' in Cologne.[10] When Maximilian Henry Archbishop of Cologne died in 1686, Louis lost a willing ally in a prime strategic location. When Louis put forward Fürstenburg as his candidate, he was opposed by Leopold's own candidate, the 17-year-old Joseph-Clément, brother of the Elector of Bavaria. Although Fürstenburg did not have the required two-thirds majority, he received more votes than Joseph-Clément. But the pope installed Joseph-Clément as the new Archbishop of Cologne. Here seemed overt proof of an anti-French conspiracy between Emperor and Pope and again of the futility of all attempts of conciliation.

Table 5.2: How Leopold provoked Louis XIV and contributed to the collapse of peace 1685–June 1688

Although Louis' own aggressive policy of Réunions and seizure of Avignon contributed to these setbacks, it seems that he did not see the connection. Instead, he clearly hoped to intimidate his enemies. He miscalculated, provoking the very kind of war he had hoped to avoid or pre-empt.

Louis outlined his perceptions regarding why he was again at war in his September 1688 *Mémoire*:

1 the rapidly changing situation in Europe posed a serious threat to French security along its eastern border on the Rhine
2 Leopold, German princes and the pope had actively aided and abetted this and were conspiring to attack France
3 it was only a matter of time before the League of Augsburg would essentially 'become Leopold's war coalition'.[11]

The speed with which Leopold led his alliance to war against France from September 1688 confirmed Louis' worst fears of Habsburg encirclement. Habsburg troops were rushed to the Upper Rhine, supported by troops from Brandenburg and Saxony along the lower Rhine. Leopold also undid Louis' efforts to keep ally Savoy on board in 1690 by offering Vittorio Amadeo imperial fiefs in Piedmont. This sparked Louvois'

ACTIVITY 5.5

Prepare a class debate on the extent to which you believe that Louis XIV was provoked into war in 1688–89. Take account of the French king's aggressive actions and their consequences, but don't neglect Leopold's role in this: did the Emperor start the Nine Years War? Was the changing state of Europe itself the root cause of conflict? Did external factors goad Louis into more desperate and aggressive decisions?

military intimidation and the escalation of a war into which Louis claimed he had been provoked.

At last, Louis was now both outnumbered and isolated by his enemies. No finer time was there for William and Leopold to put an overbearing Sun King in his rightful place. Or so it seemed.

The Nine Years War: outbreak, course and outcome

The war in Europe

France was initially outnumbered and isolated, with 220,000 troops against 250,000 Allied soldiers. Louis was now at war, in all but name, with the Elector of the Palatinate, Emperor Leopold and Bavaria from autumn 1688, and with the Dutch from November 1688.

After the Grand Alliance declared war in May 1689, Brandenburg, Sweden, Lorraine, Spain and England all joined Habsburg and German Protestant armies fighting France. Denmark, Savoy and Bavaria had formally joined them by 1690, thereby ending chances of a short war as Louis had wished. His days of lightning victories against weak hapless enemies were in the past.

Louis now faced fighting around his borders, in the Rhineland, Spanish Netherlands, Catalonia and Savoy. But his armies were neither defeated nor humiliated. The Grand Alliance was weakened by:

- its lack of unified command
- Sweden and Denmark ceasing hostile actions in 1691
- France bribing Savoy to leave the Alliance in 1696. This forced Leopold to reluctantly accept peace on the Italian peninsula.

Louis' generals Vauban and Luxembourg performed brilliantly. France was never successfully invaded and claimed many notable victories:

Year:	French success:
1690	Luxembourg defeated Dutch, Spanish, Brandenburg and English troops at Fleurus, inflicting around 10,000 enemy casualties. This prevented the Dutch from joining Brandenburg in Cleves.
1691	Vauban captured Mons.
1692	Vauban captured Namur. Louis' household infantry routed William's forces at Steenkirk.
1693	Luxembourg defeated William at Neerwinden, before taking Courtrai and Charleroi. Subsequently, William had to defend his policies in parliament. Noailles captured key Spanish garrisons at Rosas, in Catalonia.
1694	Noailles captured Ter, Palamos and Girona.
1697	Vendôme took Barcelona. Spain was forced out of the war, with losses 97% higher than France's. Subsequently, Leopold accepted that he could not: • seize Strasbourg • simultaneously fight France and the Turks.

Table 5.3: French victories on European soil during the Nine Years War

ACTIVITY 5.6

1. Do some further research on the following and write a few sentences about each of them, noting both what happened and how each impacted on the growing prospect of war in 1688:
   - Palatinate
   - Elizabeth Charlotte's claim to the Palatinate
   - Count Neuburg
   - Buda and Mohacs
   - Habsburg encirclement.
2. Make a mind map showing how Louis acted both dynastically and defensively in 1688.
3. Make a revision timeline of events 1685–88 that is themed around the following sections:
   - the increasing revulsion of German Protestant states
   - Leopold's increased willingness and ability to threaten and fight Louis
   - Spain's new found victim status and need for security
   - French aggression 1687–89.

Voices from the past

Duc de Saint-Simon

Louis de Rouvroy, the Duc de Saint-Simon (1675–1755) was a soldier, diplomat and courtier. His memoirs reported on Versailles court life, leaving a wonderfully detailed, gossipy account of strong personalities, ambition and rivalry. This was partly destroyed by the crown and only published after his death.

'Flattery fed the desire for military glory that sometimes tore him from his loves, which was how Louvois so easily involved him in major wars and persuaded him that he was a better leader and strategist than any of his generals, a theory which his officers fostered in order to please him. All their praise he took with admirable complacency and truly believed that he was what they said.'[12]

Figure 5.4: Saint-Simon

Louis' northern Italian campaign also succeeded initially, capturing Susa, Avigliana and Carmagnola and defeating Savoy at Staffarda (1690) and Marsiglia (1693). Far from being totally eclipsed by the Allies, therefore, the Sun King still had many shining military successes and averted the humiliation that had been planned for him. But Louis lacked the decisive victory or the **hegemony** that he desperately craved. France endured a grim protracted stalemate and some serious setbacks.

These included:

- William resoundingly defeating James II at the Battle of the Boyne (1690)
- futile attempts to bribe German princes (with 6 million livres) to defect to France
- Louis' failure to penetrate the Rhineland
- Savoy's invasion of Dauphiné and capture of Carmagnola (1693)
- the losses of Mainz and Bonn on the Rhine and Huy in Flanders (1694).

Such setbacks did not defeat France, but inevitably cast questions over whether Louis' enthusiasm for war was matched by his ability to successfully prosecute it.

1695 – A key turning point in the European War?

Louis needed a decisive military breakthrough in Europe but could not achieve it. France was exhausted financially and economically (see Chapter 4, The costs of wars and The impact of years of war on France in this chapter).

The necessity of peace was brought home further in 1695 when Louis lost his talismanic general Luxembourg. His replacement Villeroi lived up to his reputation as incompetent and lost Namur (1695). This loss was significant for three reasons:

1 It shattered French military prestige: Vauban's fortifications were not impregnable after all.

2 William's recapture of Namur also eased the questions being asked in England over his military leadership and gave him back the strong river barrier line of the Meuse from Namur to Maastricht. This hardened his determination to hold on for substantial gains from peace talks.

3 Nevertheless, the Allied siege of Namur in 1695 was costly and brought no major breakthrough victory: William lost 18,000–20,000 casualties compared to 8,000 French. This, along with their setbacks at sea and in the New World, made the Allies also ready to pursue peace.

ACTIVITY 5.7

For each of the following, find out more detail from further reading (e.g. Treasure, *Louis XIV*) and online research:

- Duc de Luxembourg
- Fleurus
- Mons
- Noailles
- Namur
- Villeroi.

The war at sea: mixed fortunes

Louis' navy had some surprising initial successes, claiming to have destroyed more than 5,000 Dutch and English ships. France's war at sea is detailed later in this chapter, but achieved no sustained or decisive victories.

Success at Beachy Head (1690) was offset by defeat at La Hogue (1692). With honours even, both sides were ready to negotiate for peace from a position of relative strength.

The war in North America, the Caribbean and Asia

Although the Nine Years War started within Europe, it extended to North America, the Caribbean and Asia, as some of the warring nations had colonies and trading posts in those places. This wider global conflict mirrored the European war, with setbacks and successes on both sides. In North America and the Caribbean, however, Louis had the upper military (if not moral) hand which strengthened his position in peace negotiations in 1697.

The Nine Years War in North America

France and England had long-running tensions over the economically valuable North American fur trade, competing for influence over the local Iroquois (Native Americans who controlled much of that trade). Unsurprisingly, therefore, conflict spread to North America. This mainly comprised three main theatres:

- New England, Acadia and Newfoundland
- Quebec and New York
- Hudson Bay.

Figure 5.6: The battleground of the Nine Years War

Governor General of New France, Louis de Buade de Frontenac, expanded the war by continually raiding English settlements. This:

- started what became known as 'King William's War'
- caused significant damage and disruption to English colonies.

ACTIVITY 5.8

1. Summarise the main French successes of the War in Europe as a spider diagram.
2. Read Saint-Simon's account. How convincing is this for telling us about Louis' inability to win the Nine Years War?
3. Discuss how far you agree with the view that 'The Nine Years War was a total disaster for France'.

Figure 5.5: French and English colonists fought keenly for supremacy in North America and the Caribbean during the Nine Years War

Although massively outnumbered, French colonists were supported by their Native American allies (the Algonquin and Abenaki tribes) and inflicted repeated defeats on the English, including:

- the destruction of Dover, New Hampshire (killing 20 English colonists)
- Baron de Saint Castin's capture and destruction of the English fort at Pemaquid (modern-day Bristol) and Maine in 1689; Pemaquid's fall was a serious English setback, pushing England's frontier back to Casco (now called Falmouth)
- killing 4 settlers at Saco and 25% of an English military company in 1689, forcing its retreat
- French Canadians massacring 60 settlers in a pre-dawn raid at Schenectady, New York in 1690
- Castin's destruction of English colony Salmon Falls and the battle of Fort Loyal in 1690, which killed over 200 English colonists
- killing about 100 English settlers and burning down their colonial buildings in the 1692 Candlemass Massacre
- French soldier de Villieu's raid with Abenaki natives of the English settlement of Durham, New Hampshire (the 'Oyster River Massacre'). This killed 45 inhabitants and destroyed half of the dwellings and five garrisons.

French success was neither decisive nor complete. The French failed to capture their target of Boston, and British commander, Sir William Phips captured Port Royal – the French-held capital of Acadia (Nova Scotia) and destroyed what had been begun as a garrison.

Overall, however, France won the economic war over England by:

- retaking Port Royal
- repulsing Phips' quest to seize Quebec and Montreal
- a French Canadian and native Indian force destroying every English settlement in Newfoundland and killing over 100 English settlers in 1696
- defeating three English ships in Hudson Bay in 1696.

This was insufficient to alter the outcome of the main war. European casualties overall were fairly light and the North American war was of secondary importance to the conflict in Europe. Crucially though, Louis had given England a bloody nose.

The Nine Years War in the Caribbean

So it was similarly, against Spanish interests in the Caribbean. French fortunes against the Allies were initially disappointing:

- France was repulsed from Surinam by the Dutch in 1689.
- After gaining St Christopher and St Eustatius in 1689, France lost them along with St Kitts, which the English captured in 1690.

France's fightback in the Caribbean involved Jean-Baptiste du Casse. Du Casse had considerable naval experience, and fought against the League of Augsburg and in the War of the Spanish Succession. He captured Jamaica in 1694. Additional Allied setbacks saw English commander Christopher Codrington fail to capture Guatemala and Martinique, losing two frigates.

Tit-for-tat conflict with Spain started off inconclusively. French burning of a Spanish colony in 1690 prompted Spanish retaliation by burning Cap Français in 1691. After Namur's loss in 1695, Louis had increasing interest and success pirating in the Caribbean – seizing the Spanish treasure fleet.

Initial pickings were disappointing. Spain's fleet eluded French ships and disease and malnutrition wiped out many French **privateer** sailors. However, French captain Desaugiers did succeed in capturing a Spanish galleon, with over 91,000 silver pesos and over 1.3 million livres worth of cacao on board. Although disappointed with his total haul, he did capture two warships and nearly four and a half tons of silver. French privateer Baron de Pointis also succeeded in taking an immense haul of over 10 million livres back to France (despite a three-day chase by the English) after his siege of the Spanish colony port of Cartagena, in present day Colombia. Inadvertently, the Allied pursuit of Pointis' Caribbean pirating expeditions 'enabled France to knock Spain out of the war'.[13] English concern over French plans to seize Spain's treasure fleet led to Vice-Admiral John Nevill's large and well-armed navy being diverted away from protecting the Spanish mainland to the West Indies. This was unsuccessful in its aim of catching the smaller French fleet and above all, enabled a combined French land and sea attack to seize Barcelona and knock Spain out of the war.

The Nine Years War in Asia

Conflict extended to Asia in October 1690 when French admiral Duquesne-Guitton attacked the Anglo-Dutch fleet at Madras. This started a war that went badly for French commercial interests. In 1693, 19 Dutch ships of the line carrying 1,500 coalition troops forced Governor François Martin to surrender the French garrison of Pondicherry on the south eastern coast of India.

The Peace of Ryswick 1697

Despite being outnumbered, Louis had not lost the war, and he was certainly not prepared to lose the peace. France was exhausted, but had gone beyond mere defensive goals in fighting the war and more than held his own against numerically superior enemies. Louis had succeeded in:

- defeating Spain
- not having to recognise William as King of England before hostilities stopped
- frustrating Leopold.

Thus, France would not be completely bound by the treaties of Westphalia and Nijmegen. Louis was prepared to concede on some major issues at the 1697 Peace of Ryswick to win the key things that mattered to him. He was magnanimous in defeat not because he had to be, but because he chose to be, for his eyes were on a much bigger potential prize – the Spanish Succession.

The recipe for peace was set. Louis would box cleverly and prioritise compromise over conflict to win diplomatic support and further strengthen French security. In both respects, he was moderately successful.

The key terms of Ryswick

In Europe:

- The Palatinate was returned to William of Neuburg (Louis' principle of defending his sister-in-law's rights was now conveniently forgotten).
- Louis conceded defeat over Cologne and Bavarian Joseph Clément (Leopold's candidate) was recognised as Archbishop.
- Louis recognised Protestant William's succession as King of England and promised to withdraw his support for Catholic ally James II.
- Louis returned Luxembourg, Charleroi, Ath, Mons, Courtrai and Catalonia, including Barcelona to Spain. In return, he retained control of Hainault (including Cambrai and Valenciennes) that France had gained after 1648.
- France abandoned all gains on the right of the Rhine, including Philippsburg, Breisach, Freiburg and Kehl.
- The Dutch won the right to garrison frontier towns such as Ypres, Menin, Courtrai and Luxembourg. They were also granted relaxed regulations favourable to its trade and return to the French tariff of 1664.

ACTIVITY 5.9

1. Make a summary of gains and setbacks during the war at sea, using information from this and later sections in this chapter.
2. Make a themed timeline of the War outside Europe that shows successes and setbacks in Asia, America and the Caribbean.
3. 'More successful than not'. Discuss this verdict on French involvement in the Nine Years War outside of Europe.

- France ended its 30 year occupation of Lorraine, but reserved the right to march troops through the territory.
- Louis surrendered all territories gained by Réunions to their original rulers, with the key exceptions of Strasbourg and 82 towns in lower Alsace.

Outside Europe:

- France and England exchanged all colonial territory taken from each other.
- The Spanish accepted French control of the western part of Hispaniola.
- Pondicherry was restored to France.

Reactions to the Peace of Ryswick

Reactions to the Peace of Ryswick varied, both within Europe and France. Leopold was as pleased as he was disappointed. He had gained a great deal, but nowhere near as much as he had earlier anticipated. William won the respect and backing of the English parliament for curbing French arrogance and aggression. It vaunted Ryswick as a crowning achievement and William as England and Europe's saviour. Parliament declared after the Peace of Ryswick that William 'had been given to England to hold the balance of power in Europe'.[14]

Vauban saw Ryswick as humiliating to France, especially given the devastating impact of the Nine Years War upon France's finances and socio-economic well-being. Vauban's concerns regarded perceived damage to France's level of national security and pré carré along its eastern frontiers with the Rhine and Alps. Louis' concessions aroused much resentment at court among noble families who had suffered disproportionately high casualties. This fact was echoed in a letter penned by Madame de Maintenon on 25 May 1697:

'All the restitutions offered by the King have occasioned warm debates here. They are tired of the War and yet think it a little shameful to restore what has cost so much Toil and Blood. For my Part, I think it is glorious to restore what has been taken, so long as we are not constrained to do it'.[15]

By contrast Louis saw compromise as a strength, not a weakness. Carlos II's ailing health meant that Louis needed to garner diplomatic support for his attempt to win at least a part of a bigger prize – the Spanish inheritance. The Sun King's propaganda machine therefore waxed lyrical in presenting Ryswick as a remarkable French achievement:

'The moment decreed by Heaven for the reconciliation of the nations has arrived. Europe is at peace. The ratification of the treaty which my ambassadors concluded recently with those of the Emperor and the Empire has put the seal on the re-establishment of this tranquillity which everyone has desired ... Strasbourg, one of the principal ramparts of the Empire and heresy, is united for ever with the Church and my crown; the Rhine established as the barrier between France and Germany ... these are the gains of the recent treaty'.[16]

The truth lay somewhere in between.

ACTIVITY 5.10

1. Draw up a table of Louis' gains and losses at the Peace of Ryswick.
2. Read Madame de Maintenon and Louis' accounts. Which of these is the more useful source for telling us about Louis' level of success at Ryswick in 1697? Use the sources and your own knowledge to explain your answer carefully.
3. 'The most important consequence of the Nine Years War was that French power was reduced'. How far do you agree?

The new balance of power

The position of France in relation to the European powers by 1697

In 1697, France was in a new position – parity with, not hegemony over, other European powers. Louis had ended a war without a decisive victory and needed to make big concessions. Louis had not sold out at Ryswick but the balance of power no longer weighed in France's favour.

Arguably, the loss of almost all Réunions gains weakened France's eastern frontier security. Valuable Rhine crossing points including Zweibrücken and Montbéliard were now out of French control. This left Franche-Comté, Alsace and Strasbourg more exposed to attack. So too did the ending of French occupation of Lorraine, return of Luxembourg and permanent loss of German Protestant allies in the Rhine. France's south eastern border seemed more vulnerable to attack. Savoy's invasion of Dauphiné had highlighted this, as had the high price Savoy demanded for its defection in 1696 – the return of valuable buffer zone Pinerolo to Savoy.

Ryswick also apparently undermined French prestige and Louis' reputation. He had abandoned two dynastic interests that he had previously fought for – his sister-in-law's claim to the Palatinate and his cousin James II's claim to England, Ireland and Scotland. In agreeing to the latter, he had recognised his arch nemesis the Protestant William of Orange as English King 'by the grace of God'. Economically, much had also been given away and the task of attacking the Spanish Netherlands and the United Provinces made much harder by allowing the Dutch to garrison frontier towns such as Ypres.

However, it would be wrong to exaggerate the value of all the concessions made by Louis in 1697. Recognition of William as English king was perhaps not quite the climb-down for France that many have claimed.

Firstly, Carlos' ailing health meant it tactically sensible to get William on side to support French claims regarding the Spanish inheritance. Secondly, William III had no children. So it remained perfectly feasible that, on William's death, England might invite back either James II or his son, giving the country a Catholic monarchy again thereby removing it from the Dutch orbit and making it once more a potential French ally.

There was also motive in Louis' surrendering all land captured from Spain: it manufactured an image of benevolence to bolster his claim to the Spanish inheritance. Appeasement of the English and the Dutch and return of Réunion lands to Sweden and German Princes also served a wider purpose – trying to win over support for the French claim to the Spanish inheritance from William, the Dutch government and a pro-French faction at the Spanish court. Louis made concessions because he chose to, not because he had to. Like a wily chess grandmaster, Louis had surrendered a few pieces tactically to try and win the key battle ahead that mattered to him.

The Sun King had proved that he was no pushover. Fleurus, Steenkirk and Neerwinden all attested to this. So too did Leopold's repeated failure to invade Alsace and French naval victories in 1694, including:

- pirate Jean Bart driving off a much stronger Dutch force and capturing 130 grain ships at Texel
- Vauban's triumph in repulsing a disastrous Allied attempt to land at Brest in 1694, taking a Dutch frigate, 600 prisoners and 400 Allied lives (including English General Talmach).

Louis therefore had fairly good grounds that he had held his own, and could continue to hold his own, against his wartime enemies.

The gains of lower Alsace towns and Strasbourg strengthened this perception. The League of Augsburg had failed to bind him to the treaties of Westphalia, Nijmegen and Münster. Retention of Strasbourg bolstered France's pré carré and frontier security; after three invasions of France through Strasbourg during the Dutch War, this was vital peace of mind.

Nevertheless, France's position had weakened. Gone were the days of lightning victories over the Spanish. Until 1697, French forces were too light to break through in Catalonia, which was only defended by a small Spanish force of 12,000–13,000 troops.

French commander Noailles had just 11,000–12,000 men and so avoided attacking the enemy for much of 1690, 1695 and 1696.

General Luxembourg's death in 1695 hit France hard. Leadership issues now loomed large within its military. Villeroi had fumbled and lost Namur, thereby shattering the myth of French invincibility.

England under William now seemed well placed to keep French expansion in check. His navy had frustrated plans to invade Spain (at least until 1697) and had outbuilt, if not outclassed, France's by 1697, as explained in the next section. William had improved the English artillery and army medical services. He had also found and tried his future battlefield genius, John Churchill, first Duke of Marlborough.

Marlborough had gained valuable experience commanding British troops in the Low Countries and in battle at Walcourt in 1689. Allied commander Prince Waldeck stated that:

'despite his youth he displayed greater military capacity than do most generals after a long series of wars ... He is assuredly one of the most gallant men I know.'[17]

The real game changer was finance. France relied upon declining taxation revenues and increasingly expensive loans and venality (as highlighted in Chapter 4). By contrast, the creation of the Bank of England and national debt in 1694 allowed England to borrow securely at low interest and fund wars more easily. Louis would now have to tread warily with William and try and keep him on side.

The impact of years of war on France's economic and military resources

The attritional and protracted nature of conflict 1688–97 had a seriously debilitating effect upon France's economic and military resources.

Debt, borrowing costs and taxation had all risen rapidly. This had combined with economic stagnation to exhaust France. This exhaustion arose from the size of army France needed to fight multiple enemies along different parts of its borders. This caused cutbacks to naval spending, problems of supply and high casualty rates that seriously limited Louis' ability to wage war and dominate his enemies. These impacts were partly masked by the combined talents of Luxembourg and Vauban. But the cracks in France's war-making capacity had grown considerably.

Never before had France committed so many soldiers into a war. 80,000 men fought at Fleurus and by 1694, the army had reached an estimated 400,000 strong. This placed an incredible strain on France's already depleted finances. Between 1690 and 1695, war consumed some 78% of government expenditure – a 24% increase in 1680–89 and a 36% increase in 1662–69 (Table 5.4). The threat of invasion became alarmingly real when Savoy invaded Dauphiné. This drove up fortification costs and expenditure to totally unsustainable levels, especially 1689–93, as highlighted in Table 5.4.

The devastating economic impact of the Nine Years War, both before and after 1697, is summed up brilliantly by Gary McCollim. He states that 'the last year of the war had alone cost 218,971,172 livres ... Vauban called for reducing revenues to 116,822,500 livres annually, a figure that would barely have paid for the government's expenses in 1700, the lowest amount since 1688'.[18]

Year:	Total estimate war expenditure in millions of livres:
1689	81.98
1690	84.8
1691	83.93
1692	89.13
1693	85.13
1694	78.97
1695	78.31
1696	77.85
1697	74.65

Table 5.4: Total estimate war expenditure from 1689–97

As we saw in chapter 4, exponential rises in wartime expenditure heightened pressures to increase taxation – 160 million livres' worth was collected in the war. This seriously lowered demand for industrial and agricultural goods, encouraged emigration of skilled labour and contributed significantly to the widespread economic difficulties across much of France from the late 1680s. Increasing reliance upon extraordinary sources of revenue drove up government debts. These totalled 138 million livres in 1697.

The growing expense of war coincided with declining taxation revenue and rising expenses of collection and borrowing. Something had to give. Naval expenditure – never enthusiastically endorsed by Louis – was seriously scaled back. From having the third most powerful navy in Europe in the 1670s, France fell seriously behind English and Dutch spending on its fleet.

32% more
British ship completion compared to French by the end of the Nine Years War

76% more
First-to fifth-rate ships constructed by the British and Dutch compared to the French during the war

4:1
The approximate rate at which the Allies outbuilt the French navy

Figure 5.7: The depletion of the French navy, compared to French and Dutch navies

This weakened Colbert's mercantilist goal – of increasing and protecting overseas trade growing at the expense of enemies. The decline of France's navy by 1697 was paralleled by the further decline of some overseas colonial ventures:

- French tobacco trade in Saint Domingue on Hispaniola declined; supply quickly exceeded demand as French privateers brought vast amounts of stolen English tobacco.
- The French population and colonial fishery activity at Placentia in Newfoundland 1689–98 dropped sharply.
- The number of French West-Indies sugar refineries 1687–1701 dropped by 21% and French refineries on Saint Christopher suffered a 84% collapse.

Nevertheless, the period of the Nine Years War was not continually bad news for all French overseas economic activity. Saint Domingue developed a thriving indigo trade from 1694. By 1697, France's tobacco monopoly had increased revenues paid to the crown one and a half times through foreign tobacco imports.

However, France's economy was undoubtedly harmed 1688–97. The return of all captured English and Spanish colonies in 1697 was, from a mercantilist perspective at least, a further own goal.

Financially, the Nine Years War caused France's army to expand and live well beyond its actual means. French fiscal resources simply could not keep up the rapacious demands of such a large army. In 1693, the army's *munitionnaire* (supplier) in Piedmont was still owed 2 million livres for 1692 and received inadequate funds for transporting bread and other supplies.

The Herculean effort to repel invasion along France's eastern border left its forces unable to breakthrough elsewhere, as illustrated by the example of Noailles in Catalonia. Added to this were the high casualty rates from battle. French victories did not come cheaply; some 3,000 French soldiers were killed at Fleurus and 7,000–8,000 at Neerwinden. The siege of Barcelona in 1697 lasted 12 months and cost 9,000 French lives.

France's army increased in quantity during the Nine Years War, but not in quality. Corruption through faggoting remained a serious problem; Rowlands estimates a 10%–20% difference between the army's actual size and what was recorded on paper. The army also had to change its character by increasing the number of veterans and militia units quartered upon towns (which harmed agriculture) along with naming non-noble commanders. This raised concerns about quality of the recruits. Vauban was so concerned at this at the start of the war that he said that France was only capable of fighting a defensive war. So much then for 'nec pluribus impar'.

The prospects of future wars

For all Louis' best efforts, the potential for future war remained as high as the potential for keeping peace. The Sun King had good reasons to try and avoid future conflict, militarily and financially, but the controversial issue of the Spanish inheritance was among factors that suggested that the Peace of Ryswick might not last.

By 1697, Carlos' long flirtation with death was reportedly coming to an end; at last, he was slowly but surely dying. Disease ridden and severely swollen with dropsy, Carlos (otherwise known as Charles II) had fathered no children. This raised the tricky question of who should succeed him and inherit his vast kingdom. This led to a straight contest between Louis and Leopold, and a potential French-Habsburg fight if it could not be resolved peacefully, as explained further in Chapter 6.

Louis knew that Leopold coveted the Spanish inheritance and would no longer abide by the partition treaty he had secretly agreed, although never signed, with him in 1668. He therefore may have considered future war likely and perhaps even inevitable (although not desirable), in 1697. He certainly appears to have done so by 1700.

Either way, Leopold's dogged determination to pursue his own claims to the Spanish inheritance and frustrate those of the Sun King certainly put a spanner in the works of maintaining the peace. The Habsburg Emperor's own claims were:

- through his grandson Joseph Ferdinand by his marriage to Carlos' sister and Philip IV's second daughter, Margaret Theresa
- that as the grandson of the Spanish King Philip III, he should rightfully pursue the interests of his sons from his third marriage to Eleanor of Neuburg, Joseph and Archduke Charles.

Leopold had planned for his first son Joseph to succeed him as Emperor (which happened in 1705). More ominously, Leopold had struck a deal with the English and the Dutch in 1689 to pass the entire inheritance to his second son Archduke Charles. His improving situation against the Turks also made war more likely.

All of this effectively invalidated Leopold's 1668 partition deal with Louis. It also made the prospect of a straight fight between the Bourbon and Habsburg dynasties distinctly likely in the aftermath of Carlos' apparently imminent death. Leopold's desire to take the whole inheritance and not cut any partition deal usurped Louis strong dynastic claims. Louis had had his son, Louis the Dauphin, with Maria Theresa, the first daughter of Philip IV. Spanish practice was for first daughters to inherit a throne in the absence of any surviving sons. With such a legitimate claim, Louis was hardly going to let Leopold try and take it all, especially when he had not won the last war.

Too much was at stake for Louis not to consider the prospect of having to fight again. In addition to Spain itself, the Spanish King controlled the following territories:

- Spain's Italian lands, including Milan, Naples, Genoa, Sardinia and Sicily
- the Spanish Netherlands and lands in Flanders
- the Spanish Indies
- Mexico, Central America and all South America except Brazil
- the Canary Islands and the garrisons of Oran and Cueta (in modern day Algeria and Morocco respectively) in Africa.

However, Louis had good reasons to think that he had minimised the prospects of future wars. Free of Louvois' influence, Louis was cultivating an altruistic international image – in stark contrast to 1688–9. This he felt was enough to outflank Leopold over the Spanish Succession and avoid war in one swoop. By doing so much to appease Britain, the United Provinces and Spain at Ryswick, Louis had reasonably hoped to gain William's support for his claim to the Spanish inheritance – along with that of a pro-French faction at the Spanish court – and avoid having to fight to secure it. Louis certainly appeared confident that he could win the argument by persuasion, and not have to resort to the power of his military.

Louis needed to avoid conflict. His military and financial resources had been pushed to the limit 1688–97. With his army rapidly demobilising, vast wartime debts still to pay and criticisms of Ryswick still ringing in his ears, Louis certainly had strong reasons to avoid further conflict. At Ryswick and thereafter, Louis certainly seems to have displayed a new found willingness to consider international opinion, compromise to a level inconsistent with French military conquests on the battlefield and, above all, find peaceful solutions to the Spanish Succession issue. We shall examine this in more detail in the next chapter.

Prospects of future war were also negated by Allied desperation for peace:

- In England, anti-war opposition to the financial cost of war and failure to defeat Louis outright made William less likely to wish to fight again. So too did pressure from parliament to demobilise the army and cut back on military spending.
- The resources of the Holy Roman Empire were exhausted, as Leopold was still fighting the Turks.
- Savoy was no longer a Grand Alliance member.
- Spain had effectively been defeated.

War seemed both possible and avoidable in equal measure in 1697. Louis certainly made great plans and efforts to try and avoid it after Ryswick. However, events both beyond and within his own control conspired to make war a reality again by 1702.

ACTIVITY 5.11

1. From reading this and relevant parts of chapter 4, sum up the impact of the Nine Years War upon French finances, economic growth, military and Louis' reputation.
2. Sum up the Spanish inheritance issue and why war was still possible after Ryswick.
3. Short discussion/essay task: 'In 1697, there seemed little hope of peace lasting'. How far do you agree?

Timeline

1648	Treaty of Westphalia
1678–9	Treaty of Nijmegen
1686	Formation of League of Augsburg by princes of Franconia and the Rhineland
1686	Habsburg victories over Ottoman Turks along the Danube at Buda
1687	Habsburg victories over Ottoman Turks along the Danube at Buda in Mohács
1688	James I/VII of England and Scotland overthrown in Glorious Revolution
1688	League of Augsburg included Brandenburg, Bavaria, Palatinate, Saxony, Spain, Sweden, United Provinces and Habsburg Empire
1688–1689	French soldiers capture Philippsburg and conduct scorched earth policy in the Palatinate
1689	Formation of anti-Louis Grand Alliance with England, United Provinces, Lorraine and Habsburg Empire
1689	Grand Alliance declared war in May
1689	James I/VII of England and Scotland invaded Ireland (March) with 6,000 French
1690	James I/VII of England and Scotland defeated by William (III) of Orange at Battle of the Boyne, Ireland
1690	Savoy and Spain joined the Grand Alliance
1695	Louis lost general Luxembourg; Villeroi lost Namur
1697	Peace of Ryswick

Practice essay questions

1. 'The power of France was significantly weakened by the Nine Years War between 1688–97.' Assess the validity of this view.
2. 'The most significant consequence of the Nine Years War were the concessions Louis XIV made at the Peace of Ryswick.' Assess the validity of this view.
3. 'Louis started the Nine Years War by excessive force but concluded it at Ryswick with considerable skill.' Assess the validity of this view.
4. With reference to these sources and your understanding of the historical context, assess the value of these three sources to an historian studying Louis XIV's foreign policy.

Extract A

From the memoirs of Versailles courtier Count Saint-Simon, published after Louis' death

'Flattery fed the desire for military glory that sometimes tore him from his loves, which was how Louvois so easily involved him in major wars and persuaded him that he was a better leader and strategist than any of his generals, a theory which his officers fostered in order to please him. All their praise he took with admirable complacency and truly believed that he was what they said. Hence his liking for reviews, which he carried to such lengths that he was known abroad as the 'Review King', and his preference for sieges, where he could make cheap displays of courage, be forcibly restrained, and show his ability to endure fatigue and lack of sleep.'

Count Saint-Simon, *Memoirs of Louis XI*, cited by Lucy Norton, ed. *Saint-Simon at Versailles*. New York, 1980, p. 217–226, 229–30

Extract B

William and the English parliament's declaration of war on Louis XIV in 1689, from a document entitled 'An address agreed upon at the Committee for the French War, And Read in the House of Commons April 19th 1689':

'We your Majesty's most loyal subjects, the Commons of England in Parliament assembled, have taken into our most serious consideration the condition and state of this nation, in respect of France, and foreign alliances; in order to which, we have examined the mischiefs brought upon Christendom, in late years, by the French King, who without any respect to justice, has by fraud and force, has endeavoured to subject it to an arbitrary and universal monarchy. In prosecution of this design, so pernicious to the repose and safety of Europe, he has neglected none of those means, how indirect so ever, which his ambition or avarice could suggest to him. The faith of treaties, among all princes, especially Christian princes, ever held most inviolable, has never been able to restrain him.'

The Harleian Miscellany, Volume 1, Joseph Meredith Toner Collection (Library of Congress) printed for R. Dutton, 1808

Extract C

Louis' letter written to the Archbishop of Paris for the singing of Thanksgiving in the Cathedral of Notre Dame, in gratitude of the peace concluded with the Emperor and Empire', 1698:

'The moment decreed by Heaven for the reconciliation of the nations has arrived. Europe is at peace. The ratification of the treaty which my ambassadors concluded recently with those of the Emperor and the Empire has put the seal on the re-establishment of this tranquillity which everyone has desired … Strasbourg, one of the principal ramparts of the Empire and heresy, is united for ever with the Church and my crown; the Rhine established as the barrier between France and Germany … these are the gains of the recent treaty'.

Cited by David Smith, *Louis XIV*. Cambridge: Cambridge University Press; 1992, p. 89

Chapter summary

From reading this chapter, you will be able to:

- explain why William of Orange was able to challenge Louis XIV and achieve the Dutch-English alliance after the Glorious Revolution of 1688
- judge Louis' level of responsibility for this and the formation of the Grand Alliance, the League of Augsburg and the anti-French alliance between Protestant states, the Empire and Spain
- understand the causes of the Nine Years War, know the main events of its course in Europe, North America, the Caribbean and Asia, and have insight into the terms of the Peace of Ryswick
- judge the extent of the new balance of power and French decline in relation to the European powers by 1697; the impact of years of war on France's economic and military resources; the prospects of future wars.

End notes

1 Cited by Treasure G. *Louis XIV*. Harlow: Longman; 2001. p. 243.

2 Duras to Louvois (12 May, 1689). Cited by Lynn J. A. *The Wars of Louis XIV 1667–1714*. London: Routledge; 1999. p. 197.

3 Louvois, cited in Rowlands G. Louis XIV, Vittorio Amedeo II and French military failure in Italy, 1689-96. *The English Historical Review*. 2000; 115(462): 534–569. p. 540–41.

4 Treasure G. *Seventeenth Century France*. London: Rivingtons; 1966. p. 369.

5 Pope Innocent XI, cited by Treasure G. *Louis XIV*. Harlow, England: Longman; 2001. p. 241.

6 Marquis de Chamlay, cited by Wilkinson R. *Louis XIV, France and Europe, 1661–1715*. London: Hodder & Stoughton; 1993. p. 118.

7 Louix XIV Memoire des raison du guerre — memoir of reasons for war — to the Emperor of Germany, cited from: http://babel.hathitrust.org/cgi/pt?id=uc2.ark:/13960/t2d79mp9n;view=1up;seq=7

8 The French king's memorial to the emperor of Germany. HathiTrust. 2016. Available from: http://babel.hathitrust.org/cgi/pt?id=uc2.ark:/13960/t2d79mp9n;view=1up;seq=7

9 Dagneau, cited by Lynn J. A. *The Wars of Louis XIV 1667–1714*. London: Routledge; 1999. p. 189.

10 Treasure G. *Louis XIV*. Harlow: Longman; 2001. p. 242.

11 Treasure G. *Louis XIV*. Harlow: Longman; 2001. p. 240.

12 Norton L. (ed). *Saint-Simon at Versailles*. London: Hamish Hamilton; 1980. p. 217–226, 229–30.

13 Pritchard J. *In Search of Empire: The French in the Americas, 1670≠1730*. Cambridge: Cambridge University Press; 2004. p. 330.

14 Treasure G. *Louis XIV*. Harlow: Longman; 2001. p. 256.

15 *The Letters of Madame de Maintenon*. Google Books. 2016. Available from: https://books.google.co.uk/books?id=glsyAQAAMAAJ

16 Letter by Louis XIV (1698), cited by Smith D. *Louis XIV*. Cambridge: Cambridge University Press; 1992. p. 89.

17 Hibbert C. *The Marlboroughs*. London: Penguin; 2002. p. 48.

18 McCollim G. *Louis XIV's Assault on Privilege*. Rochester, NY: University of Rochester Press; 2012. p. 142.

6 France defeated, 1697–1715

In this chapter, we will look into:

- the issue of the Spanish Succession: Louis, Leopold and Carlos; the aims and policies of France; the international response to French claims; the outbreak of war
- the War of the Spanish Succession: the war in Europe; the war in North America; the war in the Caribbean
- the Treaty of Utrecht and its impact on the balance of power in Europe
- the legacy of Louis XIV by 1715: the last years of the reign; the problem of the succession; the annulment of the King's will and the formation of the regency of Orléans

The issue of the Spanish Succession

Louis, Leopold and Carlos

Carlos II's long-expected death had never been a straightforward issue, and neither was the issue of his inheritence. At stake was control over Spain and a vast number of other territories, as outlined in chapter 5. Louis and Leopold both felt they had strong dynastic claims. Here is why:

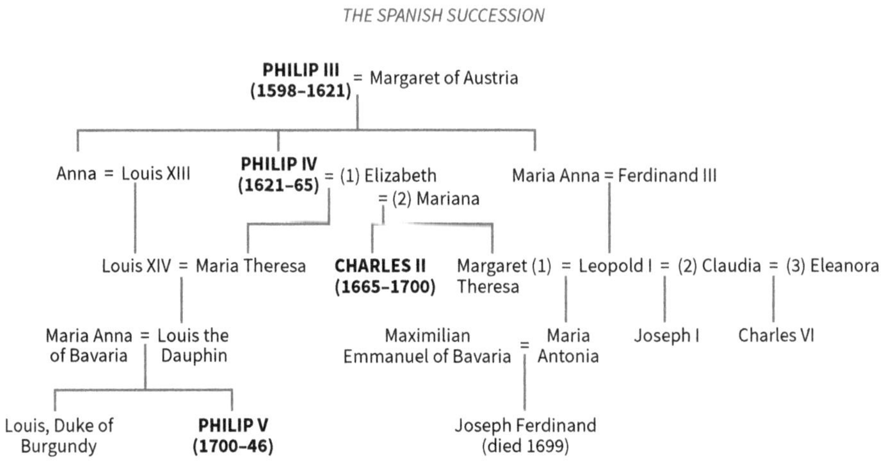

THE SPANISH SUCCESSION

PHILIP III (1598–1621) = Margaret of Austria

Anna = Louis XIII
PHILIP IV (1621–65) = (1) Elizabeth = (2) Mariana
Maria Anna = Ferdinand III

Louis XIV = Maria Theresa
CHARLES II (1665–1700)
Margaret Theresa (1) = Leopold I = (2) Claudia = (3) Eleanora

Maria Anna of Bavaria = Louis the Dauphin
Maximilian Emmanuel of Bavaria = Maria Antonia
Joseph I
Charles VI

Louis, Duke of Burgundy
PHILIP V (1700–46)
Joseph Ferdinand (died 1699)

Figure 6.1: Family connections and the Spanish succession

Spain's custom was for:

- daughters to inherit a throne in the absence of sons
- descendants of daughters to make claims.

As the family tree in Figure 6.1 shows, several people had claims based on being Philip III's descendants through one or more parents or grandparents. They were:

- Louis XIV
- Louis the Dauphin
- Louis, Duke of Burgundy
- Philip, Duke of Anjou
- Leopold I
- Joseph
- Archduke Charles
- Joseph Ferdinand.

ACTIVITY 6.1

What relation to Philip III was each of the claimants?

Louis XIV decided to pursue his son's claim rather than his own. In terms of descent, Louis the Dauphin had the best claim of anyone. Carlos left no heirs, so the strongest claims were either via his oldest sibling (the Dauphin's mother) or via Philip IV's oldest sibling (the Dauphin's grandmother).

However, there were complicating factors:

- On marrying Louis XIV, Maria Theresa had renounced her claim to the Spanish throne; this potentially affected claims by her descendants, although they had not been born when this occurred
- Philip IV affirmed this fact in his will, giving his younger daughter Margaret Theresa priority
- Maria Theresa's **renunciation** had been rewarded by a large dowry
- This had never actually been paid, so Louis saw the renunciation as void.

Leopold chose to advance the claim of his grandson Joseph Ferdinand (while not forgetting that his sons Joseph and Charles were also interested parties). This was also complicated.

Joseph Ferdinand's mother Maria Theresa's only child Maria Antonia married the Elector of Bavaria. She had renounced her claim as Philip IV's granddaughter to the Spanish throne in favour of Leopold's sons Archduke Joseph (and in case of his death, his half-brother Charles). But Leopold's sons' claims were rejected by the Spanish Council of State. It decided not to recognise Maria Antonia's renunciation and instead welcomed Leopold's grandson's claim. The Spanish Council of State decided it did not recognise the renunciation and welcomed Leopold's grandson's claim.

ACTIVITY 6.2

Looking at the family tree in Figure 6.1, and taking account of complicating factors, who do you think had the best claim and why?

The aims and policies of France

To Louis, the prospect of this inheritance bypassing France and going entirely to Leopold was clearly threatening. Without partition of the Spanish lands, Leopold's Habsburg Empire would be dominant. France would be encircled, and its overseas possessions also menaced:

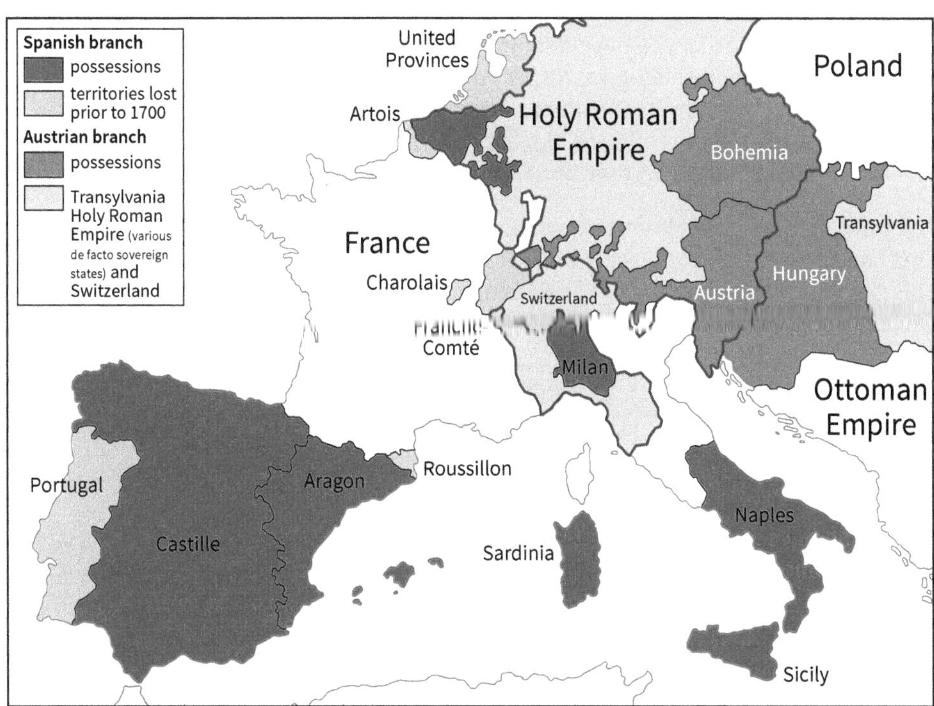

Figure 6.2: France's fear of being surrounded by her Habsburg neighbours in 1700. See also Figure 6.8

Louis aimed to:

- avert Habsburg encirclement
- secure a share of the spoils through partition of the Spanish inheritance
- exploit the split in the Spanish court over how best to resolve the Spanish Succession issue after Carlos' imminent death
- avoid war at all costs.

This was a matter of dynastic honour, as well as national security. France was in no position to fight again. Louis therefore pursued a diplomatic path by trying to:

- win over the English, Dutch and the Spanish court faction, which favoured partition
- suggest to Leopold (while Carlos was still alive) that partition was the best outcome.

The First Partition Treaty of 1698 reflected Louis' concern to find a peaceful outcome:

'The state of the King of Spain's health gives grounds for fearing that he does not have long to live.... It is essential to make plans for the event of his death because the opening of the succession question would inevitably cause another war if any of the three contenders insisted upon his claim.'[1]

Leopold's obstinacy made war more likely. Louis planned to circumvent this through self-restraint and compromise. This he hoped would leave the Spanish court and Leopold no other option but to bow to Dutch and English opinion and give France some portion of the Spanish lands without war, before Carlos died.

ACTIVITY 6.3

1 Produce a mind map of Louis' aims and policies 1697–98.

2 Why did Louis propose the First Partition Treaty in 1698?

3 Look at the source on the First Partition Treaty of 1698 and the source from Maland about 'removing all fears'. How useful are these for telling us about Louis' commitment to a peaceful solution to the Spanish Succession issue in 1698?

With this goal in mind, Louis also:

- tried 'removing all fears that Spain and France might ever be united' by instructing his ambassador in Madrid that the Dauphin would renounce his claim in favour of his own younger son, Philip, the Duc d'Anjou[2]
- showed considerable commitment and guile in prising England and The Dutch Republic away from the notion of Leopold taking the entire Spanish inheritance.

Diplomacy and scare-mongering by Colbert de Torcy (Foreign Affairs Minister 1698–1715) were both used to win over William III to the notion of partition. Torcy calmed Dutch fears that France might not respect the Dutch border by offering reassurances that it no longer bore any hostile intent. When English diplomat Portland visited at Versailles in 1698, Torcy reminded him that the Habsburgs had once before held a unified empire including German and Spanish lands.

The fruits of Louis' tireless labours were apparent by October 1698 when he agreed the First Treaty of Partition (or Treaty of The Hague) with England and the Dutch Republic. This gave the lion's share to Joseph Ferdinand, Leopold's eight-year-old grandson, while dividing the rest between Archduke Charles and the Dauphin as follows:

Joseph Ferdinand:	Archduke Charles:	Louis the Dauphin:
Spain	Milan	Sicily
Spanish Netherlands		Naples
Spanish Indies and all other colonies		Ports in Tuscany, e.g. Porto Santo Stefano
Sardinia		Towns north of the Pyrenees, e.g. San Sebastian

Table 6.1: First Partition Treaty, 1698

Louis had good reason to feel that this was a perfectly fair and workable compromise for all parties.

Joseph Ferdinand's Bavarian father was a **Wittelsbach**, not a Habsburg, so neither Habsburg nor Bourbon came out on top. Both Leopold's son and Louis' were compensated with lands in Italy. French power and security were increased by taking most of Spain's Italian land. This would secure the Dauphiné from invasion, boost trade and could be used as future bargaining counters to improve French pré carré.

As the lion's share went to Leopold's eight-year-old grandson, Louis expected this to sway Leopold towards acceptance, especially as his son was gaining Milan. The balance weighed in Leopold's favour. Louis therefore expected him to sign, and a done deal. The plan quickly hit three major problems:

1 Carlos insisted that his lands all pass undivided on his death to Joseph Ferdinand. This proposal was supported by a powerful Spanish court faction.

2 Leopold rejected both the partition treaty and Carlos' declared intentions. He was annoyed that he had not been consulted and at what he saw as the inadequate provision for his son Charles.

3 Joseph Ferdinand died before Carlos did, in February 1699.

Louis now negotiated a Second Partition Treaty with William. This offered Spain's throne and the bulk of its kingdom to Leopold's son, Archduke Charles, on the condition that he renounced all claims to being Habsburg Emperor. This was agreed in principle in June 1699 and was fully ratified in the March 1700 Treaty of London and apportioned Spanish lands as follows:

Archduke Charles:	Duke of Lorraine:	Louis the Dauphin:
Spain Low Countries Spanish Indies and other colonies	Milan	All Italian lands except Milan Lorraine

Table 6.2: Second Partition Treaty, 1700

The very wording of the Second Partition Treaty reflected Louis' national strategic interests, but also how far he was prepared to compromise in order to accommodate Leopold and avoid war in Europe:

'The Dauphin will have for his share, in full and rightful possession, and renouncing all his claims to the Spanish throne ... the kingdoms of Naples and Sicily, and the dependencies of Spain on the coast of Tuscany ... Furthermore, the lands of the Duke of Lorraine ... shall be ceded and conveyed to the Dauphin, in place of Milan, which shall be ceded and conveyed, to the Duke of Lorraine ... The Crown of Spain and the other kingdoms, islands, lands and places which the Catholic King currently possess, both within and without Europe, shall be given to Archduke Charles, second son of the Emperor ... (except ... from the Dauphin's share ...), in full and rightful possession.[3]

Even though his son was offered Spain and most of its empire, Leopold condemned the plan. He continuingly opposed partition and along with Prince Eugène of Savoy, believed there was no need to sacrifice the Italian lands. Leopold's situation was changing: after the 1699 Peace of Karlowitz with the Turks, he was freer to fight Louis. By August 1700, Habsburg troops were reported to be marching to Italy.

Carlos also fiercely opposed the Second Partition Treaty and secretly drafted a new will in October 1700. This named Louis' grandson Philip d'Anjou as his sole heir, so long as he renounced his claim to the French throne.

When Carlos died on 1 November 1700, his will took everyone, especially Louis, by complete surprise. Carlos had always loathed Louis and given his first wife Marie Louise (Louis' niece) a hard time, forging letters to prove she had committed adultery, and strangling her parrots for speaking in French.

ACTIVITY 6.4

Write a clear and precise explanation of each of the following and its contribution to the War of the Spanish Succession:

- The First Partition Treaty
- The Second Partition Treaty
- Carlos' will.

The international response to French claims

After forty years of dreaming and much deliberation, Louis could not resist a Bourbon inheritance of the entire Spanish Succession. He opted to accept Carlos' will for his grandson to become ruler of the Spanish Empire on 12 November 1700, knowing that this made war with Leopold more likely, but refusal would betray his family's interests and lead to the Spanish inheritance being offered to Leopold's son Archduke Charles. By September 1701, the Grand Alliance had reformed. By May 1702, it had formally declared war upon the Sun King. France was dragged into the very kind of prolonged and costly war that Louis had tried to avoid. How had this come about?

ACTIVITY 6.5

Louis XIV was reported as greeting his grandson's inheritance of the Spanish crown by saying: 'What rapture! The Pyrenees are no more!'[5]

1 What did he mean?

2 What will the phrase have implied for the monarchs of England, the Dutch Republic and the Holy Roman Empire?

Arguably, Louis' rash and tactless actions from November 1700 were largely to blame. He chose to ignore Tallard's advice not to:

- break his word to William about partition by formally announcing his acceptance of the will
- have a formal ceremonial acceptance of the will at Versailles by summoning the Spanish Ambassador to his court on 16 November 1700 (as depicted in Figure 6.3).

Not surprisingly, this gave William and Leopold the very idea that they had feared – that Louis would not respect Carlos' wish to separate the two kingdoms. It also raised the alarming prospect of France disrespecting Spanish neutrality and becoming too dominant within Europe, as noted by the Duc de Saint Simon:

'Gentlemen', he said, pointing to the young Anjou, 'birth has called him to the crown, and the dead King by his will. The whole nation wished for his accession and urged me to approve it; it is the will of heaven and I accede with pleasure. Then to his grandson: 'Be a good Spaniard, this is your first duty. But remember that you were born a Frenchman so that you may further unity between the two nations.'[4]

Figure 6.3: The Spanish ambassador kneels before his new king, Philip V

The manner of accepting the Spanish crown broke Louis' earlier promises of partition and outraged William. Louis still wished to avoid war, but he provoked it with two tactless and provocative steps in February 1701:

1 Louis announced that Philip d'Anjou retained his claim to the French throne and had this registered in the Paris Parlement, even though he was the new Spanish king and Carlos' will expressly forbid any union of the French and Spanish kingdoms. This added to fears of the Sun King's interference in Spain, which Louis had already stoked in 1700 by starting joint defence arrangements with Madrid.

2 Louis sent French troops to occupy Dutch garrisons in the Spanish Netherlands to force them to swear allegiance to his grandson Philip, as the Dutch States General had not yet recognised him as king of Spain. This violated the Peace of Ryswick and Louis' previous assurances to William that he would respect the neutrality of the Dutch border forts. It also fuelled perceptions of bad faith and French aggression, along with the 'universal suspicion that Louis, not Philip, would be the arbiter of Spain's fortunes'.[6] English newspapers reported a French invasion of the Dutch Republic.

Leopold responded by invading Spanish lands including Lombardy in an effort to seize Milan. The Emperor's success and demonstration of his willingness to act for himself helped to make English and Dutch opinion more pro-Habsburg. This weakened French prestige in Spain, thereby making it much harder for Louis to offer any concessions to Leopold.

This local conflict with Leopold could have been avoided or contained if Louis had acted with the respect for international opinion that he had shown before November 1700. Instead, from March 1701 the Sun King behaved recklessly, committing a series of further provocative actions which rekindled the English appetite for conflict with France. This was reflected in two key developments:

- In June 1701, the English parliament unequivocally backed William's 'defence of European liberties and attempts to reduce the excessive power of the Bourbons'.[7]
- The formation of a second Grand Alliance through the Treaty of The Hague (7 September 1701). This undertook to prevent forever the union of the French and Spanish crowns, to share Spanish colony captures between the English and Dutch and above all, to support Leopold's claim to Spain's Italian lands and the Spanish Netherlands. Louis was offered just two months to consider these terms – which were essentially William and Leopold's war manifesto.

The declaration of the Grand Alliance laid full blame on Louis XIV (as shown in Extract B).

Louis had largely brought all of this upon himself. Between March 1701 and March 1702, he exhibited increasing uninterest in negotiation and further tactless impetuosity, as shown by the following summary table:

Date:	Louis' action:	International reaction:
March 1701	Kept Dutch border fort troops captive Categorically refused English and Dutch demands to offer compensation for Leopold.	Leopold invaded northern Italy and continued to press for Milan. The Allies saw decreasing opportunity for negotiation with Louis. By April 1701, the English parliament ended its limit on military funding and by June was keenly backing Leopold.
July 1701	Refused to admit the emperor's representative to negotiations with William and recalled his ambassador to The Hague.	Leopold and William seized upon this as an opportunity to negotiate for a second Grand Alliance; arguments that could not be won by persuasion would have to be won by force.
August 1701	Ordered Philip to grant the **Asiento** – the privilege of importing slaves into South America so coveted by the English – to the French Guinea Company. Bought the right for French companies to trade in the Spanish Empire.	William had a pretext to stir up opinion against Louis, using the suspicion that he wanted to manage the Spanish Empire with Philip as his puppet. Powerful merchant houses in London and Amsterdam complained of a French fleet hampering trade by guarding Cadiz; they gave William their full support for reducing excessive Bourbon power. Helped a pro-war Whig party gain support and power in England.

Date:	**Louis' action:**	**International reaction:**
September 1701	Just nine days after the Grand Alliance was reformed, Louis seemingly willed the death of exiled James II/VII of England/ Scotland by naming his son James III before James II had died.	Offended English Protestant opinion. Increased calls to go to war to curb Louis' excessive ways and tactless violation of the Peace of Ryswick which had recognised William of Orange as rightful King of England.
October 1701	Published an edict that banned most English goods (including beer, cider, glass, bottles and wool) and put prohibitive taxes on the rest.	English merchants, politicians and press deplored a blatant violation of the spirit of Article V of the Peace of Ryswick, which promised relaxed trading conditions and much lower tariffs on English and Dutch imports. Seen by many as a near declaration of war. Helped with a pro-war Whig government being elected in England.
Autumn 1701	Sent troops to help garrison fortified towns in Cologne.	Outrage at the presence of French troops within the Empire and increased anti-French feeling.
March 1702	Insulted the Dutch by trying to use William of Orange's death to his own advantage. Informed the Dutch government that Dutch liberty was now restored and stated his assumption that the Dutch Republic would now be ready to leave the anti-French coalition.	Incensed Dutch nationalist opinion and provoked the start of a general war against Louis in April 1702, when the Allies besieged Kaiserwerth. Led to English and Dutch formal declarations of war in May 1702 and Leopold's in September 1702.

Table 6.3: Louis' provocative actions March 1701–March 1702

French ambassador in London, Tallard had warned in December 1700 that English and Dutch neutrality seemed safe, but could be threatened by any violation of Dutch security in the Low Countries and any tampering with Anglo-Dutch trade and involvement in the Asiento. This warning fell on deaf ears.

Louis continued to desire peace, but was not prepared to negotiate or act with the requisite discretion or self-restraint required to ensure it. According to M. A. Thomson, Louis 'made inevitable the very war he dreaded' and 'allowed it to happen in the most unfavourable circumstances'.[8] By the winter of 1701, William had enlisted German elector states, including the Palatinate, Brandenburg-Prussia, Münster, Baden Baden and Trier into the Grand Alliance. By 1703, Louis was fighting England, the Dutch Republic, the Empire, Savoy and Portugal.

Undeniably, Leopold provoked Louis and the war as well. Leopold rejected the Second Partition Treaty which offered him so much, even though neither of his sons had a Spanish mother. This gave Louis the idea that war was inevitable. So too did Leopold's marching of troops towards Italy in 1700, invasion in March 1701 and steadfast refusal to acknowledge Philip as Spanish king. This was reflected in Louis' edict to continue the Capitation tax in 1701:

'But the movements and preparations that are being made in Germany, England and in The Dutch Republic do not leave us any room to doubt that some princes, jealous of the new advantages of the House of France and others in the aim of colonising entire peoples that a longer peace that could have been confirmed in the rest of freedom, if they hadn't decided to restart the war'.[9]

Louis' naming of James III/VIII as king of England and Scotland probably reflected his growing despair at a mounting English-Dutch conspiracy with Leopold, especially after the impossible demands presented to him in the Grand Alliance ultimatum nine days earlier. As Vauban noted, William was committed to war.

While this may be true, the point was being missed. The return of a huge anti-French coalition and worldwide war in 1702 was largely down to the Sun King's display of arrogance and wilful disregard of international opinion in 1701–2.

The outbreak of war

Fighting started in Italy with Leopold's invasion in March 1701. It escalated with:

- the Grand Alliance's formation in September 1701
- Imperial forces crossing the Rhine near Cologne in April 1702
- formal English and Dutch declarations of war in May 1702
- Leopold following suit in September 1702.

Louis' efforts to keep the peace had been frustrated, mainly by his own provocative actions. Now Louis would be frustrated in his efforts to conclude the war quickly and fight on favourable terms. A bankrupt France with few allies faced a huge coalition which aimed to impose Leopold's son Archduke Charles as Spanish King.

Louis faced war on four fronts: in Italy, Spain, the Rhine and Flanders. By 1703, Savoy and Portugal had deserted him. Bavaria was his only ally until 1704, when it was knocked out of the war. France faced its toughest military struggle yet. Unprepared for war and unsupported, France seemed ripe for the taking.

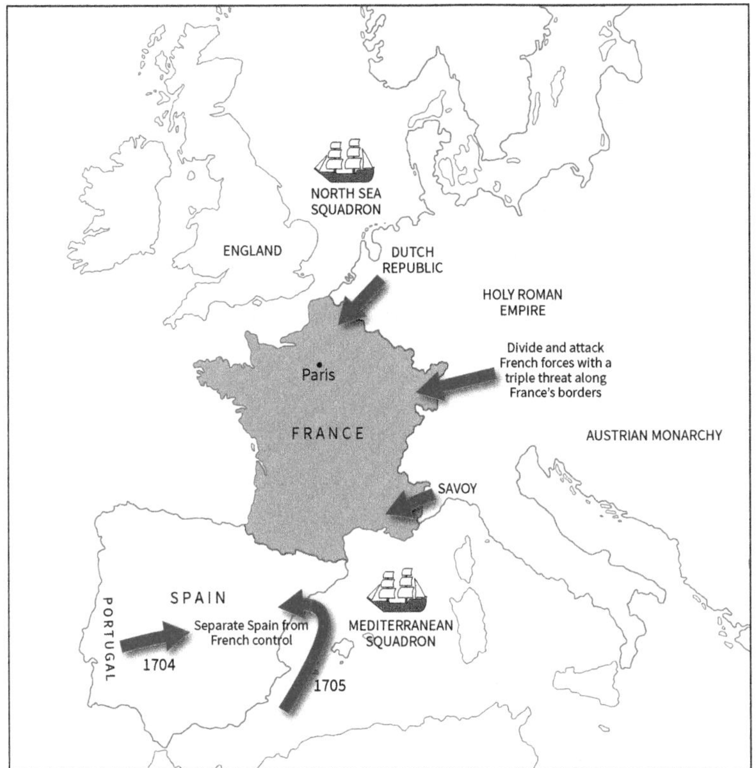

Figure 6.4: At the start of the Spanish Succession War, France faced enemies on four fronts

ACTIVITY 6.6

Write a clear and precise explanation of each of the following terms that shows their significance as to why war started in 1702:

- Asiento
- Grand Alliance.

ACTIVITY 6.7

1. Why did Louis XIV's acceptance of Carlos II's will cause so many problems?
2. To what extent were Louis' problems following Carlos II's death of his own making? Explain your answer carefully.
3. Make notes on the written sources cited in this section, considering how useful they are for telling us about why Louis XIV found himself at war with the Grand Alliance by 1702.

The War of the Spanish Succession

France suffered a level of ignominy and defeat from 1702 that had not previously been seen during Louis' reign. By 1706, France had been knocked out of the war in Italy and much of the Spanish Netherlands. By 1709, it had suffered foreign invasion and Louis was begging for peace.

The war in Europe

Talented English commander-in-chief John Churchill, who became Duke of Marlborough, led Allied defeats of France's army. Between 1702–11, he:

- captured over 30 enemy fortresses, including Kaiserwerth, Venlo, Roermond and Liege in 1702, and Huy and Limbourg in 1703
- led four key battleground victories over France: Blenheim 1704, Ramillies 1706, Oudenarde 1708 and Malplaquet 1709.

These victories altered the war's course. Until Blenheim, Austria was threatened by being forced to surrender because of a powerful Hungarian rebellion and a planned French-Bavarian march on Vienna. Marching his men 250 miles in just five weeks, Marlborough:

- killed half of French forces at Donauwörth to cross the Danube
- crushed Louis' army at Blenheim.

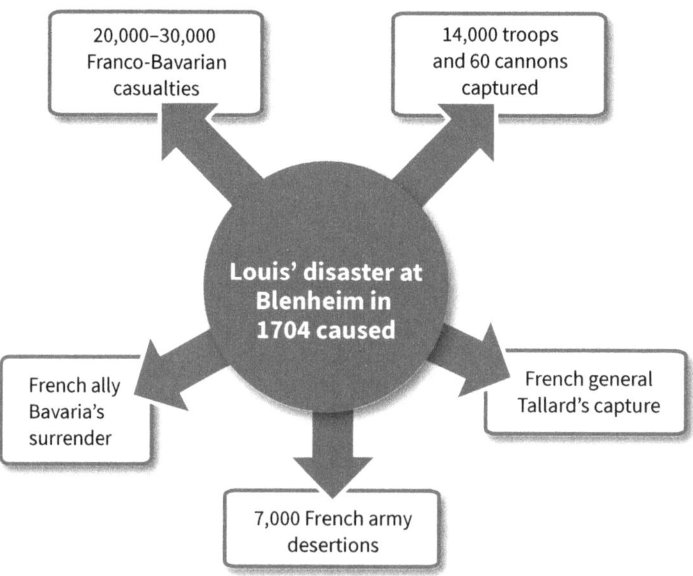

Figure 6.5: The disaster at Blenheim, 1704

France lost:

- its aura of invincibility
- garrisons at Landau, Laubanie, Trier and Trarbach
- a fabulous opportunity to defeat Leopold; his forces were diverted to fight Rákóczi's rebellion, which had overrun two thirds of Hungary
- Bavaria's assistance in November 1704.

Marlborough also routed Louis' finest troops and General Villeroi at Ramillies in May 1706, with 12,000 French casualties and 6,000 captured. Marlborough exploited this by seizing Ghent, Brussels, Bruges, Damme, Oudenarde, Antwerp, Ath and more crucially, Menin – fortified by Vauban and on French soil.

At Oudenarde (1708), Louis' army suffered 5,000 desertions and 12,000–15,000 casualties – over three times the Allied total. This caused Lille's capture and the expulsion of French forces from almost all the Spanish Netherlands. At Malplaquet (1709), French general Villars had his knee shattered. Marlborough captured Mons afterwards.

Figure 6.6: Soundly defeated, Louis XIV's army lost its aura of invincibility at Blenheim

The spectre of French defeat within Europe prevented Louis from securing peace in 1706.

French defeats in Spain and Italy and securing peace 1702–9

Marlborough's victories were crowned by:

- British capture of Gibraltar in 1704
- Allied soldiers marching on Madrid in 1706.

In northern Italy, Leopold's general Prince Eugène and Vittorio Amedeo of Savoy led the 1706 Siege of Turin. This cost France:

- 9,000 troops (25% of its entire army in Turin)
- commander Marsin
- all its siege equipment
- control of Italy.

By 1707, French fortresses Pavia, Alesandria and Casale were lost along with Milan, Nice and Cannes. The Allies gained control of the entire Po Valley, leaving south-eastern France open to invasion. That same year, Austrians stood on French soil after besieging Toulon.

By 1709, France was on its knees. Louis' surrender terms included:

- withdrawing Philip from Spain's throne
- giving Archduke Charles II all Spanish lands
- surrendering Strasbourg and territory in Flanders including Lille and Ypres
- recognising Protestant Queen Anne as successor to England's throne
- James III/VIII's expulsion from France
- two million livres for Marlborough.

Voices from the past

Marlborough sent this report to his wife's close friend Queen Anne after his victory at Ramillies:

'I humbly beg leave to congratulate your [Royal Highness] upon the success of [Her Majesty's] arms and those of her allies, God Almighty having blessed us yesterday with a complete victory over the enemy'.[10]

If these had been accepted and not rejected in 1709, then French defeat and humiliation would have been complete. But Allied greed prevented Louis from securing the peace he craved since 1706. When he was asked to invade Spain to help depose his grandson Philip, Louis had no option but to continue fighting.

French defeat: neither completely losing the war nor the peace

J. H. Shennan argues that the Succession War 'went disastrously for Louis everywhere except in Spain' and that his problem was being 'up against two of the greatest soldiers of the century'.[11]

These claims have some validity, but seem fairly simplistic, perhaps even slightly jingoistic. This is because:

1 France's defeats were at least partly self-inflicted rather than the result of enemy leadership genius.
2 France was never completely defeated 1702–13 or forced to surrender through invasion, as Marlborough had wished – allied setbacks, greed, a loss of domestic support and improving French fortunes from 1709 prevented this. Geographically and chronologically, French military performance varied.
3 Diplomatically, Louis certainly surrendered much at Utrecht in 1713, but also secured a substantial amount that never seemed possible in 1709, mainly down to Torcy's negotiating skill.

France's defeats 1702–13 were caused by its own problems, not just brilliant enemy leadership. The 1702–5 Huguenot Cévennes revolt deprived France of Villars, probably its best general, and 20,000 troops at Blenheim. If Villeroi had been less impetuous at Ramillies and waited for Marsin's reinforcements, then he would have outnumbered and not equalled the enemy's fighting strength. He also allowed most of his army to be immobilised behind a marsh.

Some of Louis' generals lacked their predecessors' talents: Vendôme's replacement of Villeroi in 1706 left the ineffective Marsin and Orléans commanding France's army in Turin. La Feuillade diverted some of these troops to chase Vittorio Amadeus in the mountains. At Oudenarde in 1708, Vendôme failed to attack Marlborough's troops crossing the Scheldt and was let down by the inexperienced Duke of Burgundy, Louis' grandson. Burgundy ignored repeated requests to assist Vendôme in supporting an attack, losing an excellent chance of destroying the Allied right flank. Unable to see the battlefield whatsoever from his headquarters, Burgundy decided to retreat to Ghent, which encouraged a rout.

Moreover, Louis' desperation for peace emanated from France's increasingly grim financial and socio-economic situation, not just defeats. As explained in Chapter 4, France's financial exhaustion and profligacy increased exponentially, undermining its war-making capacity. By 1707, Chamillart, Louis' War Secretary and Controlleur-Général, was begging Villars' assistance in plundering Germany. No wonder; by 1708, debt had tripled from 1699.

Additional peace pressures in 1708–9 came from devastating famine and winter. As Madame de Maintenon noted:

'How can you say that God has not declared Himself against us, when He sends us a winter such as he has not seen for five or six hundred years?'[12]

Yet, despite several heavy losses, France was never actually defeated on all four battlefronts or forced to surrender by a successful Allied invasion. Marlborough failed to bring about a complete and decisive French defeat because:

- Blenheim (1704) was partially offset by French success in Italy. Vendôme captured Milan, Turin, Ivrea and Verrua, thereby encircling the Duke of Savoy.
- French general Berwick (James II's illegitimate son and coincidentally Marlborough's nephew), assisted Philip V in securing victories on the Portuguese border. With Salvatierra, Pena Garcia, Castelo Branco and Portalegre all gained in 1704, the Allies were not much closer to deposing Philip V as Spanish king.

Marlborough could not sustain his momentum of victory and cut a fairly frustrated figure. In 1705, his assault on Louvain was delayed by Villeroi and a lack of Dutch support. Louis described Marlborough's subsequent withdrawal as 'a shameful retreat'. After waiting two weeks for a siege train in 1706, Marlborough complained that: 'We can advance no farther till we have our cannon'.[13]

In 1706, the Allies failed to maintain their armies so deep in Spain and fulfil their key overall objective – overthrowing Louis' grandson Philip V. The majority of Spanish people remained loyal to him. Subsequently:

- the Allies abandoned Madrid and retreated
- Berwick recaptured fortresses Castile and Murcia
- Philip recovered from a major setback and remained king of Spain.

In 1707, Marlborough was exasperated by missed opportunities for ending the war. The Dutch vetoed his planned attack on the Moselle. The alternative major Allied assault – Eugène's attack on Toulon failed. Stern resistance by Tessé cost 10,000 of Eugène's troops, thereby depriving Marlborough of the requisite fighting strength to defeat France in Flanders. With 24 fewer battalions than the French, he complained: '... that my hopes are not great for this front'.[14]

1707 also saw notable French victories. Villars broke the supposedly impregnable Allied lines at Stollhofen without casualties and made invaded populations contribute to French war expenses. Württemberg paid 2.2 million livres. Milan's loss was also offset by a stunning victory in Spain at Alamanza. This inflicted over 50% Allied army casualties and strengthened Philip's hold on most of Spain. Valencia, Xàtiva, Saragossa and Aragon were all regained.

Marlborough continued to struggle to invade France:

- At Lille in 1708, he lost five times more casualties than at Oudenarde.
- The battle of Malplaquet left his army too depleted to advance beyond Mons, with 5,000 Dutch killed in the first half hour and 21,000 casualties overall – 25% of all his force.

By 1709, therefore, France had been saved, its morale transformed and Allied armies greatly weakened.

Allied greed in peace negotiations in 1709–10 prevented France from being disgraced diplomatically. By continuingly demanding that Louis personally help to remove Philip from Spain and turning down his 500,000 livres offer to help subsidise the cost of his grandson's removal, the allies dealt Louis a last card and a justification to continue fighting through an impassioned backs-to-the-wall rallying call:

'Although my affection is no less than I feel for my own children and although I share all the sufferings inflicted by war upon my faithful subjects, and have shown plainly to all of Europe that I wish sincerely that they should enjoy peace, I am convinced that they themselves would scorn to receive it on conditions so contrary to justice and to the honour of the French name'.[15]

ACTIVITY 6.8

1. When and how did each of the following contribute to French defeat after 1702:
   - inept French leadership?
   - inadequate French finances?
   - famine and winter?
2. Prepare plans for each of the following essay questions:
   - To what extent did the changing balance of power within Europe bring about French defeat 1702–13?
   - To what extent do you think Louis lost the War of the Spanish Succession but in 1713 won the peace?
   - How far was the War of the Spanish Succession in Europe a failure for Louis XIV?
3. Make notes on Marlborough's and Madame de Maintenon's responses to the Battle of Malplaquet. How useful are these sources for explaining why the Allies failed fully to defeat France, 1702–13?

So, the changing state of Europe did not guarantee French defeat 1702–13. The opportunity to disgrace France was missed. The state of Europe and war actually changed in Louis' favour from 1710 onwards, as Table 6.4 shows:

Year:	Allied setback:
1710	Sweeping victories ended the Allied threat in Spain. Guerrilla warfare and Franco-Spanish successes at Villaviciosa and Brihuega destroyed most of the 12,000 Allied invasion troops. After two surrenders, the Allies were ousted from Spain's central provinces permanently. This ended their threat to Castille and Aragon and hopes of overthrowing Philip V.
1710	The Tories took over England's government and committed themselves to ending the increasingly costly European war; this allowed Torcy to negotiate much better peace terms.
April 1711	Emperor Joseph I died (after succeeding Leopold who had died in 1705). His brother now becoming Charles VI undermined the Allied war rationale: if Emperor Charles was made Spanish king, the Habsburg Empire would be too strong. This softened attitudes towards coming to a negotiated settlement with Louis XIV over the Spanish inheritance.
December 1711	Marlborough was discredited, accused by the Tories of pursuing the war for his own gain and sacked; Louis' new arch-nemesis and the most talented Allied general was gone.
1712	Villars defeated Eugène at Denain, suffering only a third of the Allies' 6,500 casualties. Subsequent French victory at Marchiennes led to 7,000–9,000 Allied troops and 100 cannon being lost, and put an end to the threat of enemy invasion from Flanders. The retaking of Douai, Quesnoy and Bouchain restored France's pré carré and strengthened Louis' hand for negotiating peace.

Table 6.4: Improving war fortunes in Europe 1710–13

Thus, it is possible to question the extent of French military defeat in Europe. By hook and crook, dogged resistance and some considerable luck, Louis was going to salvage some successes from the war; he had been dealt a last chance and seized it with both hands.

Figure 6.7: Native Americans fought on both sides of the War of the Spanish Succession

The war in North America

The Spanish Succession war was not just an issue of 'whether France would gain hegemony in Europe', but was also about colonial and trading supremacy in America.[16] This was enshrined in the sixth article of the Treaty of Grand Alliance. This stated that the English and Dutch were legally entitled to seize parts of Spanish America and secure economic and territorial advantage in the national interest at France's expense. War could be for Anglo-Dutch profit if it could pay for itself and lost for France if it was denied its ability to fund conflict (chiefly through Spanish bullion). Possession of Spanish American wealth and French colonies, therefore, were key components of England's strategy to defeat France.

Queen Anne's War

Fierce fighting erupted in North America 1702–13. This war was much smaller in its impact upon European lives than the European war:

- the French and Spanish lost no more than 60 killed
- New England lost 200 dead
- about 150 were killed from local Carolina militia.

Commonly known as 'Queen Anne's War' or the 'Third Indian War', this essentially involved conflict in three key areas:

1. Spanish Florida and the English province of Carolina
2. New England – English colonists fought with French and Native American forces in Acadia and Canada
3. Newfoundland – mutual English and French attempts to ruin local trading economies.

French and Spanish North American colonies were vulnerable due to the French navy's continual decline. Between 1695 and 1715, the number of French ships fell by over 50%. This, and an acute shortage of overseas funding, meant that France's policy was to protect and exploit Spanish America rather than defend its own colonies.

This left French and Spanish territories open to attack, as demonstrated by the war in Spanish Florida and English Carolina. In January 1702, French Canadian colonist d'Iberville proposed to:

- arm the Apalachee Native Americans to attack the English and their Native American allies
- gain control of the Mississippi river, a lucrative trade route.

The plan badly backfired. 500 Spanish-led Native Americans were killed or captured. Thereafter, Franco-Spanish interests suffered multiple setbacks:

- English governor George Moore seized and burnt the Spanish Florida trading town of St Augustine with 500 English militia and 300 Native Americans
- The genocidal impact of Moore's 1704 Apalachee massacre upon the native Apalachee and Timucua populations, depriving France and Spain of foot soldiers to lead against the English.
- An English-led army of 3,000–4,000 Chickasaw Native Americans committed great destruction to France's Choctaw allies near the Mississippi river, thereby extending English influence from the Atlantic seaboard. Subsequent attacks by 1706 left France having to support a native war against English-backed Chickasaws.
- A French-Spanish attack on the South Carolina capital Charles Town failed in 1706. Invading Spanish soldiers were surprised while eating by English captain Fenwick on James Island, leading to 12 being killed, 60 captured and wholescale retreat. English governor Sir Nathaniel Johnson's garrison killed 30 and captured 320 invading soldiers in just four days.
- An English-led Talapoosan attack in 1707 on the Spanish settlement of Santa Maria de Galve at Penascola Bay, Florida, killed 11 Spaniards.

The American conflict showed France's failure to dominate the continent from 1702. To defend their Native American allies, French colonists at Mobile were sucked into a proxy war which almost wiped out the entire native population of Spanish Florida.

But England also gained no significant advantage or any major territorial gains. George Moore failed to take the main fortress of St Augustine and withdrew in 1706 after a Spanish fleet arrived from Havana. French imperial ambitions in North America after 1702 were largely thwarted, but were not entirely defeated.

The war in New England

War in New England also led to French disappointment but no major defeat, despite threadbare colonial defences. England's minor successes included:

- disrupting French trade to Canada and other northern colonies
- in 1704, capturing the French ship *La Seine* containing an estimated 1.3 million livres of provisions
- Colonel Benjamin Church's maritime expeditions.

In 1704 Church destroyed the Acadian settlements of Grand Pré, Pigiquit and Cobequid in the Minas Basin. In 1707 Church also led English retaliatory raids on French Grand Pré and Chignecto. In 1710 English forces captured Port Royal, the capital of Acadia, thereby ending French control of the peninsular part of Acadia (modern-day Nova Scotia). French governor Subercase had under 300 men to Sir Francis Nicholson's English fleet of 34 vessels including seven warships and a 1,500-man landing force.

Were the French defeated?

Overall, France was defeated in North America, but the Allies hardly enjoyed continuous victories. Rather, France's colonists, left largely on their own, successfully defended their lands against superior English numbers. The English experienced numerous setbacks, including:

- Subercase routing two New England assaults (1707)
- French Canadian and Native American attacks on New English settlements between Wells and Falmouth (1703). These were destructive, capturing 300 English colonists
- the destruction of the English Deerfield settlement in Massachusetts Bay in 1704; 54 English colonists were killed and 120 taken captive.

Similar raids persisted in 1705 and continued until 1713, often taking English colonists by surprise. By 1709, Philippe de Rigaud Vaudreuil, governor of New France, claimed that two-thirds of fields north of Boston were untended.

English investment in New England colonial warfare from 1710 and gain of Port Royal was too little too late:

- Twice in 1704 and 1707, the English had failed to attack Port Royal when it was so lightly defended.
- Acadia was not lost to the English.
- Ile de Saint Jean remained in French hands.
- Acadia between present-day Maine and New Brunswick remained disputed territory.
- Bad weather and poor piloting prevented the English from reaching the town of Quebec. They only reached the mouth of the St Lawrence River with eight transport ships and 900 men lost.

Neither New France nor New England had triumphed overall. It is also debatable whether the war in Newfoundland ended in French defeat.

Tit-for-tat raids on trading communities saw no decisive defeat or advantage for England or France. John Leake attacked outskirt French communities, sinking 51 French vessels and levelling several settlements. Anglo-Dutch attacks destroyed many French fishing outposts in northern Newfoundland; it suffered an estimated 52% decline in fishing vessel numbers during the war. Trade to Newfoundland also suffered, with 70% less ships departing than from 1698–1702. France's failure to capture Saint John's in 1705 reflected its limited imperial clout after 1702. Eventual French capture of the town and destruction of its fortifications in 1708 proved a Pyrrhic victory. Lacking the resources to hold St John's, the French had to withdraw, allowing Britain to recapture it in 1709.

However, France was not decisively defeated and held its own in the war in Newfoundland. In 1705, severe damage was done to English colonial settlements at Conception and Trinity bays. This destroyed all English outposts as far as Bonavista, except Carbonear, causing an estimated 4 million livres' worth of damage. The 1705 French campaign against Saint John ruined several hundred boats, destroyed 40 cannon, captured 1,200 English colonists and caused £188,000 of claimed damages. The English repeatedly failed to:

- attack Placentia
- venture beyond their fortified colonial strongpoints.

ACTIVITY 6.9

1. Prepare a summary of French setbacks in the War of Spanish Succession in North America.
2. Prepare a summary of French successes in the War of Spanish Succession in North America.
3. Where was the war in North America least AND most successful for France and why?
4. Make a revision timeline of the War of the Spanish Succession in North America.

This negates the notion of French defeat. English strategy in Newfoundland backfired, inflicting more damage to English than to French fishing. This is illustrated by:

- the 77% fall in the number of English fishing vessels compared to peacetime
- the highest annual English catch volume (1702–7) was less than half the lowest volume during the last four years' of peace.

As with other sectors of the Spanish Succession war, therefore, conflict in Newfoundland was anything but a clear cut French defeat.

The War in the Caribbean

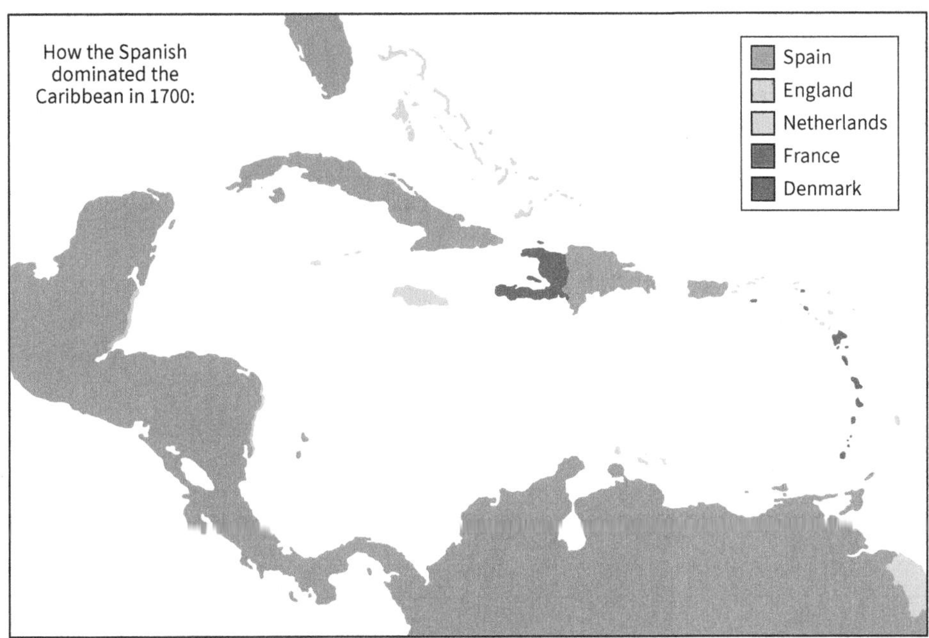

Figure 6.8: Spanish territories in the Caribbean in 1700

English successes in the Caribbean have also been overstated. French setbacks included:

- 2,500 English troops (led by Captain General Christopher Codrington and Major General Walter Hamilton) capturing St Christopher (Kitts) from French governor the Comte de Gennes without a single shot being fired (July 1702)
- Vice Admiral John Benbow running the 600-ton French troop transport Gironde aground at Haiti
- Admiral Charles Wager's 1708 attack on Spanish galleons near Cartagena on Colombia's Caribbean coast. This destroyed three ships and some gold and silver crossing the sea to fund the French-Spanish war effort. An estimated 7–11 million pesos on board the *San Jose* was blown up
- the capture, three miles off Havana, of the 550 ton French ship *Thetis* (1711)
- 600 English reinforcements repulsing a French attack on English Antigua (July 1712).

However, notions of French defeat in the Caribbean are misleading. France's Caribbean stronghold and economic interests were actually strengthened. St Christopher was no great loss and was easily replaced by expanding French West Indian sugar production elsewhere. France's sugar works grew by 30% in Martinique, 39% in Guadeloupe and by one and a half times on Saint Domingue (Haiti). Far from being destroyed, France's Caribbean trading assets were thriving after 1702.

Moreover, for all their build-up and high profile, English attacks on French and Spanish ships and colonies largely lacked an end product. In 1702, an attempted English landing in Puerto Rico ended in failure, with 40 killed compared to just one Spaniard. The English also failed off Colombia's Santa Marta 1702. Despite vastly superior numbers, Benbow failed to stop French commodore Jean Baptiste Du Casse from transporting troops to Cartagena on the Spanish mainland to force it to swear allegiance to Phillip.

French glee was as well-deserved as English disappointment. Benbow was severely injured in the leg and later died. He was also let down by the captains of the *Defiance, Greenwich, Windsor and Pendennis.* They refused to chase and deserted (leading to two death sentences) from the scene of conflict with specious excuses from ammunition shortages, to exhaustion to bad weather. This started an overall trend of English failures against the French, as summarised in Table 6.5:

Date:	English Caribbean setback:
1703	Despite a 4,000-man and six-warship invasion force, the English abandoned a plan to capture Martinique after 25% died of disease, scurvy or drink after reaching Barbados. Codrington and English commodore Hovenden Walker's attempt to capture Guadeloupe failed; 4,000 men were driven off by disease, hunger and Jean Gabaret, French lieutenant general for the West Indies who arrived with three warships and 820 men from Martinique.
Oct 1703	A Franco-Spanish attack on English-held Bahamas destroyed the capital Nassau, with over 40% of English settlers massacred, 22 guns and 80–100 captured, including English governor Ellis Lightwood.
1704	English captain Henry Lawrence allowed the French to capture the 48-gun, 670-ton HMS *Coventry* and was court martialled in 1705.
1706	Captain Henri-Louis de Chavagnac, captain of the King's ships, spent a week devastating St Christopher and pillaging considerable booty, including 300 black slaves. Captain Henri-Louis de Chavagnac and French commander Pierre le Moyne d'Iberville invaded English-held Nevis unopposed with 3,000 men, landing near the capital Charlestown. English governor Abbot surrendered. They torched two-thirds of Charlestown, ruined plantations and took considerable plunder, including 3,000–5,000 slaves.
1708	Wager's failed to capture Spanish galleon bullion. He captured the *Santa Cruz*, with no government treasure on board and just 13 chests of pieces of eight and 14 pigs of silver. He failed to catch and pursue the *San Joaquin*, mainly down to the inertia of captains Bridges and Windsor, who were both court martialled. This key target escaped with 5 million pesos aboard with the rest of the Spanish fleet to Cartagena. 12 English boats were intercepted by the Spanish at Cape San Antonio; half of the convoy was carried off to Veracruz (Mexico).
1709	The 36-gun *La Valeur* captured the 44-gun HMS *Adventure* off Martinique

Table 6.5: Summary of English setbacks against the French in the Caribbean

French privateering in the Caribbean from 1702 caused significant damage in a very short space of time to Anglo-Dutch imperial economic interests:

- In just 3 months in 1702, almost 600 slaves were taken from the English entering Martinique.
- In 1704, 82% of English West Indian plantation ships had been seized.

- An estimated 130 English vessels had been taken by the French since 1702.
- English merchants estimated £380,000 of costs for a single year.

French dominance in the Caribbean War from 1702 was further shown in its four invasions of the English colony of Montserrat (1707, 1708, 1710 and 1711). The latter invasion significantly damaged England's economic interests, causing £180,000 of damage and taking 1,200–1,400 slaves, a third of Montserrat's black population. Dutch interests were also harmed:

- French buccaneers forced Dutch mass-emigration from Sint Maartin in 1703.
- Curaçao was bombarded and a heavy ransom yielded in 1708 and in 1712.
- Nantes privateer Jacques Cassard attacked Surinam, seizing 700,000 florins of sugar and 730 slaves. In total, Cassard inflicted losses on English, Dutch and Portuguese colonies estimated at 30 million livres.

English financial losses heightened anti-war feeling, as this grumble from English politician James Vernon in 1706 shows:

'Money is so scarce that unless a trade can be opened with the Spanish West Indies, and that we have bullion, we shall be reduced to barter commodities for want of current coin in the market.'[17]

French defeat in the Caribbean remained a pipe dream. Talk of English naval and imperial dominance was hubris. Louis had not decisively lost the war, and he was not prepared to lose the peace.

ACTIVITY 6.10

1 Take notes on the French setbacks and successes of the War of the Spanish Succession in the Caribbean.

2 What proof is there that France did not lose this war?

3 Plan essay answers to the following questions:
   - 'The War of the Spanish Succession outside of Europe was a disaster for France.' How far do you agree?
   - To what extent did France fail in its wars in North America and the Caribbean between 1688 and 1713? Explain your answer carefully.

The Treaty of Utrecht and its impact on the balance of power in Europe

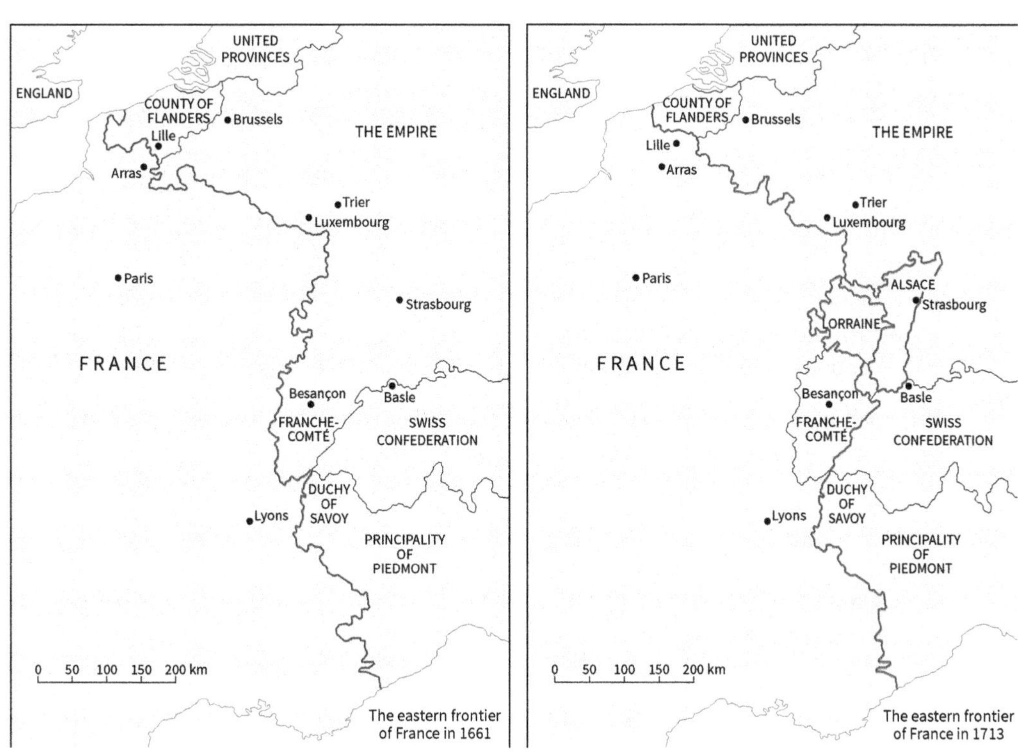

Figure 6.9: France's border in 1661, and after the 1713 Treaty of Utrecht

It is true that French ambitions of territorial hegemony within Europe were checked significantly at the Treaty of Utrecht in 1713. Compared to 1661, the balance of power among the major powers was much more equal. French power and borders were limited, as shown in Figure 6.10:

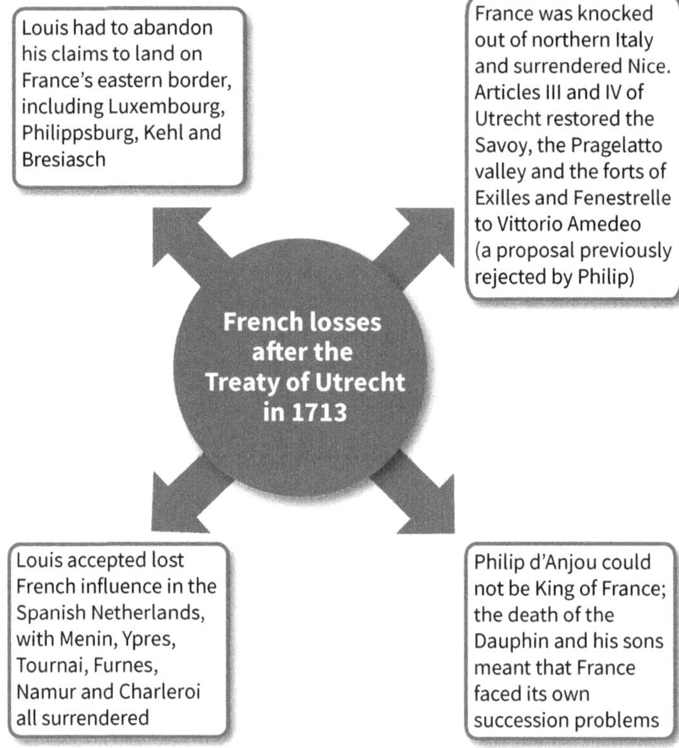

Figure 6.10: French losses after the Peace Treaty of Utrecht in 1713

A changing balance of power: the case for

There were other checks to French power made obvious during 1713–14. Agreeing to end French occupations of Savoy and Lorraine ended Louis' dreams of annexing these two duchies. Lorraine's future was left entirely unclear. It was not mentioned in the treaties and remained a future potential security threat to Alsace. To some extent, the pendulum of power had swung away from both Spain and France towards Britain, both economically and imperially. Britain benefited considerably at Spain's expense, gaining:

- Minorca
- Gibraltar
- the asiento; this was a valuable source of Britain's growing wealth, with British transatlantic ships carrying 3 million slaves during the eighteenth century.

Britain also gained from France a level of colonial territory that was well above its actual military dominance within America and the Caribbean. It received:

- Hudson Bay
- Newfoundland
- Acadia
- St Kitts
- trading rights over the Iroquois Native Americans
- control of most of the eastern Atlantic seaboard down to South Carolina.

Demolition of the French fort at Dunkirk and Austria's gains at the 1714 Peace of Rastatt also suggested that the Sun King's influence over Europe was now starting to fade. Rastatt gave Austria's Habsburg Empire its largest territorial extent in its history and made it a major power in western, southern and central Europe. Emperor Charles received:

- Spanish territory in Italy, including Milan, Sardinia and Naples
- the Spanish Low Countries
- Freiburg.

A changing balance of power: the case against

However, the notion of French defeat in 1713–14 is easily overstated. In reality, the peace terms represented a mixed bag, both for France and for Europe's balance of power.

Firstly, Louis did much better than he previously thought possible. Philip remained King of Spain, which was more than Louis had offered in both partition treaties and in 1709. A Bourbon Spanish king represented Allied failure; the Grand Alliance's chief war aim had been to establish Archduke Charles as Spanish king. France also retained:

- Strasbourg, which Louis had offered to surrender in 1709, and had been the source of three attacks upon France 1672–9
- Alsace
- Franche Comté
- Lille, Aire and Bethune
- Dunkirk.

Utrecht and Rastatt may have denied French territorial hegemony, but they preserved its national integrity and security. Louis' pré carré had not been entirely lost.

To have gained all of this against a vast international enemy force was arguably a remarkable achievement. The idea that Louis 'had not succeeded in any of his aims' and capitulated seems as exaggerated as does talk of a new balance of power that totally favoured France's enemies. Louis had lost a few things that were no longer important to him, but had also won many things that were.

Louis gave very little away to his arch-enemy the Dutch, aside from the right to some garrison forts along the River Scheldt border. These could easily be overrun, as in 1701, and seemed scant consolation for the commercial supremacy and financial strength sacrificed by the Dutch in the war. Dutch debts rocketed by 83% between 1700 and 1713.

Louis had strengthened both his dynastic influence and frontier against Habsburg invasion. He secured Landau from the Habsburgs and the lands he ceded to Emperor Charles could not deter the Emperor from feeling cheated of his main aim – the Spanish crown. In exchange for relinquishing its grip on Savoy, France gained the Barcelonnette valley – a more logical and defendable natural border along the Alps.

Lorraine's ambiguous future and Savoy's restoration were neither preventable nor major setbacks to Louis. Louis managed to circumvent a British proposal during the negotiations for the Utrecht Treaty for Philip exchanging Spain for Savoy and Piedmont, and Vittorio Amedeo becoming King of Spain. He also lacked a preconceived or uniform policy on frontier occupation. This begs the question whether Louis actually lost out and actually wanted to keep Lorraine and Savoy. Arguably, he no longer did and had succeeded in shedding potential frontier liabilities in 1713–14. After all, Lorraine had contributed very little to the costs of its occupation and war. Abandoning French claims to north Italy also seemed a logical and realistic step given the severe bandit problems in Savoy, 1704–6. French occupation of Nice was also unsustainable; a French memorandum of 1707 recommended abandoning the county as the costs of occupation were three times the amount taken in revenues.

Colonial losses were Louis' bargaining counter at Utrecht and were not as decisive as many have claimed. St Kitts was no great loss at all economically to French West Indian sugar production. In North America, France had lost Port Royal, but did not technically lose Acadia. Article 12 invited future dispute and only limited British control along 'ancient boundaries'. Moreover, section 14 of Utrecht prevented full English control of the Acadian population, by stating that 'the subjects of the said king may have liberty to remove themselves within a year to any other place'. Britain's new trading rights over the Iroquois assumed that trade would be welcomed, which was not always the case. In Newfoundland, France preserved its fishing rights from

ACTIVITY 6.11

1 Draw up a two-column table, listing in the left-hand column reasons for seeing the treaties of Utrecht and Rastatt as being French defeats and in the right-hand one, French successes.

2 If these are the answers, what are the questions?
- North Italy and Spanish Netherlands
- because his grandson could not be King of France
- Ypres and Menin
- Asiento
- St Kitts
- because Britain had proposed making Vittorio Amedeo King of Spain
- 3 times more than amounts taken in revenues
- Strasbourg, Franche Comté and Alsace
- Bonavista to Pointe Riche
- because sugar production rocketed in Martinique and Guadeloupe.

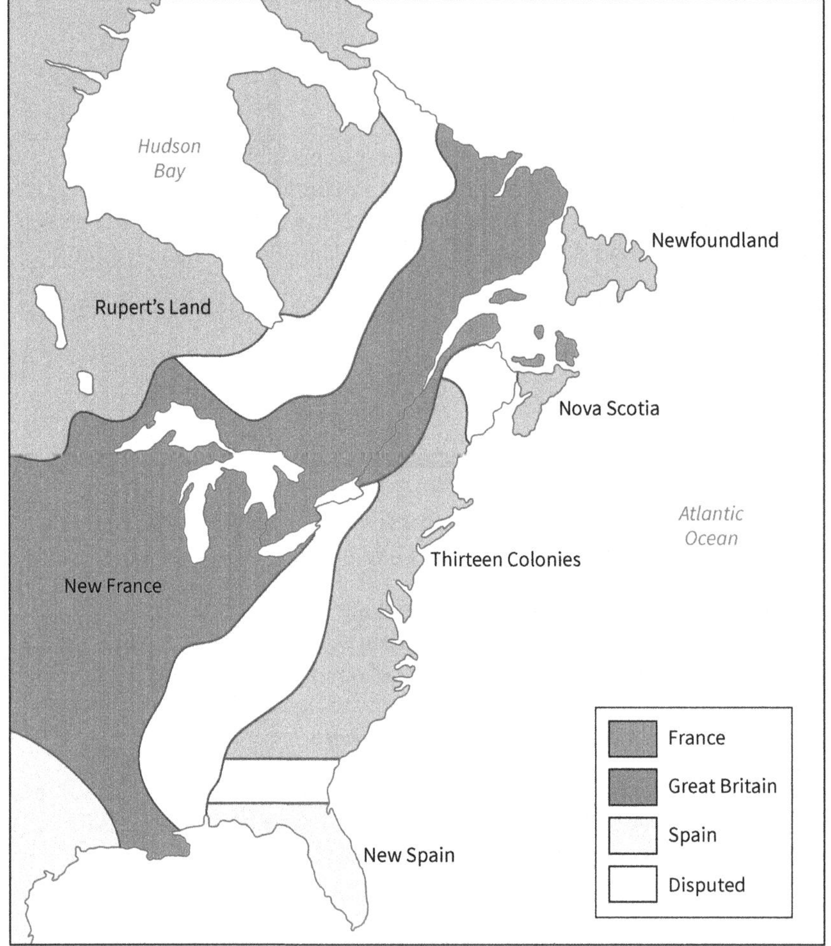

Figure 6.11: Colonies in North America, 1713

Bonavista along the north coast to Point Riche on the west coast. The loss of fishing rights on the south coast was easily offset by French occupation of Cape Breton Island. France also retained all the islands in the Gulf of St Lawrence thereby protecting French interests in Canada.

Both continentally and colonially, the cords of French influence had been stretched, but not broken. Louis had won neither the war nor the peace, but it remains doubtful that he fully lost either. French defeat was neither complete militarily nor diplomatically.

The legacy of Louis XIV by 1715

The last years of the reign

By August 1715, Louis had gangrene in his left leg and was dying. As Colin Jones suggests, living to 76 was quite an innings given his childhood bout of smallpox, youthful gonorrhea, near death with an anal fistula in 1686 and the average life expectancy of 30 years at the time. Nevertheless, Louis appeared pretty rueful six days before he died and reportedly warned his great grandson (the five-year-old future Louis XV) against making the same mistakes that he himself had made:

'Your happiness depends on your submission to God and the care you will take on your people. To achieve this task, you have to avoid war as much as you can, war is the ruin of the people. Do not follow the terrible example I gave you on this matter, I too often waged war without much forethought and continued it due to vanity. Do not imitate me, be a pacifist prince and make your principal care the relief of your subjects.'[18]

Underpinning this belated capacity for self-reflection were a number of problems that Louis knew he was bequeathing his successors. As we have already seen earlier in Chapter 4, after 1685 French society and economy had been badly neglected. France suffered depopulation through a severe famine, run-away wheat price hyperinflation and a severe winter during 1708–9. In northern France, a doubling of wheat prices in 1708 caused more than a doubling of deaths in 1709. Equally problematic was the increasing vitriol of critics of Louis XIV, such as Fénelon and courtiers such as Saint-Simon. Appalled at what he saw as an erosion of the prestige, privileges and power of noblesse de robe (nobles with judicial and administrative powers), Saint-Simon even could not resist having a dig at the Sun King upon his death:

'The King was little regretted....The provinces, in despair at their ruin and annihilation breathed again and leaped for joy; and the Parlement and the robe destroyed by edicts and by revolutions…the people ruined, overwhelmed, desperate, gave thanks to God…for deliverance'.[19]

Such negativity may have been alluding to the perceived loss of remonstrance in 1667 and 1673 and tax exemption (at least in principle through the 1695 Capitation and Dixième in 1710). Louis was possibly unaware of the scale of this problem, but he must have had some inkling of the grim financial situation he left in 1715. State expenditure had risen from 175 million livres in 1702 to 264 million in 1711. Two thirds of this had to be covered by resorting to offices and borrowing, as tax revenues were so poor. Even after the war:

- net tax revenue remained half of expenditure
- state debt had soared to 2 billion livres, with 90 million spent just on annual interest payments.

Small wonder, therefore, that the following concern was bemoaned by Regency Council Finance Council President Noailles in 1715:

'The Treasury is absolutely empty and loans made by the Receivers General are such that the Royal Treasury is almost entirely owned by them up to 1718'.[20]

Louis' wars had broken the bank. A shortage of specie (or hard coinage) made further profligate borrowing both appealing and addictive. Louis had reportedly borrowed 32 million in billets (paper credit money) from Samuel Bernard to borrow 8 million livres in coinage. The Sun King was unable to pay his creditors and left debts estimated to be at least 83% of GDP.

ACTIVITY 6.12

Write short notes on the 1710 *Dixième* and Vauban's *Dixme* mentioned in Chapter 4.

The problem of the succession

Worse still was a looming Bourbon dynastic emergency from 1711. Within three years, the loss of Louis' son, two grandsons and a great grandson raised the chilling prospect of the War of Spanish Succession being followed by a War of French Succession.

This unexpected turn of events made the denial of Philip d'Anjou's inheritance rights to the French crown at Utrecht a distinct problem. Louis d'Anjou himself (the future Louis XV) had nearly died of smallpox (or measles) along with his parents and an older brother in 1712. D'Anjou's protection against the doctors' well-intentioned, but fatal, bloodletting treatment may have helped save his life. Louis d'Anjou became heir to the throne upon the death of his brother the Duc de Bretagne in 1712, when he was two years old. After Berry's death in 1714, the now four-year-old Dauphin was Louis XIV's only surviving legitimate descendant who could claim the throne. It also left as the sole candidate as regent, the Sun King's power-hungry, hedonist nephew, Philippe duc d'Orléans, who Louis rightly suspected would not protect the interests of the crown and the young duc d'Anjou.

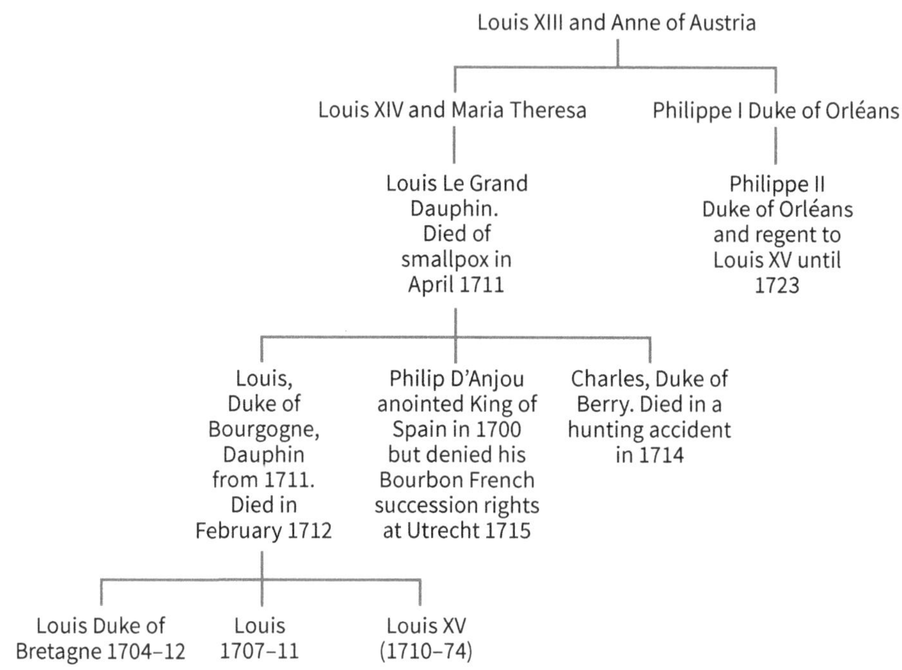

Figure 6. 12: Louis XIV's dynastic crisis and looming succession problem from 1711

France's Bourbon monarchy was now hanging by a thread: Louis planned his will accordingly. His aim was simple – to prevent Philippe duc d'Orléans' influence as regent. To this end, he tried to give a veneer of legitimacy to all his illegitimate children by his mistresses Louise de La Vallière and Madame de Montespan by marrying them into the most powerful noble families within France and anointing them as 'Princes of the Blood'. He also made a very divisive will to act as a brake on Orléans subverting the regency for his own ends. This stated that:

- Louis' illegitimate son, the Duc du Maine, would act as Louis XV's guardian and superintendent of his education, and Commander of the Royal Guards.
- Orléans was not to be sole regent, but only head of a regency council.

Figure 6.13: The Anointing of Louis XV

The annulment of the King's will and formation of the regency of Orléans.

As often happens with the best laid plans, Louis' scheme to restrict Orléans' influence did not work. The following account by the Duc de Saint-Simon usefully highlights the sense of outrage and disgrace felt by many courtiers at the announcement of Maine as a Prince of the blood, and part of the reason why Louis' plan to restrict the power of Orléans within the Regency Council essentially backfired:

'I will content myself with a few reflections upon this most monstrous, outstanding and frightful determination of the King. I will simply say that it is impossible not to see it as an attack upon the Crown, contempt for the entire nation, whose rights are trodden under foot by it; insult to all the Princes of the blood; in fact, the crime of high treason in its most rash and most criminal extent.'[21]

Orléans himself also played an active role within the subversion of the dead King's wishes. The day after Louis died, Orléans asked the Paris Parlement to overturn the parts of the will that restricted his power and ever the skilled manipulator, presented the ultimate win-win scenario; if the Parlement acquiesced and named him with full powers as regent (rather than just head of a regency council) then he would restore their right to remonstrance taken by Louis in 1667 and 1673. The Parlement accepted. Orléans further consolidated his power by by banning the use of external mail and couriers to keep Philip V of Spain in the dark about his actions. He also tactically included Louis XIV's and Montespan's grandson in his council, though without intending him to have any influence. This allowed him to relieve the Duc du Maine of his military command and prevent Philip V of Spain from playing any role in France's succession, thereby maintaining the new balance of power that had been agreed at Utrecht in 1713. It also seems, if we believe Saint-Simon, that he just stamped his authority over the Duc du Maine;

'The Duc du Maine wished to speak. As he was about to do so, M. le Duc d'Orléans put his head in front of M. le Duc and said … "Monsieur, you will speak in turn". In one moment, the affair turned according to the desires of M. le Duc d'Orléans. The power of the Council of the regency and its composition just fell … Thus all favours and punishments were in the hands of the Duc d'Orléans alone … the Duc du Maine did not dare say a word'.[22]

Orléans' position as regent was of immense significance. Not only did he return the Parlement's right of remonstrance, he allowed them to revoke the 1713 Bull Unigenitus, which Louis had forced through by lit de justice hoping it would end the challenge of Jansenism.

With Louis XIV dead, his grandson and illegitimate sons were quickly marginalised. Louis' dreams had been frustrated, and not for the first time.

Timeline

1698	First Partition Treaty
1698–1715	Colbert de Torcy French Foreign Affairs Minister
1699	Death of Joseph Ferdinand (February)
1699	Peace of Karlowitz between Habsburg Empire and Ottoman Turks
1700	Carlos died 1 November
1700	Carlos II drafted a will naming Louis' grandson Philip d'Anjou as his sole heir (October)
1700	Louis XIV accepted Carlos II's will 12 November
1700	Treaty of London, Second Partition Treaty (March)
1701	The English parliament backed William III against Bourbon France
1701	Fighting in Italy following Leopold's invasion part of the War of the Spanish Succession (March)
1701	Grand Alliance reformed (September)
1701	Louis sent French troops to occupy garrisons in the Spanish Netherlands
1701	Louis XIV announced that Philip d'Anjou retained his claim to the French throne (February)
1701	Treaty of The Hague refounds Grand Alliance (7 September)
1701	William III persuaded German elector states, Palatinate, Brandenburg, Prussia, Münster, Baden Baden and Trier to join Grand Alliance (winter)
1702	Grand Alliance declared war on France (May)
1702	Imperial forces crossed the Rhine near Cologne (April)
1702	John Churchill commanded forces in victories at Kaiserwerth, Venlo, Roermond and Liege and Huy and Limbourg
1702–13	Queen Anne's War or Third Indian War
1703	John Churchill commanded forces in victories at Huy and Limbourg
1704	British capture of Gibraltar
1704	John Churchill commanded forces in victory at Blenheim
1706	Allied soldiers marching on Madrid
1706	John Churchill commanded forces in victory at Ramillies
1706	Siege of Turin
1707	Villars led French forces to victory at Stollhofen
1708	John Churchill commanded forces in victory at Oudenarde
1709	John Churchill commanded forces in victory at Malplaquet
1712	Death of the Duc de Bretagne
1713	Treaty of Utrecht
1714	Death of the Duc de Berry

Practice essay questions

1. ‘Louis XIV was primarily responsible for the outbreak of the Spanish Succession War in 1702.’ Assess the validity of this view.
2. ‘Ambition totally outran achievement in Louis’ foreign policy in the period 1704–12.’ Assess the validity of this view.
3. ‘The most significant consequence of the Spanish Succession War was the collapse of French military prestige and security by 1715.’ Assess the validity of this view.
4. ‘The peace treaties of 1713–14 were an absolute disaster for Louis XIV.’ Assess the validity of this view
5. With reference to these sources and your understanding of the historical context, assess the value of these sources for studying Louis XIV’s foreign policy.

Extract A

From a satirical English pamphlet published in 1703 in London called ‘The King of France his catechism: Written at Paris, and licens'd by Father La Chese, the French King's confessor’.

Question: Which are your Majesty’s principal virtues?

Answer: To oppress my own subjects and threaten all my neighbours, to disturb all Europe with my unjust wars and increase my dominions by a devious peace, to covet universal monarchy as much as I did in the Spanish Netherlands. To keep no oath farther than my own interest and to be wholly governed by the secret councils of Madame de Maintenon.

Question: How did your majesty acquire the name of Louis the Great?

Answer: By tyranny and unjust conquests; I seized upon those principalities that adjoined my own and gave a reason for it by the mouths of my invincible Dragoons.

Question: Which is the greatest check to your Majesty's ambition?

Answer: Those troublesome English, that fought so like devils at Liege and Vigo, damned fellows that swallow smoke and gun-powder like beef and pudding.

‘The King of France His Cathechism’ (London 1703)

Extract B

The Declaration of the Grand Alliance issued by Great Britain, the United Provinces and the Habsburg Emperor on 7 September 1701. This set about implementing the Second Partition Treaty and followed Louis XIV’s grandson Philip V’s refusal to leave Spanish territory:

‘Louis XIV … has usurped the possession of the entire …. Spanish monarchy for the aforesaid Duke of Anjou … The kingdoms of France and Spain are (now) so closely united and cemented that they may seem henceforward … as one of the same kingdom … So it appears, unless timely care be taken, that his Imperial Majesty will be destitute of all hopes of ever receiving … the fiefs belonging to him in Italy and the Spanish Netherlands … and that the French and Spaniards, being thus united, will within a short time become so formidable to all that they may assume themselves the dominion over all Europe. The Emperor, King of Great Britain and the United Provinces have therefore thought strict conjunction and alliance between themselves necessary for repelling the greatness of the common danger.'

The declaration of the Grand Alliance, 7 September 1701, cited by David Smith, *Louis XIV*. Cambridge: Cambridge University Press; 1992, p. 94-95

Extract C

From an open letter to his subjects 12 June 1709, by Louis XIV, to be read aloud by the parish priest in every church during attempts to open peace negotiations with France's enemies in the War of the Spanish Succession:

'The more I have testified my willingness to remove the alleged fears of my enemies about my designs to extend my power, the more they add new demands to their original ones and, making use of the name of the Duke of Savoy or of the interests of the Princes of the Empire, they have led me to realise that their intention was only to strengthen themselves in the states bordering my dominions, at my expense; and to open for themselves an easy path to penetrate into the interior of my kingdom at any time it might suit their interests. But, although my tenderness for my people is as strong as that which I have for my children; although I share in all the evil that the war inflicts on such faithful subjects and that I have shown all Europe that I sincerely desired them to enjoy peace, I am persuaded that the French people would oppose themselves to conditions so contrary to justice and the honour of Frenchmen.'

Open Letter of Louis XIV, 12 June 1709, in Recueil de diverses pièces touchant les préliminaires de paix proposez par les allies et rejettez par le Roy (Paris, 1709)

Chapter summary

You should now have a good understanding of the causes, course and consequences of the War of the Spanish Succession. From reading this chapter, you will have grasped:

- the issue of the Spanish Succession, the aims and policies of France, international response to this and why war broke out in 1702
- why the 1698 and 1700 partition treaties failed to prevent war
- Louis' level of responsibility for this and the reformation of the 'Grand Alliance'
- the main events and details of the War of the Spanish Succession in Europe, North America and Caribbean, and of the Treaty of Utrecht in 1713
- the extent to which French defeats were caused by a new balance of power and of French decline in relation to the European powers by 1714
- the problem of Louis' legacy, the succession, annulment of the King's will and formation of Orléans' regency.

End notes

1 The First Partition Treaty (11 October 1698). Cited by Smith D. *Louis XIV*. Cambridge: Cambridge University Press; 1992. p. 92.

2 Maland D. *Europe in the Seventeenth Century*. London: Macmillan Education; 1983. p. 356.

3 The Second Partition Treaty (March 1700). Cited by Smith D. *Louis XIV*. Cambridge: Cambridge University Press; 1992. p. 92.

4 Saint-Simon, cited by Treasure G. *Louis XIV*. Harlow: Longman; 2001. p. 264.

5 Ibid.

6 Maland D. *Europe in the Seventeenth Century*. London: Macmillan Education; 1983. p. 360.

7 The Spanish Succession 1701. Spanishsuccession.nl. 2016. Available from: http://www.spanishsuccession.nl/1701.html

8 Thomson, M. Louis XIV and the Origins of the War of the Spanish Succession. *Transactions of the Royal Historical Society*. 1954; 4:111. p. 134

9 Thomson M. Louis XIV and the Origins of the War of the Spanish Succession. *Transactions of the Royal Historical Society*. 1954; 4:111. p. 121–2.

10 The Duke of Marlborough to the Prince of Denmark after the Battle of Ramillies, (May, 1706). Murray G. *The Letters and Dispatches of John Churchill, First Duke of Marlborough, from 1702 to 1712*. London: John Murray, Albemarle Street; 1845. p. 521.

11 Shennan J. *Louis XIV (Lancaster Pamphlets)*. London: Methuen; 1993. p.44

12 Madame de Maintenon to the Princesse des Ursins (1709). Cited by Treasure G. *Louis XIV*. Harlow: Longman; 2001. p. 281.

13 Lynn J. A. *The Wars of Louis XIV 1667–1714*. London: Routledge; 1999. p. 299 & 307.

14 Letter from Marlborough to the Duke of Savoy (December 1706). Murray G. *The Letters and Dispatches of John Churchill, First Duke of Marlborough, from 1702 to 1712*. London: John Murray, Albemarle Street; 1845. p. 268–9.

15 Louis XIV's open letter of 1709. Cited by Treasure G. *Louis XIV*. Harlow: Longman; 2001. p. 284.

16 Pritchard J. *In Search of Empire: The French in the Americas, 1670–1730*. Cambridge: Cambridge University Press; 2004. p. 358.

17 James Vernon, cited by Satsuma S. *Britain and Colonial Maritime War in the Early Eighteenth Century*. Woodbridge: Boydell & Brewer; 2013. p. 57.

18 Philippe de Courcillon, Marquis de Dangeau. Louis XIV of France [Internet]. Hoocher.com. 2016. Available from: http://hoocher.com/Louis_XIV/Louis_XIV.htm; Aldridge P, Aldridge P. Louis XV Part I : Childhood and early reign. News and information from France. 2014. Available from: http://www.france-pub.com/forum/2014/03/06/louis-xv/

19 Memoirs of Louis XIV and His Court and of the Regency, by Duc de Saint Simon. Guttenburg.org. 2016. Available from: http://www.guttenburg.org/files/3875/3875-h/3875-h.htm

20 Louis Antoine de Noailles. Wikipedia. 2016 [cited 15 April 2016]. Available from: http://en.wikipedia.org/wiki/Louis_Antoine_de_Noailles

21 Duc de Saint Simon. *Memoirs of Louis XIV and His Court and of the Regency, Vol.9*. New York City: Wallachia Publishers; 2015.

22 Ibid.

Glossary

Académie Française: An organisation established in 1635 to enhance France's artistic, linguistic and intellectual prestige that propagated royal propaganda and presented government opinion as perceived wisdom and fact.

Academy of Sciences: Established by Louis as a government advisory body on scientific matters and means of self-promotion, royal patronage of the Academy of Sciences reinforced his cultivated image and perceived academic acumen.

Advocate General: The Paris Parlement's legal adviser to the government.

Affaires extraordinaires: another name for extraordinary revenues or monies secured through selling contracts to financiers to collect ad hoc taxes and venal offices.

Aides: A wide range of indirect taxes, mainly on drink and salt, levied by the state.

Asiento: The privilege of importing slaves into South America.

Assiette: The basic assessment of the main direct tax, the taille.

Bailiffs: Local government officers employed to collect taxes and if necessary, arrest non payers.

Bourbon: A member of the European royal family line that ruled France from 1589 to 1793 (when Louis XVI was executed by the revolutionaries). Restored in 1815, the Bourbon lineage continued to rule in its Orleans branch from 1830 until 1848.

Bourgeoisie: Middle class or non-noble members of rural and urban society that were wealthy enough not to have to work with their hands, including merchants.

Burgundian Chain: The Spanish/Habsburg military supply network or line of military communications that stretched from Spain's northern Italian lands to the Spanish Netherlands.

Calvinism: A major branch of Protestantism that follows the teachings of theologian John Calvin.

Camisard: Hugeunots (French Protestants) from the isolated and mountainous Cévennes region of southern-central France, who revolted against the increased anti-Huguenot persecutions following the Edict of Fontainbleau.

Cardinal: A leading dignitary of the Roman Catholic Church, appointed by the Pope.

Chambre de Justice: A special royal tribunal established to investigate the conduct of money lenders with the power to imprison, fine and issue the death penalty to anyone it found guilty of wrong-doing.

Chambre St-Louis: A united committee of the parlement that formed in 1648, composed of members of all the sovereign courts of Paris. They condemned previous royal financial edicts and demanded acceptance of a scheme of constitutional reforms that they had framed.

Chambres de L'Edits: Courts which protected Huguenot interests established by the Edict of Nantes and contained a number of Protestant magistrates who would judge all cases involving Huguenots.

Chambres de Requêtes: Civil appeal courts.

Chambres des Comptes: Sovereign courts specialising in financial affairs.

Chambres de Réunions: Special law courts established as part of Louis' Réunions policy (1681-4) to investigate French claims to different territories. This included researching their status as dependencies under different rulers and powers, sometimes over periods extending back into the Middle Ages.

Charlemagne: Legendary King of the Franks 768–814 and Holy Roman emperor (as Charles I) 800–14. As the first Holy Roman emperor Charlemagne promoted the arts and education and became known as Charles the Great.

Coalition: A group whose members unite together in a common interest or cause.

Commissaries: Special royal representatives or officials.

Concordat of Bologna: An agreement made in 1516 between French king Francis I and Pope Leo X. This permitted the Pope to collect all the income that the Catholic Church made in France, and confirmed the King of France's right to tax the clerics, restrict their right of appeal to Rome and above all, to nominate appointments (archbishops, bishops, abbots and priors). This gave the French King effective control over the leadership of the French Church.

Conseil des depêches: Part of the King's Council, the Council of Dispatches oversaw the entire administration of ecclesiastical, judicial, provincial and municipal affairs.

Conseil d'en haut: (Ministerial council of state), an informal branch of the King's Council made up of his most trusted advisors on political, foreign and ecclesiastical affairs.

Constitutional powers: An individual of a state's inherent right to govern as justified by fundamental principles.

Controlleur-Général: A chief minister in the royal government of 17th and 18th century France in charge of finances.

Corsican guards incident: A confrontation between Pope Alexander VII's Corsican guards and Frenchmen guarding the French embassy in Rome, that Louis XIV used to impose his power over and humiliate the Pope.

Corvée: A month's forced labour on highway maintenance.

Council of State: Louis' Conseil d'État – a division of the King's Council comprising legal advisers and experts that heard claims affecting the crown's non-financial interests.

Cours des Aides: Sovereign courts of appeal primarily concerned with customs, but also other matters of public finance. They exercised some control over certain excise taxes and octroy duties, which were regarded as of a different nature from the taille, the gabelle, and the general imposts of the kingdom.

Cum nuper: papal bull issued in 1703 by Pope Clement XI. This condemned the Jansenists' claim to right to respectful silence which had been supported by members of the Sorbonne in the Case of Conscience.

Dauphin: The title of the heir to the French throne. The title was held by four different people during Louis XIV's reign: the eldest son Louis who was dubbed the 'Grand Dauphin' after the birth of his son, Louis Duke of Burgundy the 'Petit Dauphin', Louis Duke of Brittany, oldest son of the Petit Dauphin, and Louis the 'bien aimé' to whom the title passed when his brother died, and who lived to became Louis XV.

Decree: A royal judgement, ruling or law.

Deficit: A shortfall, as when a government is taking in less money in taxes than it is spending.

Dévot: Religious faction, a loose grouping of people who zealously supported monarchy and Roman Catholicism, and opposed Protestants and French participation in the Thirty Years War.

Diaspora: The dispersion or spread of any people from their original homeland.

Dissident: Rebellious or nonconforming.

Don gratuit: The name for the Church's 'free gift' or granting of an amount of revenue to the king after much negotiation.

Dyke: A natural or artificial slope or wall used to regulate water levels.

Écu: Gold and silver coins used in Louis XIV's reign.

Edict: A permanent law on a single issue.

Edict of Fontainbleau: The royal edict in 1685 by which Louis XIV revoked the Edict of Nantes (1598) and ended Huguenot freedom of worship and freedom from persecution.

Edict of Grace: (Or 'of Alès') 1629, a treaty negotiated by Cardinal Richelieu with Huguenot leaders and signed by King Louis XIII of France on 27 September 1629. This ended the previous religious warring between Huguenots and Catholics and confirmed the basic principles of amnesty and toleration of Huguenot worship (as previously granted by the 1598 Edict of Nantes). It also ended Huguenots' political rights and demanded the immediate handing over and destruction of their cities and fortresses.

Edict of Nantes: the decree passed by Louis XIV's grandfather Henri IV that granted Huguenots freedom of public worship, within certain areas of France (away from court, Paris, areas surrounding Paris and the armed forces). It granted Huguenots full civil rights, including access to education, and established a special court, the ***Chambre de l'Édit***, made up of both Protestants and Catholics, to resolve disputes arising from the edict. The Edict of Nantes also stated that the state should pay Huguenot priests and costs of garrisoning military strongholds for eight years.

Embezzlement: The practice of not handing over, of keeping or stealing money.

Excommunication: A kind of banishment, a punishment that is handed out by a church when one of its members breaks some important church rule.

Exemption: Immunity from taxation (the right not to pay it).

Faggots: Men drafted in temporarily (often through bribes) to exaggerate army regiment numbers when intendants tried calculating a regiment's size; army captains did this for financial gain, as they were paid according to how many men they commanded.

First Estate: The clergy. They fulfilled a spiritual role in society and so were exempted from taxation.

First President: The most senior judge in France and head of the Paris parlement nominated by the King.

Formulary: A prepared document like a modern form with gaps for individuals to add their names, the date and other specifics.

Four Gallican Articles: Statements drafted by Bishop Bossuet and passed by Louis' Assembly of Clergy. These reaffirmed Louis' rights over the Pope on theological issues and allowed papal rulings to be altered if they did not have the support of General Councils.

Franc-fief tax: A fee owed by commoners who held noble land.

Francophobic: Fearing, disliking or hating France.

Gabelle: Hated tax levied on salt, of which a fixed minimum amount was supposedly bought. This brought in 23.7 million livres when leased in 1687. Salt prices differed significantly due to regional variations, exemptions and privileges.

Garrison: A group of troops stationed in a fortress or town to defend it.

Généralités: Administrative districts of France established in the 14th century to organise royal revenue collection

Gloire: (Glory), reputation for glory, greatness and noble deeds with contemporaries and future generations.

Grand couvert: The name for the formal dining part of Louis XIV's day at Versailles, observed by courtiers and part of habitual self-displaying at court.

Hegemony: Dominance or supremacy, taking a leadership role.

Iconography: The imagery and pictorial representations of an individual or event.

Imperial diet (assembly): The general assembly of the various Imperial Estates of the Holy Roman Empire.

Inflation: The process by which prices go up over time.

Intendants: Officials who supervised judicial affairs, presided over civil cases and oversaw tax collection, army training, billeting and the enforcement of royal edicts. They regularly reported back to Colbert.

Jansenism: A school of thought within Roman Catholicism that man was hopelessly sinful and therefore could only be saved by God's grace.

Jesuit: A Roman Catholic religious order, Jesuits tended to be strongly ultramontanist.

Judicial: Relating to courts of law, judges and the administration of justice.

L'affaire des importants: The name for the aristocratic conspiracy, led by the Duc de Beaufort, to murder Mazarin between 1643 and 1644.

Laissez-faire: The policy of minimising state or government interference in the economy, allowing producers and customers to negotiate the quantity, quality and prices of products and services.

League of Augsburg: A defensive alliance formed by the princes of Franconia and the Rhineland in 1686. By 1688, it included Brandenburg, Bavaria, The Elector of the Palatinate, Saxony, Spain, Sweden, the United Provinces and the Emperor.

League of German Princes: 1658, a diplomatic alliance secured by Mazarin and German elector princes. This afforded France the right to 'protect' long stretches of the Rhineland, thereby strengthening its border and opportunity for pre-emptive military action.

Lettres de cachet: Letters signed by the king imposing edicts, preventing assemblies and imprisoning individuals without trial.

Lettres Provinciales: Satirical letters written by Jansenist Blaise-Pascal that attacked the laxity of Jesuit doctrine.

Lieutenant-General: A high rank of officer in the army, above major general and below general.

Livres: The French currency from 781 to 1794, consisting of 20 sous.

Madame: Title given to Elizabeth Charlotte, Princess Palatine and wife of Louis' homosexual brother Philippe duc d'Orléans ('Monsieur'). Madame de Chevreuse – or Marie de Rohan was a French aristocrat (1600–79) and daughter of the Duke of Montbazon (who possessed great estates in Anjou and Brittany and enjyed a princely rank at court). She was involved peace negotiations with Lorraine and Spain during the 1630's (leading to her exile in 1637), the 1641 Soissons conspiracy, the Cable des Importants (after which she fled again) and despite her intial support for Mazarin during 1649–50, the aristocratic Frondes from 1651.

Maîtres des requêtes: Masters of requests or royal judges attached to the King's council (often intendants and venal office holders).

Mars Christianissimus: 'Most Christian God of War', parody of Louis' official title as French king, 'Rex Christianissimus' (most Christian king, a title awarded to his ancestors by the pope).

Mazarinades: Defamatory anti-government pamphlets published in mid-seventeenth century France, so-called due to their fixation upon Jules Mazarin. Allegations included Mazarin's low birth, greed, lechery, scrounging, alleged shameful personal tastes, financial mismanagement, embezzlement and sexual relations with Anne of Austria.

Minority: Youth or name for a time when a king was considered too young to rule himself.

Monsieur: Traditional title of a French king's brother, applied to Philippe duc d'Orléans.

Most Christian King: The title and reputational status across Europe sought by Louis so that he could potentially be elected as Holy Roman Emperor in the event of Leopold's death.

Most Christian Turk: Parody of Louis' official title as French king, 'Rex Christianissimus' (most Christian king, a title awarded to his ancestors by the pope) referring to his attacking the Hapsburgs just when they were under pressure from the Ottoman empire.

Muster rolls: Lists of soldiers in troops, used as the basis of calculating pay.

Native Americans: Descendants of those people who were in the Americas before the arrival of settlers from other parts of the world, including Europe – often mistakenly called 'Indians'.

Noblesse d'épée: (Or sword nobility), sword nobles were those privileged through feudal or military service.

Noblesse de robe: (Robe nobility), those who achieved nobility from serving in the higher ranks of judicial and administrative office.

Nuncio: A papal ambassador to a foreign court or government.

Occitan: The historic language of southern France, related to French but also to Catalan.

Octroys: Urban sales taxes.

Office system: The government system of selling jobs in the government service to raise money.

Officiers: Office holders or officials in the royal administration. They were exempt from taxation and had responsibilities for tax collection and judicial affairs.

Palais de Justice: A court of law in Paris.

Pancarte: Sales tax.

Panegyric: A published piece of writing or public speech which praises someone or something.

Papacy: The office or authority of the Pope.

Papal: Relating to the pope.

Papal bull: A formal letter from the pope. It has some of the qualities and status of a contract. Bulls take their name from the 'bulla' or a lead seal which identifies them as genuine.

Partitioning: Dividing into separate parts.

Patronage: The power to control appointments to office or the right to privileges.

Paulette: (Or droit annuel) was the annual payment of money from office-holders to the crown. This was one sixtieth of the officer's estimated value and was in return for the right of an officer to transfer his office to another (often a son).

Pays d'élection: Districts for financial administration that were told by Paris exactly how much they had to pay and that nothing less would be accepted.

Pays d'états: Newly acquired and often semi-autonomous territories; they formed a third of France land-wise, but only paid a tenth of all taxes.

Péages: Tolls

Peasantry: The social class made up of peasants (or members of a traditional class of farm labourers or small farm owners).

Petit coucher: Louis' observed routine of going to bed, in which selected people attended to his final needs of the day.

Petit lever: Louis' observed morning wake up routine, in which selected people attended to help him get dressed.

Pope: The Bishop of Rome as head of the Roman Catholic Church.

Positive representational culture: Propaganda and the art of promoting Louis XIV in the most favourable light, using a wide range of written and artistic media.

Pretext: An excuse or smokescreen for an underlying motive.

Princes of the blood: Members of the royal family.

Privateer: A privately owned ship or sailor that a government allows to wage war on and capture the ships of an enemy country, thereby weakening its colonial economic power.

Projet d'une Dîme Royale: A book written by Sébastien Le Prestre de Vauban with his secretary, Father Vincent Ragot de Beaumont and published in 1707 that was highly critical of government policies and called for a Capitation tax along with other means of addressing France's financial and socio-economic difficulties.

Propaganda: Information and images designed to promote a specific political viewpoint and condition people to think, often favourably towards government policies.

Reaction: A response that seeks to reverse recent changes and restore the situation that existed before them.

Reform: A response to a dangerous or unjust situation that makes changes intended to improve it.

Régale: The King's right from the 1516 Concordat of Bologna to collect revenue from empty dioceses in northern France.

Regent: An individual who is appointed or assumes power to rule on behalf of an heir who is too young to do so after the death of the last king (and heir's father).

[illegible] [illegible]

Remonstrance: The right of the Paris Parlement to protest against and delay a royal edict.

Rentier: A money lender to the crown/buyer of government bonds.

Renunciation: The formal rejection of something, typically a belief, claim, or course of action.

Réunions: Louis' policy from 1680-84 of using military force to seize border territories for strategic reasons, alongside legalistic investigation to allege that France had acquired certain territories under the terms of previous treaties.

Robe nobility: See noblesse de robe.

Roman Catholic: The branch of Christianity headed by the pope.

Royal prerogative: Traditional, unrestricted powers.

Sabotier rebellion: A peasant rebellion in Sologne incited by Huguenot the Marquis de Bonnesson and involving several other Huguenots in 1659. Bonnesson was beheaded as a warning to others.

Salients: Small territorial bulges or areas of land that protrude out into enemy territory, leaving civilian populations and defending soldiers exposed to attack from more than one direction.

Schism: A split, rift or break up between members of a group.

Scorched earth policy: A military tactic of destroying all materials (including buildings, crops and livestock) that might prove useful to an enemy when withdrawing from a region. The intention is to leave an advancing enemy in control of territory as near a desert as possible.

Second Estate: The nobility who were traditionally exempt from taxation.

See: A bishop's diocese, bishopric or parish or area.

Sorbonne: Part of the University of Paris, established in 1253 as a theological college.

Sovereignty: Supreme power or authority. National sovereignty means the authority of a state to govern itself or another state.

Spanish Netherlands: The southern area of the Low Countries (modern Belgium and The Netherlands) under Spanish rule from 1581 to 1713.

Spanish Road: The route Spanish troops took to the Spanish Netherlands, running from its northern Italian lands alongside France's eastern border.

Specie: Money in the form of coins rather than bank notes.

St Clovis: Clovis I was the first king of the Franks (from 481 to 511) to unite all the Frankish tribes into one kingdom and was seen as the founder of the Merovingian dynasty which ruled France until the 8th century and the French kingdom's politics and religion.

Subsistence: A tax paid by townspeople that exempted them from troop billeting.

Succession: The right, act, or process, by which one person succeeds to the throne, office, rank, estate, or the like, of another.

Surintendant: Superintendant or person who managed an area of responsibility.

Surintendant des finances: The finance minister and head of the financial administration within France.

Tariff: A tax on goods that a country imports or exports.

Testament Politique: Richelieu's self-congratulatory account of his achievements and legacy as Louis XIII's Chief Minister; a masterpiece of blowing his own trumpet.

Third Estate: The common people of France before the French Revolution, or all French citizens who did not possess a noble title and were not ordained by the Church. The third estate included the bourgeoisie, workers and at the very bottom, peasants.

Thirty Years War: A series of wars in Central Europe between 1618 and 1648 involving the Holy Roman Empire and Spain, supported by Bavaria (from 1620), Denmark 1643–45 against Saxony, the United Provinces, Brandenburg-Prussia, Sweden (from 1630) and France (from 1635).

Tithe: 10% tax of income paid to the church.

Toisé: A tax on houses built near the walls of Paris.

Toll: A charge payable to use a road, bridge or river.

Tory: A member of the Conservative party.

Traitants: The government's tax collecting and office-selling financiers.

Traits: Government taxes on internal goods, often levied more than once on a single journey.

Usurp: Take (a position of importance or power) illegally or by force, thereby infringing and encroaching upon someone's rights.

Usurpation: The act of doing the above.

Ustencile: A tax paid in cash and kind levied at a local level that was due to army units as an allowance for additional living-expenses.

Venal: Capable of being bought, inherited, corrupted or bribed.

Wittelsbach: German noble family and dynasty who reigned as Dukes, Electors and Kings of Bavaria.

Bibliography

Abbott J. *Louis XIV. Makers of History Series.* F Q Books; 2010.

Ashley M. *Louis XIV and the Greatness of France.* New York: Free Press; 1965.

Beard C. *Port-Royal: A Contribution to the History of Religion and Literature in France, Volume 2.* University of Michigan Library; 1873.

Beik W. *Urban Protest in Seventeenth-Century France.* Cambridge: Cambridge University Press; 1997.

Bergin J. *The Politics of Religion in Early Modern France.* New Haven: Yale University Press; 2014.

Bien D, Schwartz R, Schneider R. *Tocqueville and Beyond: Essays on the Old Regime.* Newark: University of Delaware Press; 2003.

Binisti T. *Versailles: The Dream of a King.* Les Films d'Ici; 2009.

Blanning T. *The Pursuit of Glory.* London: Penguin; 2008.

Blaufarb R. *The Politics of Fiscal Privilege in Provence, 1530s–1830s.* Washington, DC: The Catholic University of America Press; 2012.

Bonney R. The Secret Expenses of Richelieu and Mazarin, 1624–1661. *The English Historical Review.* 1976; Vol.91, No.361.

Bonney R. Absolutism: What's in a name? *French History Review*: 1987; 1(1):93–117.

Bonney R. *Political Change in France under Richelieu and Mazarin, 1624–1661.* Oxford: Oxford University Press; 1978.

Bonney R. The Paradox of Mazarin. *History Today.* 1982; Volume 32, Issue 2.

Bossenga G. H-France Review of 'Expansion and Crisis in Louis XIV's France: Franche-Comté and Absolute Monarchy, 1674–1715'. *Society of French Historical Studies.* 2010; Vol.10, No.60.

Bossuet J.B. Political Treatise 1679 cited by History.hanover.edu. *Extracts from Bossuet's work on kingship.* Available at: https://history.hanover.edu/texts/bossuet.html

Bourque B. All the Abbe's Women: *Power and Misogyny in Seventeenth-Century France.* Germany: Deutsche Nationalbibliothek; 2015. Available at: https://books.google.co.uk/

Bouton C. *The Flour War: Gender, Class and Community in Late Ancient Regime French Society.* University Park: Pennsylvania State University Press; 1993.

Brakshian A. Turenne: Marshal General of France Part 1. *History Today.* 1974; Vol. 24, Issue 7.

Bryant M. 'Partner, Matriarch, and Minister: Mme de Maintenon of France, Clandestine Consort 1680–1715' in Orr C. *Queenship in Europe, 1660–1815.* Cambridge: Cambridge University Press; 2004.

Chéruel A. *Mémoires sur la vie publique et privée de Fouquet, surintendant de finances.* Paris: Charpentier; 1862.

Church W.F. *Richelieu and Reason of State.* Princetown: Princetown University Press; 2015.

Coleman F. *Neither Angel Nor Beast: The Life and Work of Blaise Pascal.* New York: Routledge & Kegan Paul; 1986.

Cooper J. *The Decline of Spain and the Thirty Years War, 1609–59.* New York: Cambridge University Press; 1970.

Darby G. Pope Innocent XI: The Saviour of Christendom? *History Today.* 2011; Volume 61. Issue 5.

Darby G. *Spain in the Seventeenth Century.* London: Routledge; 1994.

Dee D. *Expansion and Crisis in Louis XIV's France.* Rochester, NY: University of Rochester Press; 2009.

Devlin E.L. The Corsican Affair. *History Today.* 2013; Volume 63. Issue 5.

Doyle W. *Venality and the Sale of Offices in Eighteenth Century France.* Oxford: Clarendon; 1996.

Durrand G. What is Absolutism? In Louis XIV And Absolutism (ed. Hatton R, Fox P.W.). *The Canadian Journal of Economics and Political Science.* 1960; Vol. 26. No. 1.

Engel C.E. English Visitors at Louis XIV's Court. *History Today.* 1959; Vol. 9. Issue 6.

Fisher J.R. *The Economic Aspects of Spanish Imperialism in South America 1492–1810.* Liverpool: Liverpool University Press; 1997.

Goubert P. *The Course of French History.* London: Routledge; 2002.

Grose C.L. Louis XIV's Financial Relations with Charles II and the English Parliament. *The Journal of Modern History.* 1929. Volume 1, No.2: 177–204.

Harleian Miscellany: A collection of scarce, curious, and entertaining pamphlets and tracts, as well in manuscript as in print, found in the late earl of Oxford's library, interspersed with historical, political, and critical notes. Volume 1, Joseph Meredith Toner Collection (Library of Congress). Printed for R. Dutton, 1808.

Henshall N. *The Myth of Absolutism, Change and Continuity in Early Modern Monarchy.* London: Routledge; 2014.

Hockey T. (ed). *The Biographical Encyclopedia of Astronomers.* New York: Springer; 2007.

Hockey T, Trimble V, Bracher K. *The Biographical Encyclopaedia of Astronomers.* New York: Springer; 2007.

Höfer B. *Psychosomatic Disorders in Seventeenth Century French Literature.* Farnham: Ashgate; 2009.

Hudgins E.L. *Freedom to Trade: Refuting the New Protectionism.* Washington, DC: Cato Institute; 1997.

Hunt M. *Women in 18th Century Europe.* London: Routledge; 2014.

Hurt J. Louis XIV and the Parlements: *The Assertion of Royal Authority.* Manchester: Manchester University Press; 2002.

James A. *The Origins of French Absolutism, 1558–1661.* London: Routledge; 2006.

Jarvis W.H. *The Gallician Church: A History of the Church of France from the Concordat of Bologna, 1516 to the Revolution.* Volume 1. 1872. Cornell University Library; 2009.

Jones C. *The Great Nation: France from Louis XV to Napoleon: The New Penguin History of France.* London: Penguin; 2003.

Kettering S. Brokerage at the Court of Louis XIV. *The Historical Journal.* 1993; 36(01):69.

Lee S.J. *Aspects of European History, 1489–1789.* London:Routledge; 1984.

Leibniz G, Riley P. *The Political Writings of Leibniz*. Cambridge: Cambridge University Press; 1998.

Livi-Bacci M. *Population and Nutrition: An Essay on European Demographic History*. Cambridge: Cambridge University Press; 1991.

Louis, Longnon J. ed *Memoires de Louis XIV*. Paris: Jules Tallandler; 1927.

Marley D. *Wars of the Americas: A Chronology of Armed Conflict in the Western Hemisphere, 1492 to the Present*. ABC-CLIO Interactive; 2008.

McClain J, Merriman J, Ugawa K. *Edo and Paris*: Urban Life and State in the Early Modern Era. Ithaca: Cornell University Press; 1994.

McCluskey P. Absolute Monarchy on the Frontiers: Louis XIV's Military Occupations of Lorraine and Savoy. *The English Historical Review*. 2016; 131(548):191–193.

McCullough R. *Coercion, Conversion and Counterinsurgency in Louis XIV's France*. Leiden: Brill; 2007.

McLachlan J.O. *Trade and Peace with Old Spain, 1667–1750: A Study of the Influence of Commerce on Anglo-Spanish Diplomacy in the First Half of the Eighteenth Century*. Cambridge: Cambridge University Press; 1940. (new edn 2015)

McNeese T. *The Age of Absolutism*. St. Louis: Milliken Pub.; 2000.

Mettam R. *Power and Faction in Louis XIV's France*. Oxford: B. Blackwell; 1988.

Mitford N. St. Cyr: Madame de Maintenon as Educationalist. *History Today*. 1965; Volume 15.

Monahan W.G. Lyon in the Crisis of 1709: Royal Absolutism, Administrative Innovation and Regional Politics. *French Historical Studies*. 1990; Volume 16, No.4: 837–848.

Moote A. *Louis XIII, The Just*. Berkeley: University of California Press; 1989.

Murphy A. *John Law*. Oxford: Clarendon Press; 1997.

Olson T. *Poussin and France: Painting, Humanism, and the Politics of Style*. New Haven: Yale University Press; 2002.

Parrott D. *Richelieu's Army: War, Government and Society in France, 1624–1642*. Cambridge: Cambridge University Press; 2001.

Peck A, Bogansky A. *Interwoven Globe*. New York: Metropolitan Museum of Art; 2013.

Pritchard J. The French West Indies during the Nine Years War, 1688–97: A Review and Reappraisal. *French Colonial History*. Vol. 2. Michigan State University Press; 2002.

Ranum O. Richelieu and the Great Nobility: Some Aspects of Early Modern Political Motives. *French Historical Studies*. 1963; Vol.3 No.2.

Riding A. At Versailles: The Hall of Mirrors, almost good as new. Nytimes.com. 2007. Available from: http://www.nytimes.com/2007/06/26/arts/26iht-mirrors.1.6333443.html?_r=0.

Riley P.F. *A Lust For Virtue: Louis XIV's Attack On Sin in C17th France*. Praeger; 2001.

Ronning C. *Diplomatic Asylum: Legal Norms and Political Reality in Latin American Relations*. The Hague: M. Nijhoff; 1965.

Root H. *The Fountain of Privilege*. Berkeley: University of California Press; 1994.

Rowlands G. *The Dynastic State and the Army under Louis XIV: Royal Service and Private Interest 1661–1701*. Cambridge: Cambridge University Press; 2002.

Rowlands G. *The Financial Decline of A Great Power: War, Influence and Money in Louis XIV's France*. Oxford: Oxford University Press; 2012.

Rowlands G. Louis XIV, Vittorio Amedeo II and French Military Failure in Italy, 1689–96. *English Historical Review*. 2000; Vol. 115, No. 462.

Salmon J.H.M. The King and His Conscience: the Religious Problems of Louis XIV. *History Today*. 1965; Volume 15, Issue 4.

Schmidt L. This is Versailles: The Lack of Toilets. Thisisversaillesmadame.blogspot.co.uk. 2014. Available from: http://thisisversaillesmadame.blogspot.co.uk/2014/04/the-lack-of-toilets.html

Scoville W.C. *The Persecution of Huguenots and French Economic Development, 1680–1720*. Berkeley: University of California Press; 1960.

Sluga G. James C. *Women, Diplomacy and International Politics since 1500*. London: Routledge; 2015.

Smith E.G. *The Performance of Male Nobility in Molière's Comédies-Ballets*. Farnham: Ashgate; 2005.

Sternberg G. *Status Interaction During The Reign of Louis XIV*. Oxford: Oxford University Press; 2014.

Stewart Saunders E. Louis XIV: Patron of Science and Technology. *Libraries Research Publications*. 1984; Paper 46.

Stradling R. Spain's Struggle for Europe, 1598–1668. London: Hambledon Press; 1994.

Sturdy D. *Science and Social Status: The Members of the Academie Des Sciences, 1666–1750*. Woodbridge: Boydell & Brewer; 1995.

Sturdy D. *Richelieu and Mazarin*. New York: Palgrave Macmillan; 2004.

Swann J. *Provincial Power and Absolute Monarchy: The Estates General of Burgundy 1661–1790*. Cambridge: Cambridge University Press; 2003.

The King of France: His Catechism. London: 1703.

Thackeray F.W. Findling J.E. *Events That Formed the Modern World*. Santa Barbara: ABC-CLIO; 2012.

Thomson M.A. Louis XIV and the Origins of the War of the Spanish Succession. *Transactions of the Royal Historical Society*. 1954; Vol.4.

Vecchio J. Vaux-le-Vicomte: The History of Chateau and its Owner, Nicolas Fouquet. Bonjour Paris. 2003. Available from: https://bonjourparis.com/archives/vaux-le-vicomte-the-history-of-a-chateau/

Walker W. *A History of the Christian Church*. New York: Ulan Press, 2012.

Wilkinson R. Cardinal Mazarin. *History Today*. 1996; Volume 46, Issue 4.

Winn C, Kuizenga D. *Women Writers in Pre-Revolutionary France*. New York: Garland Pub.; 1997.

Young W. *International Politics and Warfare in the Age of Louis XIV and Peter the Great*. New York: iUniverse; 2004.

Zagorin P. *Rebels and Rulers, 1500–1600*. Vol.2, *Provincial Rebellion*. Cambridge: Cambridge University Press; 1982.

Additional websites:

L'Observatoire de Paris: https://www.obspm.fr/

Chateau de Versailles: http://en.chateauversailles.fr/history/

History Learning Site: http://www.historylearningsite.co.uk/

Mises Institute: https://mises.org/

New Advent : http://www.newadvent.org/

Acknowledgements

The authors and publishers acknowledge the following sources of copyright material and are grateful for the permissions granted. While every effort has been made, it has not always been possible to identify the sources of all the material used, or to trace all copyright holders. If any omissions are brought to our notice, we will be happy to include the appropriate acknowledgements on reprinting.

The publisher would like to thank the following for permission to reproduce their photographs (numbers refer to figure numbers, unless otherwise stated):

Cover: Farzan Bilimoria/Getty Images, **page 1:** Episode of the Fronde at the Faubourg Saint-Antoine by the Walls of the Bastille, c.1648 (oil on canvas), French School, (17th century) / Château de Versailles, France / Bridgeman Images, **figure 1.1**: Peter Horree / Alamy Stock Photo, **page 35:** The Artchives / Alamy Stock Photo, **figure 2.1:** United Archives GmbH / Alamy Stock Photo, **figure 2.2:** Invictus SARL / Alamy Stock Photo, **figure 2.3:** Jean Baptiste Colbert (1619-83) presents the map of the Canal du Languedoc to Louis XIV, engraved by Jean Baptiste Morret (fl.1790-1820), 1788 (colour litho), Sergent-Marceau, Antoine Louis Francois (1751-1847) (after) / Private Collection / The Stapleton Collection / Bridgeman Images, **figure 2.8:** Missions of the 17th Century: The Missionary Dragoon forcing a Huguenot to Sign his Conversion to Catholicism, exact copy after an original drawing of 1686 (engraving), Engelmann, Gottfried or Godefroy (1788-1839) / Bibliotheque Nationale, Paris, France / Bridgeman Images, **Page 62:** Granger, NYC. / Alamy Stock, **figure 3.10:** Peter Horree / Alamy Stock Photo, **figure 3.11:** Lebrecht Music and Arts Photo Library / Alamy Stock Photo, **figure 4.1:** FORGET Patrick/SAGAPHOTO. COM / Alamy Stock Photo, **figure 4.5:** War of the Camisards (Protestant insurgents of the Cevennes south of France who resisted the violence of the dragonnades after the revocation of the edict of Nantes) : renewed fanaticism in 1703, engraving by L. David / Photo © Tallandier / Bridgeman Images, **figure 4.7:** The Art Archive / Alamy Stock Photo, **Page 125:** Archive Images / Alamy Stock Photo, **figure 5.3:** DEA / A. DAGLI ORTI / Getty Images, **figure 5.4:** Portrait of the Duc de Saint-Simon (1675-1755) after a portrait by Hyacinthe Rigaud (1659-1743) 1887 (oil on canvas), Viger, Perrine (d.1894) / Chateau de Versailles, France / Bridgeman Images, **figure 5.5:** Mary Evans Picture Library / Alamy Stock Photo, **Page 149:** World History Archive / Alamy Stock Photo, **figure 6.3:** The Art Archive / Alamy Stock Photo, **figure 6.6:** Print Collector / Getty Images, **figure 6.7:** Glasshouse Images / Alamy Stock Photo, **figure 6.13:** Coronation of Louis XIV at Reims, June 7, 1654, 17th century French tapestry by Jean Mozin's workshop, manufacture of Gobelins, from the series Story of the King. / De Agostini Picture Library / Bridgeman Images.

Index

Lightning Source UK Ltd.
Milton Keynes UK
UKOW07f1244120716

278156UK00008B/34/P